SPIRIT OF THE BLUE

SPIRIT OF THE BLUE

Peter Ayerst – A Fighter Pilot's Story

HUGH THOMAS

Foreword by Alex Henshaw

SUTTON PUBLISHING

This book was first published in 2004 by
Sutton Publishing Limited · Phoenix Mill
Thrupp · Stroud · Gloucestershire · GL5 2BU

This paperback edition first published in 2005

British Library Cataloguing in Publication Data
A catalogue record for this book is available from the British
Library.

ISBN 0 7509 4253 3

Typeset in 10/12.5pt Iowan.
Typesetting and origination by
Sutton Publishing Limited.
Printed and bound in Great Britain by
J.H. Haynes & Co. Ltd, Sparkford.

Contents

Acknowledgements

I would like to thank the following people for their cooperation in the writing of this book: Andy Sephton and the pilots from the Shuttleworth Collection at Old Warden in Bedfordshire for their hospitality during the training week in May 2003, especially Peter Holloway for making his Miles Magister available; particular thanks go to Ian Frimston for organising the logistics; Alan and Valerie Byfield for their hospitality and Alan's recollections of Peter at Westcliff School; Dev and Pat Deverson for their generosity and Dev's memories of Peter in The Three Compasses; Tom and Jack Ayerst together with their sister, Peg Taylor, for their recollections of family life at Westcliff.

Finally, sincere thanks go to Peter for enduring numerous hours of interviews, helping me to piece his life together and for keeping me well plied with plenty of black coffee and beer.

Hugh Thomas, 2004

Foreword

Only those who experienced life during those dramatic early years of conflict can appreciate the heartache, the pain and the trauma suffered by almost every family in this tiny island of ours. We had been kicked out of Norway, experienced almost total disaster at Dunkirk and desperate retreats from North Africa, were shamed and overrun by the Japanese – both the *Prince of Wales* and the *Repulse* were sunk – and we faced an invasion that all knew would be a gruesome final effort.

Churchill spoke to the nation as only he could. With dramatic rhetoric, he told the world where we stood and how we should respond. This united us as never before.

If we were going to be defeated, then we would go down fighting.

Peter was typical of the splendid young men who were to meet the massive assault as it crossed the Channel and, in spite of being outnumbered, gave the enemy a painful taste of what to expect. Peter was also to make a contribution not always recognised by those on the ground.

Having been in the RAF since 1938, he was an experienced and competent pilot who was able to impart confidence and assistance to those young boys, many of whom had never sat in a Spitfire until they were posted to their first squadron.

Peter was selected for duty as assistant test pilot in 1945 and was the youngest of my group of RAF bomber and fighter production test pilots at Castle Bromwich.

Each pilot was chosen not only because he was above average in flying ability but also because he had the experience and intellect to understand engineering and aerodynamic problems, as well as being articulate enough to express problems related to his work with which the technicians and ground staff could deal.

The pressure of this type of flying was very different to that demanded in the RAF. Without radio or navigational and landing aids, pilots were expected to test aircraft up to heights of over 40,000ft each and every day. The location of Castle Bromwich in low marshland and in the heart of the Black Country, meant that winter and summer conditions were worse than in other parts of the country. It required unusual skill and ability day in and day out to deal with 320 Spitfires each month, as well as Avro Lancaster bombers and those at dispersal units.

This narration of Peter's life in *Spirit of the Blue* will give a greater insight into both his work with the RAF and also that more exclusive field of flying and testing the weapons of war that could mean our defeat or victory.

I would commend this excellent story to young and old if they wish to have an accurate and truthful account of someone whose knowledge, experience and integrity will convey, particularly to younger readers, the courage and qualities that were the making of the free world as we enjoy it today.

Alex Henshaw
Chief Test Pilot, Vickers-Armstrong

Introduction

Peter Ayerst is not your average fighter pilot. Most fighter pilots have one logbook to record their flights. Peter Ayerst has six.

His life is the stuff of a combination of Biggles and Frederick Forsyth – official fighter pilot ace, Vickers test pilot, NATO Action Man, senior Air Ministry staff officer – his tale is quite unlike any other.

Peter flew more than three operational campaigns during the Second World War – including the Battle of France, the Battle of Britain, El Alamein, Normandy landings and Arnhem, Ruhr offensive sweeps – from the outbreak to the close of the war. Many fighter pilots were killed on their first operational flight. Those who survived flew a further tour. Thereafter they were considered to be 'time-expired', taken off operational flying completely.

The odds of survival for a fighter pilot returning from a campaign were low. But what were the odds of survival for the entire war? Despite being shot down, hit by flak and chased by more than two squadrons of enemy aircraft and flying secret missions behind enemy lines, incredibly, Peter survived six intense years, continuing his love of flying as a Vickers-Armstrong test pilot, working with the legendary Alex Henshaw.

In a flying career that spanned thirty-five years, Peter Ayerst's story is unique for two reasons. His flying is significant historically but there is also the human side: a pilot's love of life, people, partying and enjoyment. What made this pilot tick and how did he manage to survive the war? Can it be explained rationally by luck and fate or is there perhaps a more spiritual account, where unseen and divine forces were responsible for the protection and endurance of certain pilots battling in the skies?

With contributions from friends, family and Peter himself, here is an unusual and exceptional story of an incredible man who holds a unique place in aviation history.

ONE

Spirit of Youth

26 APRIL 1973

The thin rubber tyres of English Electric Lightning XS 459 touched down on the cold, grey tarmac runway at RAF Wattisham. The scream from the two Rolls-Royce Avon engines, which were burning fiercely, dulled to a throaty whine as the throttles were pulled back. The aircraft taxied in and slowly, very slowly, it came to a halt. The two pilots looked ahead for a second, catching their breath, then looked at each other. Sitting on the left was the station commander, Gp Capt Ken Goodwin.

'Congratulations', he muttered.

'Hmm,' the other pilot in the right-hand seat grunted in acknowledgement. 'Well, I suppose that's it. The last time.' A slight melancholy crept into his voice. As the tyres met the Suffolk runway, Wg Cdr Peter Ayerst DFC had just flown his last sortie with the Royal Air Force.

It had been the stuff of Biggles; a life of flying that even the best adventure authors would have had trouble writing. Over the past thirty-five years he had battled with enemy aircraft, fighting in numerous dogfights in skies over the green fields of France to the breathtaking golden expanse of the Libyan desert; been hit by flak, narrowly avoiding a minefield; flown a vast array of aircraft and seen the transition from piston to jet aircraft; he had been one of a handful of elite pilots test-flying Spitfires for Vickers-Armstrong under Alex Henshaw. During those years, he had felt every emotion: anticipation, alarm,

1

elation, desperation, exhilaration, distress, panic. But what years! What flying! An array of characters in the guise of pilots had flown with him; their ghosts had come and gone. Now, at fifty-three, his own flying career high up in the blue had come to an end. Ken Goodwin turned in the cockpit. 'So, Pete, what have you got lined up? Pipe and slippers? Reading the papers and a bit of pruning in the garden? A long and graceful retirement?'

The chin jutted forward, the blue eyes were suddenly alert and there was the flash of a wry smile. The indefatigable spirit, the restless determination that had been ever-present in his life, especially throughout six years of wartime flying, came to the surface. The spirit of the blue . . . 'Not bloody likely . . .!'

In the third decade of the twentieth century, a new dawn began to break in Britain; an era dedicated to harmony and peace slowly emerged from a war-torn and ravaged country that was still trying to make sense of it all. The dust and debris that had ripped through families and damaged towns and villages for four long and horrific years was beginning to settle. Those four years from 1914 to 1918 had seen the highest death-toll of casualties in the history of mankind. Perceptions about warfare, life and death had changed for good. Although the scars of those four years ran deep for soldiers, sailors, pilots and their families alike, entering the 1920s was a time to leave the nightmare of the First World War well and truly in the past. Society had changed for ever. Mothers and daughters, wives and fiancées now strove for an opportunity to work for a living as they had done by making shells in the munitions factories, constructing aeroplanes with canvas stretched over wooden wings made of spruce. There was an increasing interest in spiritualism as mothers, fathers and fiancées tried to contact their loved ones in the afterlife. There was a new outlook in Britain and the old guard had been consigned to the last post. Above all, society wanted fun with plenty of dancing, living and loving. It was for time for the 'twenties' to roar.

Samuel and Hazel Ayerst lived in the seaside resort of Westcliff-on-Sea. In the 1920s it was a rural backwater on the Essex coast. The pair had met on the pier at nearby Southend, a popular place to encounter a potential spouse in pre-war England. Friendship blossomed into romance and thence to marriage soon after in 1914. Now thirty-two, Samuel Ayerst commuted each weekday into the City of London where he worked as a claims assessor for Red Star, an insurance company with a highly profitable and relatively new product: motor insurance. It was a far cry from his work as an orderly in the Medical Corps during the war when, on leave, he would take Hazel along the promenade at Southend.

With a young family to look after, Samuel kept to the daily journey to London, remaining with the company until his retirement. Gentle and jovial, he was big and tall with a cigarette permanently attached to one hand. Happy-go-lucky in character, he was a firm believer in letting things be.

His one joy in life was his cigarettes, much to the annoyance of Hazel. As soon as he returned home, he would sit down at his desk, light up and begin to flick the ash into his turn-ups, using them as an impromptu ashtray which he thought Hazel wouldn't notice. In terms of character, Hazel was very much the opposite. It was Hazel who took hold of the reins of the family and was directly responsible for the shaping and moulding of the children's attitudes.

Before she had met Samuel, Hazel Maud Sloman had worked as a teacher in Norfolk at Methwold primary school in the tranquil, sleepy backwaters of the fenlands, to the north-east of Newmarket. Hazel's intelligence and determination were evident from an early age and she was keen to make the most of women's new-found independence, catching the train from Westcliff to Brandon, the nearest station to the school. Once she had arrived at Brandon, she would cycle the remaining 5 miles through the fenlands and forest of Thetford to reach the school. It was a journey of some distance, so Hazel arranged digs with the local vicar during the week, returning each weekend. She was a woman of her time. It was this drive and spirit of independence, as well as a joy in cycling, that Hazel passed to Peter.

In the middle of the war in 1916 Hazel gave birth to Tom, the first of their four children. Being the first-born, Tom had his parents' undivided attention during this time, particularly from Hazel.

It may also have been due to her background in teaching, combined with her characteristic drive and determination, that explains why Hazel was extremely keen for Tom to spend much of his time with books.

He was considered to be bright academically, especially at French and German, but his brother and sister, twins Jack and Patricia, suggest that he never had the opportunity to enjoy his child-hood as they did because Hazel taught him to concentrate on his studies, almost to the point where she overwhelmed him. The 1920s began with a perfect answer. On 4 November 1920 Hazel gave birth to their second son, Peter. Throughout his childhood he was to encapsulate the very essence of the twenties, a love for life.

The Ayerst family was completed by the birth of Jack and Patricia in January 1923. Jack took after his father, matching Samuel in physical stature. Patricia shared her name with the family dog. There were now two Pats in the household, and to avoid any further confusion in the future, it was felt that they should use her middle name, Margaret, which in turn was abbreviated to Peggy. Over the years, the name stuck. To this day, Tom, Peter and Jack know Pat as Peg.

The children grew up in a house called Newenden, a smart semi-detached villa in Southbourne Grove, Westcliff. The name of the house was taken from the village of Newenden in Kent from where many ancestors of the Ayerst family had originated and were now buried, around Newenden and the village of Hawkhurst: a Kentish house-name for a Kentish family living in Essex. For centuries, the family name was linked with the church. One particular ancestor in the eighteenth century, William Ayerst, had been buried in Canterbury cathedral, and had held the eminent title of Doctor of Divinity to Queen Anne. Direct links to the Ayerst family tree can still be traced back and connected to other members around the world. Ayersts have emigrated to far-flung parts of the globe and have been responsible for coordinating large corporate pharmaceutical companies in Canada, the States, Australia and New Zealand. Samuel's mother had originally come from Ireland. Before she married an Ayerst her surname was Vigne. The name itself originates from France, as did her father. Samuel and Hazel continued the name at Peter's christening, when he was duly named Peter Vigne Ayerst.

Southbourne Grove ran for about a mile where Chalkwell Park lay adjacent to the London Road, which was one of the main thoroughfares leading to the centre of Westcliff. Most of Southbourne Grove had been filled with tarmac except for the last 400yds at the bottom, which was where the family lived. As a consequence, the road became exceptionally muddy, particularly with the onset of winter when it filled up quickly with rain, and it did not take very long for the Grove to turn into a quagmire. Peter felt particularly sorry for the delivery people; one of his first memories is of the horses dragging milk-wagons behind them, making their deliveries while wading through the mud.

All the children remember Samuel as a kind, affectionate, jovial father who always had a joke to tell. Unfortunately, his big problem was telling them. He'd start to laugh before he got anywhere near the end, which rather ruined the punchline. He was in many ways quite unconventional in his *laissez-faire* approach to parenting, letting his children do pretty much what they wanted and leaving them – and Hazel – to get on with the small matter of their education. He never really took control if the children, especially Peter, got out of hand. By the standards of the day, Samuel would have been deemed somewhat relaxed in his parental duties, and raising Tom, Peter, Jack and Peg was really left to Hazel. Although he cared for his children passionately, it was Hazel who was to be the main driving force in the children's life; it was down to her to make sure that her three sons and daughter did the best they possibly could.

Hazel was the boss; she wore the trousers. Reflecting the spirit of women's emancipation, Hazel was the first lady to drive a car in Southend. Reliable and intellectual, she put absolutely everything into bringing up her children. Peg says that they have many things to thank her for, not least her patience in bringing up Peter. Jack and Peg say that he was a bit of a rebel and remember Hazel chasing him around the garden. The restless spirit that was to become an integral part of his character had started early.

It is true to say that Hazel had plenty of family support in raising the children. Nurse Tether, a middle-aged lady who had been a friend of the family for many years, gave invaluable advice and assistance. In addition Hazel had the confidence to bring up her children through their formative years because she knew her parents would assist in providing additional support and cooperation. Her mother and father, Agnes and Tom Sloman, lived 400yds away at the bottom of Southbourne Grove, in a large house called Haslemere.

Tom, a little man who habitually wore a pair of pince-nez, had taken over the running of the family business, managing a large property development firm which was involved in the construction and development of residential properties. The company, established by his father, specialised in procuring and developing properties with 99-year leases, which produced a significant amount of profit. One project, for example, consisted of the construction of up to 360 houses and shops, and Tom bought land in Camberwell and the Old Kent Road, where he had an office situated in the Walworth Road. Tom gave much of the profit from this business to his children: Hazel was one of seven beneficiaries, along with Arthur, Hedley, Nelly, Rene, Eric and Doris. Growth and development was taking place in the suburbs, where towns and cities expanded at an incredible rate. However, the business was not centred exclusively on projects in London, and Sloman's company also built properties as far north as Ely. Peter remembers that his grandfather had built and developed houses in Westcliff:

My grandfather's firm built properties locally on the esplanade at Westcliff, as well as in Southend. We were living fairly close to them, in a row of houses that he had built. There was a large detached house, followed by two bungalows where one of my uncles lived. Adjoining these was Newenden, a semi-detached house that I grew up in. In the other half lived one of my aunts who stayed while her husband was alive but when he died, she let the property out. A bungalow followed Newenden, tacked on to the end.

When Samuel and Hazel were married, Tom had given each of his children a house that he had built – together with a piano. So about seven houses at the bottom of Southbourne Grove had been built by Sloman and now belonged to members of the family.

Having retreated from the hubbub of London for the weekend, Sloman enjoyed the peace and surroundings that were afforded to him by Haslemere. It must have been impressive: a large detached house that required six members of staff to run it successfully. Peter remembers that there were three housemaids and perhaps three gardeners, necessary to maintain the manicured five-acre garden.

For the children, Haslemere was an Aladdin's Cave: a cornucopia of rooms to explore, lawns to play on and places to act in. There were the huge greenhouses where the whole family spent much of their time together, with croquet and bowls played on the lawn. It really was a wonderful house for the children and all of them retain happy memories of their time there.

Sloman had a penchant for cars, so much so that he acquired three, an indication of how profitable his company had become in an age when most families could just about afford one. His favourite was a maroon Sunbeam with a black sunroof. Peter remembers that Sunbeam cars ranked alongside Rolls-Royce as the first choice in opulence and elegance. His next car, an Austin, was used by Doris, Hazel's youngest sister who lived with her parents, while his third was a little Austin Seven which his aunt used as a runabout, whistling into and around town. Sloman's wife Agnes, the children's grandmother, was kind, generous and benevolent. She helped voluntary organisations, including the WI, contributing whatever she could, whenever she could. An example of her charitable nature was her support in assisting a small group of Belgians who had arrived in Britain during the First World War. Perhaps they had fled from persecution, but whatever the reason, Agnes made sure that they well catered for with provisions and accommodation.

By all accounts, Sloman was indeed a busy man. In addition to the running of his business, he was a Freemason, connected to a variety of lodges, including the Royal Lodge, but because of his various activities there were compromises. He was frequently away from Agnes, living in London during the week and returning to Westcliff for the weekends. As the years wore on, the visits to Westcliff became less frequent: he lived with Agnes's niece in Wimbledon. This was something which Agnes never truly came to terms with, but she eventually grew to tolerate her husband's absence. She was not the sort of lady to let the grass grow under her feet, however. It would be fair to say that she made the most out of life, putting her focus into helping voluntary organisations; she became a woman Freemason and she took cruises, regularly travelling abroad. She made sure that her husband looked after her financially and she found a companion who cared for her and drove her everywhere. Right up to her death in 1939 Agnes resented the fact that her husband had been duplicitous. Tom married Agnes's niece but died a year later.

Every Sunday teatime, the entire Sloman family, including aunts and uncles, descended upon Haslemere on the corner of

Southbourne Grove to the delight of their grandparents. It was a family ritual that, despite the modernity of the age, seems rather Victorian. After tea, the men retired to the billiard room, where there was a full-sized table with benches along the side, and they remained there for the rest of the evening. As Tom, Peter and Jack grew older, they made good use of the table. Agnes was a great card-player and especially fond of patience. She was also very good at needlework, and Peter remembers her creating some marvellous patterns. Everyone took it in turns to provide a little entertainment at these family gatherings, but he recalls his uncle and aunt, Arthur and Rene, being excellent singers who often took part in Westcliff amateur operatic society shows. Arthur had a pleasant tenor voice which he put to good use by singing arias and popular songs at various public functions, trying to amuse the rest of the family as he stood with Hazel who accompanied him on the pianola. Peter, Jack and Peg would all try and hammer out something on this pianola, squabbling and arguing. Consequently, it took quite a battering. Eventually, Agnes got fed up with them and told them to do something else.

One of Peter's earliest recollections is also an indication of his spirited childhood. His twin brother and sister were then eighteen months old and Peter was about three or four, on a visit to their grandparents one Sunday afternoon. Samuel and Hazel had a huge pram that had two hoods, one at either end. Jack had been positioned under one hood, Peg at the other and Peter had been plonked in the middle. Peter has often been reminded about this incident when Jack and Peg were screaming their heads off and, as he says, he was getting an earful from each side. In due course, he got fed up with this and decided to put an end to it. 'Shaddup!' he bellowed, and suddenly a fist flashed out towards each side of the hood. He can't remember whether that was enough to stop them, but it was an early indication that he could diffuse a situation with his fists if provoked. It was not to be the last time. Early recollections of his siblings are understandably sketchy, but Peter remembers that Tom was a model child – seen but never heard. Peter says Tom was far more academic than he and sailed through his matriculation, school exams and sixth form before joining the National Provincial bank in the City. He can never recall Jack and Peg misbehaving either, probably because they were too young to take him on.

In bringing up four children, Hazel must have looked back to her days of teaching at Methwold with great satisfaction, drawing upon her experience in teaching. She subsequently employed at home the same invaluable techniques as she had used in the classroom.

The atmosphere at Newenden was consequently less that of a home on occasions and more that of a school. Hazel was a matriarchal figure, insisting on absolute perfect manners when it came to the dinner table. Peter can testify that it was very hard to pull the wool over her eyes, especially when things became rowdy. In his words, he used to 'bugger about a bit'. He was quite fiery, constantly restless – the spirit of youth – wanting to get up and go exploring somewhere.

The Ayersts had a huge dining table at home, where their mother sat at the top and Samuel at the other end, with the children on each side. Peter was always placed next to Hazel so that she could keep a beady eye on him, and he was within striking distance if he did decide to misbehave. Behind her seat was an old-fashioned bookcase where a small penny cane hung. Hazel could easily reach behind and grab the cane, if she needed to. Peter thinks he must have been 'buggering about' when he heard the familiar, stern schoolteacher-voice of his mother and knew what to expect. The cane had been removed from the bookcase. 'Hands, Peter!' He lifted his hands slowly, gingerly, in front of him, so that the backs rested on the edge of the table. Before he knew it, there was an almighty WHACK! A little chastened, with his fingers smarting, he would try to pick up his knife and fork. 'Now you behave yourself!' Hazel said. And Peter did – for ten minutes.

Hazel was the eldest of seven children. Her second brother,

Hedley, married his Irish bride Esther in 1924, and the Ayersts were naturally invited to their wedding. Peter was given the role of pageboy. The ceremony had come and gone, and everyone was now attending the reception, a well-to-do affair where the guests sat respectfully at their respective tables. The main course had come and gone and the dessert, consisting of ice-cream, had just been served. There was a contented, quiet, civil atmosphere as Hedley, Esther and assorted guests consumed the latter part of the meal.

The official role and function of a pageboy is described as a youth in attendance at official functions or ceremonies, employed to run errands or carry messages. Quite conscientiously as a pageboy, Peter warmed to his task. He had a message of his own to carry. Shattering the atmosphere, he broke the silence by proclaiming in a loud voice from his seat: 'I like *my* ice-cream hot!' Quite where he got the notion of warm ice-cream no one really discovered, but aunts in particular took a shine to him – possibly because of his notions concerning warm ice-cream, but more probably owing to the fact that he had so much energy and vitality; he was the Ayerst with bags of character. It was his unique drive, determination and independent spirit that set him apart. Whereas Tom was academically diligent and the twins were still finding their own way in life, Peter was filling the role of the wild one. He was evidence that the second child in many families tends to have a little more personality and character.

Tom, Peter and Jack were sent to Chalkwell Hall School, Westcliff. Here, for the first time, they came across elements of life that were far from happy. Some of the boys were pretty rough, their clothes matching their surly, dishevelled characters. It was all a far cry from Peter's happy childhood, but the brothers took an entrance exam and all of them went to the grammar school. He met a lifelong friend, Alan 'Beefy' Byfield, who lived just around the corner from Southbourne Grove. Alan recalls Peter spending many hours at the Byfields' house in Cardigan Avenue, where Alan's mother treated him like a second son. He thinks Peter often visited Cardigan Avenue because it provided a welcome relief from Hazel's strict regimen of discipline. On their way to school together, Alan and Peter used to meet a third friend, Jim Crowe, who would wait for them at the bottom of the road; but Peter and Alan complemented each other. Alan remembers that Peter was the type of bloke he wanted to be with; Peter had the character he wanted to be: independent and aggressive. In Alan's words, he was a milder version of Peter. He could be aggressive too but he lacked the ruthless drive. The pair joined the local Cub pack; their reputation began to spread. Alan recalls a Girl Guide camp taking place one summer on the Isle of Wight. Two Cubs could join the girls' camp but only if they were under twelve years old, limiting the possibility of any 'interest' between the girls and boys. Peter and Alan immediately put their hands up. 'No, not you two!' said Brown Owl.

In 1931, Peter and Alan passed their eleven plus exams and went to Westcliff High School for Boys, following in Tom's footsteps. The building was in the form of two quadrangles, with the headmaster's study, gym and classrooms overlooking a small grass courtyard. Here Peter had the opportunity to channel his temperament positively, developing his character and his interests. In keeping with many of the best fighter pilots of the Second World War, Peter excelled in activities that took place outside the classroom. In his words, he did not set the academic world alight: 'I just couldn't stand some lessons that seemed to go on endlessly. Another example I suppose, of not being able to sit still. I hated Latin; I could never get on with that. I didn't mind straight maths or trigonometry or, for that matter, French.' As he says, you can't win 'em all! But he loved PE. Tom recalls he was very good at sport. The gym and the field were where Peter grasped the chance to use his restlessness constructively, exhausting his tireless reserves of energy.

In many ways, Westcliff was just right for him. He got his school colours at both rugby as a centre three-quarter and athletics. Much of Peter's achievement must be due to the influence of the headmaster, Billy Williams, who himself had been a rugby international player for Wales.

Peter always thought Westcliff had the edge over Southend High School; in fact, Southend wasn't a patch on Westcliff. Southend played soccer but Westcliff played rugby.

It wasn't only Billy Williams who influenced Peter on the rugby field. The gym master, Harry Crabtree, was also an excellent all-rounder at sport. He played rugby for Richmond, then one of the largest and best rugby clubs in the country, and for the Eastern Counties as well as the Barbarians and a trial for England. He was also a fantastic gymnast, having trained in Denmark which, in the 1930s, was considered the home of gymnastics.

However, the gymnastics at Westcliff High fared somewhat differently. Lessons could best be euphemistically described as 'character-building.' When the boys were in the gym at Westcliff, they wore shorts and plimsoles but never tops.

Harry also kept a cricket bat. In addition to rugby and gymnastics he was also a good cricketer, having played for Essex and the MCC at Lords. Harry used this bat to good effect on the pupils if they were slow or had done something stupid around the gym.

Peter remembers one incident in the gym:

I must have been slow, or done something stupid on one occasion. I knew what was going to happen. First, there would be the summons. 'Come here, Ayerst!' The slow humiliation of having to traipse over to him in front of all the others had begun, followed by the anticipation as he'd tell you to bend over and finally the pain emanating from your cheeks as the bat made sound contact. It certainly made you try harder the next time. Harry wouldn't have got away with it today, of course.

Alan also remembers Crabtree brandishing the cricket bat, especially on Mondays: 'Now boys, who played for the Junior XV on Saturday?' A few hands went up. 'What was the score?'

'Oh Sir, we lost, 15–3.'

'What's three from fifteen?'

'Twelve, Sir.'

'Right! Bend over!'

It had the desired effect. Alan says the team never lost a game afterwards.

For all his questionable methods of motivation, however, Crabtree was a great rugby coach, and Westcliff built a solid reputation when it came to playing other schools. He wasn't present at his team's victories as he was busy playing for Richmond, but Peter and the others in the team travelled to London on the school bus on Saturday afternoons, playing various sides – and, as he says, beat everyone along the way. Colchester Royal Grammar School, who were supposed to be good themselves, were 'stuffed'. The list of losers grew, as did the reputation of Peter's team: Chelmsford, Wanstead County High, Tottenham High – they beat them all. Peter was also good at athletics, especially the 100-yard sprints and the 220 yards, becoming school junior champion at fourteen, winning the cup for the high jump, long jump, putting the weight, javelin and sprints as well as the 440 yards.

Peter's prowess at sports must have been particularly difficult for Hazel. Having sent Peg to St Bernard's Convent, and with her strict teaching background, she thought Peter should have done better at his studies and follow in the steps of his elder brother. The boundless energy that Peter possessed was still in abundance once the school day had finished. Hazel had hoped that he would spend his evenings studying hard indoors, but Peter found it monotonous with three, perhaps four, hours of homework each night. All he wanted to do – and often did – was get out and about. Almost always, he'd bump into his mother when he returned from some extracurricular excursion. If Hazel guessed where he had been, she never let on:

'Where have you been today?'

'Oh, 15 miles away. Cycling on the river, by the coast.'

'You've been WHERE?' Hazel said in surprise. 'Oh Peter, you really must learn to concentrate on your studies.'

He had a bicycle which he used to good effect by travelling for miles, north of Westcliff through Rochford and the village of Ballards Gore, heading for a little creek that met the River Crouch, opposite Burnham-on-Crouch. It was known then as Creeksea, and it was here that he would go exploring to his heart's content. Sometimes he headed eastwards towards Foulness Island, where his grandfather owned land on which a large shoot would be organised. Eventually this land was to be requisitioned by the Army for a very different and much larger shooting party! When Peter was allowed to attend Sloman's shoots, he collected rabbits and the odd game bird and carried these home, where his mother made a stew. Out of all of the children, Peter admits that he was probably the one who caused Hazel more than a few headaches.

Hazel was also academically intellectual. In addition to making sure that the children were brought up well, she tried to help them all with their homework. Jack says that he was terrible with his, especially maths. He just couldn't understand algebra and geometry so he was quite happy to write down the first thing that came to him, as any pupil would. Hazel, on the other hand, knowing and understanding the intricacies of algebra and geometry, got to grips with his homework and insisted that he fill in the correct answers. Jack often gave up, leaving Hazel to complete his homework for him. Hazel's commitment to her children's homework is borne out when during one Easter term at Westcliff the maths master, Jasper Woods, having marked the class's papers, noticed that Jack had done especially well; normally he was to be found in the bottom two. 'Ayerst,' he roared, 'your mother's come third this term!' Incidentally, Woods was also responsible for giving Alan his nickname of 'Beefy' on his second day in form 2A. Woods looked at Alan, who was especially large for his size, and the name has stuck ever since.

Alan says if you wanted to find Peter, he was often standing outside the headmaster's study, waiting to be punished for some misdemeanour. His streak of independence flourished. One day Peter was told by Billy Williams to hold out his hand flat and wait for the cane. Just as Williams brought down the cane, Peter whipped his hand away and the cane crashed downwards, hitting the headmaster on the thigh. Alan also remembers that they only ever had one fight. Peter was a good boxer and reached out towards Alan with his fists. Alan knew nothing about boxing and dived towards Peter's legs, preferring to bite his ankle, another indication that Peter could defend himself if necessary.

Much of Peter's energy and time was diverted from the track and rugby field by a neighbour, Tony Bunker, who became his friend. The Bunker family had six children – Roger, Joan, Peter, Pauline, John and finally Tony. Mr Bunker, who reminded Jack of Charlie Chaplin because he was small with a moustache, ran a printing firm in Southend. Mrs Bunker was a big, fat, jovial, kind lady. The eldest son, Roger, ran a successful stamp shop in an arcade in Southend. Eventually, he joined the RAF to fly Hurricanes. He was posted to Norway in 1940 as a member of No. 46 Squadron, where he was to join HMS *Glorious*. It may have been coincidence but Peter was to become closely involved with the same squadron and the *Glorious* a few years later . . .

Tom dated Joan Bunker for a while. Alan refers to Tony as crazy because he loved to ride his bike into the sea. Peter and Tony cycled everywhere, often heading for the Essex coastline, anywhere outside Westcliff.

Peter, Alan and Tony also showed their resourceful streak in a more cerebral form of Knockdown Ginger. Why knock on one house door when you can go for two, they thought? They tied a piece of string to the knocker of one door in Southbourne Grove, then marched across the street where they tied the other end of the string to a knocker of a house on the other side. Standing in the middle of the road, they pulled the centre of the string so that both knockers were raised. Poised in readiness, they let go so that both knockers firmly and loudly rapped on each door. Hurriedly, they made their escape – to see both homeowners standing at each respective front door trying to work out what had happened. Trying to work out who had perpetrated the incident was often much easier! Soon girls began to play a part. Alan says that his friend could never be described as a womaniser but he did see a young lady, Bobbie Fellowes, for a short time. Before long, her father called him in and told him to stop it. Whatever 'it' was, we don't know, but Alan is certain it wasn't much because Peter was more interested in sports.

There used to be a huge orchard full of apples and plums between Haslemere and the Ayersts' house, acres and acres with a long hedge surrounding it. When evening fell, Peter, Jack and Peg crept out of the house and stole into the orchard, where they proceeded to make themselves sick by eating too many plums. Tony and Peter bored their way through the hedge and often went scrumping – carefully putting their trophies inside their shirts – and came back by the same hole in the hedge. Because the hedge was so vast, the pair had been resourceful – they had made a nookery, a hideaway where no one would find them, and they used to spend the rest of the day eating the sweet apples and donating the sour ones to the birds! They were chased by someone one day but didn't get caught. Perhaps it was Harry Crabtree with his cricket bat! Peter has his athletics to thank for their swift escape.

For about six weeks during the years leading up to the war the family rented two huts on the beach at Thorpe Bay. Their Uncle Hedley and Auntie Esther rented a hut a couple of doors further along, where Esther made and brought wonderful apple pies. Aunt Doris, who was now dating Ron Cockburn, a relation of the Port shipping family, lived not far away. The children, now late adolescents, spent all day every day on the beach. Twenty, maybe thirty, people took part in huge cricket and rounders parties held on the sand that caught the attention of passers-by on the promenade, who cheered when the tennis ball was hit high into the air. Jack and Peg, then sixteen, had great fun at these parties.

Uncle Hedley helped Peter to build a canoe. The restless spirit of his youth was now turning into stubborn impatience and aggression, with a strong, deeply independent trait, which was borne out when Tom was swimming in the bay, head down, unable to see who or what was coming. Paddling in his canoe, Peter was unaware of Tom in the water, with the result that swimmer and canoe collided. Tom cut his eye and was promptly rushed to hospital.

All good things come to an end, and so it was for Peter at Westcliff High School. He had failed his matriculation and had not pursued taking his higher qualifications, knowing it was all rather futile. He knew he was not cut out to be an academic like his brother Tom. To him, there was little point struggling for his Highers. The realities of work were calling, and at seventeen he followed his elder brother, who was already working in the City, and went to work for a shipping company. He had a very junior role at W.A. Sparrow & Sons, 14 St Mary Axe, right in the heart of the City, and commuted for about eighteen months. The company consisted of about forty people dealing with the export of goods to Britain's Empire countries – Africa, Rhodesia, South Africa, Australia and New Zealand. Peter started by producing invoices, and it was here that he learnt his two-finger typing. He spent some time in the shipping department dealing with matters concerning shipping insurance, looking after bills of lading. Mr Ellis, the managing director, was kind to him – probably, Peter thinks, because the eldest of his two sons, Stuart, was the same age and Mr Ellis realised Peter might be a good friend for his son. As Peter says, the two got on like a house on fire. Working for W.A. Sparrow was to stand Peter in good stead later on in his flying career because it gave him a taste of the real world. According to Peter, 'I had had some work experience, so I was more worldly than some who had joined the Air Force straight out of school. At least when I joined, I wasn't totally bloody green.'

When asked what got them interested in flying, most fighter pilots of the Second World War state that once they witnessed the beauty, majesty and sheer power of an aeroplane in flight for the first time, they didn't want to do anything else; for them, there was only one thing in the world to do and that was to fly. Unusually for an up-and-coming fighter pilot ace, although he was interested in watching the aircraft take off and land from Southend aerodrome, Peter at this stage certainly hadn't thought about flying as a career. The change in Peter's life was due to a family friend, Don Wallace, who, with his older brother, visited the Ayersts' house regularly on Sunday mornings. It was a lively affair: darts were thrown and beers consumed. Wallace was a private pilot and he had learned to fly at Southend in the mid- to late thirties. Having acquired a private pilot's licence, he decided to continue his flying training with a B licence, which entitled him to fly commercially. Wallace was a couple of years older than Peter. They got talking over a game of darts: 'Come flying with me, Pete. Come down to Southend.' Peter's first-ever flight was in an old Avro biplane with a radial engine. After fifteen minutes, Wallace shouted to Peter via the intercom tube: 'Right! Let's do a loop!' The ancient Avro aeroplane circled over the Essex countryside. The flight lasted no more than thirty minutes, but in that time Peter was hooked. After that, Peter flew with Wallace as often as he could, usually at weekends. His interest in flying developed.

Holding a commercial licence, Wallace took passengers up on pleasure flights at nearby Romford. Peter assisted him by taking their money, helping them into the spare seat and strapping them in securely and he became a regular fixture at Romford aerodrome when the weather was fine. He loved it. This, he says, was when he first got the bug for flying. What was it that hooked him? In his words, it was the whole thing – the exhilaration, anticipation and sheer thrill of flying. It was a unique experience and it enveloped him to the extent that he knew this was what he wanted to do with his life.

He realised that neither he nor his parents had the revenue to pay for flights privately – as Wallace had done – but he came to the conclusion that one door was open to him: fly with the

Royal Air Force. If he was commissioned into the service, they would pay for his training. He therefore applied for a short-service commission, in June 1938, and was asked to attend an Air Ministry interview at Adastral House in Kingsway. He arrived for his initial medical; only those candidates who passed their medical went on to the next stage of the interview. Those who suffered from colour blindness, bad eyesight or high blood pressure would fail the medical and be told they would not be required to attend the interview. Peter went before a formidable-looking board of five men in civilian suits who asked him a number of direct and intimidating questions which he answered as best he could. Two weeks later he received a letter informing him that he had been accepted. He was asked to report to No. 19 Elementary and Reserve Flying Training School at Gatwick.

Britain's young men and women were being called up to join the services. It was time to fight for their country. Among hundreds of thousands of others, the Ayerst family did their bit. Tom had originally joined the Territorial Army before war had been declared but subsequently joined the RAF, ending up in the Fleet Air Arm, where he got a commission to Airfield Control. Later on, Jack joined the army and Peg joined the WAAF.

The twins agree that during their early days it was Peter who had the drive in the family – a determined, restless, independent spirit of youth that spurred him on. Much of this spirit was an influence from Hazel, who was broadly similar in character – firm, strong-minded and unwavering. It was a spirit that was to serve him well throughout his life.

TWO

Best Days of Your Life

6 OCTOBER 1938

Autumn had arrived. The air was clean and crisp with a biting snap. The leaves were turning to various shades of brown, russet and scarlet red. The seasons were changing once more and the onset of a cold, dark winter loomed. It threatened to be cold, dark and long in more ways than one. These were times during which the Royal Air Force had been forced to modernise because of the storm clouds of war that had been ever-present for the past three years. In accordance with the preparations pioneered by the soon-to-be Commander-in-Chief of Fighter Command, Hugh Dowding, who had pushed ahead the plans adopted hastily by the Air Defence of Great Britain in 1936, a grim acceptance and subsequent alacrity had been adopted by the RAF. Everything concerning the logistics, support and welfare of the Air Force was quickly stepped up in preparation for any German threat. The increase in aircraft production, radio direction finding (or radar as it became known) and airfields was rushed ahead. Plans to increase personnel, both ground- and aircrew, for fighters were essential to Dowding's plans. Elementary and advanced courses at training schools were no exception. Such aircrew courses were implemented hastily throughout 1938 and 1939, and this in turn required more resources, the building of more accommodation and the addition of new airfields around the country.

The date of 6 October 1938 was Peter's first day of his *ab initio* elementary pilot training course at one of the civil

21

airfields that had recently been requisitioned by the RAF. The grass airfield, located on the county border between Surrey and Sussex, had been known as Gatwick; it was now known as RAF Gatwick. Peter was one of twenty-two other young, green aviators about to embark on a brand-new RAF training course, which was held at a new location, flying brand-new aircraft. No. 19 Elementary and Reserve Flying Training School (E&RFTS) was the first course ever to be established at this new location. When he first arrived there on that autumnal day, Gatwick was anything but a bustling hive of activity; there had been just three scheduled flights operated by civil airlines per week. During his time there, the RAF shared flying facilties with the civil aviation authorities. A few ancient training aircraft with RAF markings were scattered about: several Hawker Harts belonging to the RAF Volunteer Reserve along with a few de Havilland Tiger Moths that were particularly popular at the weekend. The Volunteer Reserve had already stamped their authority on this quiet, civil aerodrome by flying would-be part-time pilots at the weekends. This was enough for the RAF authorities to establish a full-time elementary course for regular pilots.

The course was significant because, in addition to its new status, Peter was going to fly new training aircraft that were the first monoplane trainers used by the RAF for elementary training. They were built by the Miles company at Woodley, near Reading and were officially called M 14 Magisters. The pupil pilots called them Maggies. The Magisters were important because they had dual controls, ideal for training. Moreover, they were monoplanes, a relatively new concept in RAF training circles. They were, in essence, similar to the Tiger Moth biplanes which the RAF had used previously – without the upper wing. It was a revolution in training terms. The first Magisters were delivered to the training schools in 1938.

Eighteen-year-old Plt Off Ayerst arrived at Gatwick around mid-morning from London Victoria railway station and reported straight for duty. The rail service had been direct to Gatwick from

London. Little was he to know that by 2 p.m. that day he would be on his first training flight at 4,000ft in a Magister. His feet hadn't touched the ground – he hadn't even been to see his lodgings! No. 19 Elementary course was overseen by the Chief Flying Instructor, A. Kingwill, who had had a successful career in the RAF. He was responsible for a total of five instructors at Gatwick, all of whom had volunteered for the post after having completed their short-service commissions and were accountable to the Chief Instructor, A.D. Bennett.

Peter discovered that the key to learning the art of flying lies in a good instructor. The instructors at Gatwick came in all shapes and sizes, with a variety of characters and personalities to match. There were those who believed the best way to get the most out of their pupils was by adopting an easygoing and mild-mannered approach, praising their pupils when they could, letting the pupil relax with the aircraft accordingly. There were those who believed that all this was stuff and nonsense; the only way to teach a pupil the harsh realities of flying was to send the pupil up in the cockpit as soon as possible. If pupils were unlucky enough to have this type as their instructor, they soon found that no matter how hard they tried in their flying, they could never please or satisfy them. Who taught you was in the hands of the Gods.

Peter was fortunate. He was paired with a particularly efficient and effective instructor by the name of Flt Lt Burnett, a very competent and experienced pilot. Peter liked him; Burnett was a 'hell of a nice chap'. About thirty years in age and, like Peter, on a short-service commission, Flt Lt Burnett took a serious approach to flying and the art of instructing pupils: not for him the school of harsh realities. Burnett was to be Peter's instructor for the duration of the course at Gatwick until mid-December. In the space of ten weeks or thereabouts, Peter was to complete about fifty hours' worth of flying. Considering the conditions at this time of the year, short days, the increase in wet and windy weather, combined with his lack of flying, the fact that Peter managed to put in as many hours as he did was in no small part due to Flt Lt Burnett. This experience provided Peter with a solid flying platform on which to improve and build upon his skills. That he flew so many hours at such a crucial period in his training must be one of the factors in his ability to survive so many operational missions. Peter considers that the training given by the RAF was the best in the world. For him, it gave young, green pilots a high standard of confidence when flying, high standards in liaising with others, as well as high standards from their kit.

Twenty-two other pilots were also taking their *ab initio* flights alongside Peter in the autumn of 1938. They were in their late teens and early twenties. They were looking for fun and excitement, for girls and good times. Yes, they were aware of a German threat that could have implications on their lives, but that wasn't going to get in the way of making the most out of life – while they still could.

Their backgrounds were broadly similar to Peter's in the sense that they came from financially comfortable families. Pupils came to Gatwick from all over the world, bringing diverse characters and varied opinions. All of them had to adapt to and adopt service life as quickly as possible. Peter recalls they were quite a good crowd and they all got on pretty well: Buchanan, who came from a baronial family in Ireland; Charles Green, a Rhodesian who became a group captain; Walker, a Canadian; Ron Woods, who shared digs with Peter in Crawley; Derek Sheed; Nolan Neylan; Talbot 'Tolly' Rothwell, who became a prisoner of war and afterwards a TV producer; Victor Penney, a rogue if ever there was one, with a hell of a loud laugh, constantly borrowing money; Derek Forde; Jack Shaw, with whom Peter became very friendly. Three or four of the twenty-two pilots were LACs: leading aircraftmen, who had transferred to Peter's course. Although officially in the RAF, these LACs still dressed in civilian clothes but had been selected for aircrew training.

Generally, Peter thinks that all the boys behaved themselves because they were all new to the service and wanted to show to Kingwill, Bennett *et al* that they were worth the money the RAF had been spending on them. Although the Royal Air Force had spent time and money on their training, it did not wish to spend hundreds of pounds on uniforms for pupils only to discover that they did not pass their flying and theory examinations and were consequently asked to leave. Peter and his colleagues wore civilian clothing during their time at Gatwick, which acted as a sobering reminder that they were not part of the RAF quite yet; it was very much touch and go as to whether they would succeed in making the grade.

There were no facilities or resources for accommodation on the airfield. Accordingly, the pupil pilots were billeted in and around nearby towns, namely Crawley and Horley. Most pilots managed to find digs in Crawley.

Peter was allocated accommodation with fellow pupil Ron Woods. He and Woods walked to the railway station at Crawley, which was five minutes from their digs, to get on a train and travel the short journey to Three Bridges. They changed there for the train service to Gatwick station, which had been designated a mainline station because it was hoped that the airfield nearby would develop commercially with facilities for civil airliners that would otherwise have had to resort to flying from Croydon in the early 1930s.

Familiarisation Flight – 6 October

The afternoon of 6 October presented Peter with his first flight in a Magister, his first time in the RAF's first monoplane trainer. The lightweight de Havilland Gipsy Major engine began to purr as Flt Lt Burnett pressed the magnetos and the two-bladed wooden propeller started to rotate, faster and faster, ending in a blur. Instructor and pilot, safely strapped in, taxied over the green grass of the small Gatwick airfield. The yellow aircraft paused for a second before Flt Lt Burnett pushed the throttles forward and the gentle purr from the Gipsy Major turned into a roar. The Magister accelerated until 200yds later it was airborne.

Burnett gave Peter a few minutes to take the scene in, the airfield below them, the greens and browns of the autumn countryside. The flight was relatively low-key, lasting no more than twenty-five minutes in the air; Flt Lt Burnett aimed to familiarise Peter with the sensation of flying in the Maggie; it was nothing more than experience in the air. Burnett demonstrated what happened to the Magister if he pushed the joystick forward or back, left or right. Because the Magister was equipped with dual controls, Peter could follow what was happening to the stick. 'Take hold of the controls!' Burnett shouted. Peter took hold of the controls. He was able to appreciate just what an aircraft like this could actually do. This monoplane was new, sleek and seemed exceptionally fast for its time. The odd flight he had made in his friend's aircraft was nothing compared to this. At half past two that October afternoon, Flt Lt Burnett had brought the Magister back to earth and taxied in. Instructor and pupil clambered out of the little trainer. His first flight with the RAF had been completed and he was exhilarated though not overwhelmed. Not a bad life for an eighteen-year-old, Plt Off Ayerst thought. The first step in a career that was to last thirty-five years had just begun.

No. 19 E&FTS Course was divided into two – 'A' Flight and 'B' Flight. Daily routine depended on which Flight pupils were posted. If, for example, pupils were posted to 'A' Flight, they could expect to fly in the morning, weather permitting, and then after lunch attend study lectures on theory in the classroom. For pupils in 'B' Flight, the roles would be reversed. Theory and the classroom took place in the morning, while after lunch – if the weather held – they could squeeze in some flying in the afternoon. The focal point of the No. 19 Elementary Course was a building known as 'The Beehive' because of its unusual art deco, dome-like structure consisting of several annexes protruding out from where airliners docked, allowing passengers to board and alight. It was here that the pupils shared the Hive with the remaining civil operators who still operated from Gatwick in the days before the war. The

RAF used the space for almost all of its requirements: lecture rooms; flight offices where flying kit was kept in lockers; a dining room where the pupils ate very good food; along with a mess-room or anteroom which was comfortable. It really was a beehive of activity, with the civil Tiger Moths working in conjunction with the RAF's Magisters, and the odd Hawker Hart buzzing over the Surrey/Sussex countryside.

When the course had finished for the day, Peter and Woods would jump on the train bound for Three Bridges, changing there for Crawley. As their digs were less than five minutes from the centre of Crawley and as they were teenagers enjoying the best days of their lives, the pair would cross the level-crossing close to the station and head towards the town, where they had found a lovely pub. Peter recalls it was a very comfortable place with a good bar where they often stayed to have a beer or two. Once they had finished, he and Woods would return over the level-crossing towards their digs. About half-way between the level-crossing and their digs was a very pleasant little restaurant built in the style of a country cottage. It served excellent food and the boys would stay there, chatting to the people who ran it and eventually getting to know the owners quite well. Once back in their digs, it would be time for them to knuckle down to their studies. Peter freely admits there were times when he found it very difficult to concentrate – he was not a born academic – but he, Woods and the rest of the pupils on the course were fully aware of the consequences if they failed. None of the boys relished the prospect of being kicked off the course; the incentive to pass was clear. During the ten weeks of No. 19 E&RFTS, Peter found time to meet his brother Jack. Together with a couple of other pilots from the course and an old friend, Doug Kearey, Jack recalls them eagerly climbing into Kearey's car and making a beeline for Brighton, where all four spent the day ice-skating.

Over the next eight days, Flt Lt Burnett took Peter through the art of stalling, climbing and gliding in addition to straight and level flying. By his third flight, Burnett was demonstrating the finer points of aerobatics, putting the aeroplane into a number of spins. There were medium turns, with and without engine; taxiing and handling the engine; approaches and landings; taking off into wind; emergency action in the event of fire – including stopping and starting the engine in the air. This was pretty nerve-wracking because Peter found that he had to put the Maggie into a dive, pull back on the stick and switch the magnetos off, then switch them on again and push the stick forward, so the pilot sensed that the aircraft was picking up speed, hoping all the while that the airscrew automatically started. All in all, it was pretty risky. As a fledgling pilot, Peter learnt that he really had to concentrate hard on these manoeuvres because it was down to him to get the instructor, the aircraft and himself back in one piece.

There was another manoeuvre that all the pupils had to learn and master in detail – spins.

This was essential training for any pilot, especially in the Magisters. The first production batch of Magister aircraft to leave the Miles factory had design flaws. If an instructor and pilot were unlucky enough to go into a spin, it would be almost impossible to recover. Proof of this came in the loss of several from the first production batch, with two fatal accidents. As a consequence, the designers at Miles redesigned the whole of the empennage by extending the tailplane and heightening the fin and rudder, as well as increasing the control surfaces. As production of the Miles M 14As went ahead, there were no reports of any spinning accidents.

It was the redesigned M 14A Magister that Peter, Woods and the others were flying at Gatwick.

The history of the aircraft was no secret to them; they were told in no uncertain terms about the Magister's chequered past. It may well have been the folly or pride of youth, but Peter recalls that none of them was worried. The errors had been rectified, and in any case, Bennet, Burnett and the rest of the instructors had flown and spun them. As the instructors were still in one piece and continued to fly the aircraft, it was taken as evidence that nothing untoward would happen.

It was on 14 October that Flt Lt Burnett took Peter off for his first spin. He pulled back on the stick so that all he could see was sky and cloud, then let the aircraft nose fall into a stall. The forces of gravity were pulling them towards the earth. 'Don't forget what I told you,' shouted Burnett, 'if you push your feet to the left of the rudder bar, the plane will spin to the left; if you push them to the right, the plane will move in the opposite direction.' Peter pushed the stick back, remembering what Burnett had told him. They were suddenly going round and round, hurtling towards the earth, at an alarming speed . . . Peter could just make out Burnett's voice: 'Right! Recover the plane! Push the stick forward and move your feet quickly over to the opposite direction.' The rudder shifted accordingly. The plane recovered from the spin. Burnett then told Peter to centralise the rudder, easing back on the stick. Peter did as he was told. He felt that his first spin had gone pretty well.

By 21 October, Peter had clocked up about twelve hours' dual instruction and his instructor felt that he had enough hours in the air to make his first solo flight. It lasted ten minutes. Burnett briefed him on a circuit that he wanted Peter to stick to: 'This'll be quite simple! All I want you to do is to take off, fly one circuit and come in, that's it. No more. Understand?'

'Just one circuit, sir?' Peter queried. 'Should I repeat the take-offs? I know that you place particular emphasis on the importance of a good take-off and landing.'

'No, just one. You've only flown twelve hours; you've got a long way to go! Right, away you go.' Wearing a Sidcot suit and leather flying helmet, Peter stayed in the cockpit while Burnett nimbly descended, the engine still ticking over. The butterflies in Peter's stomach flew off as he taxied over the grass field, focused on the job in hand. Just one circuit. He took off (just the once), covered the circuit and came back in again. All in all, it was rather uneventful, but he had achieved everything that Flt Lt Burnett had asked. As such, he had achieved his first solo. A few days later, he was back in the air concentrating on improving all aspects of his flying, working on techniques such as steep turns, side-slipping, more spins and more take-offs, followed by more landings. As Burnett had told him before his solo, he remembers practising a tedious number of take-offs, approaches and landings.

The pupils began to study more advanced aspects of the course, such as navigation, which led to numerous solo cross-country flights to other airfields. They were told to take off from Gatwick, putting into practise the navigational techniques they had learnt on the course. The instructors gave them a location where each pupil had to land. Once they had landed, they then took off again to fly over various landmarks, fields, towns and villages on to the next destination, where they were asked to land. They were to take off for a third time and fly to a final airfield before making their way back to Gatwick.

It was almost like an aerial join-the-dots exercise. Each pupil held the map in the direction they were heading and, with a bit of luck, they arrived at one pencil point. They'd pick up the next by holding the map in another direction until the next point, and so on. Every map was carefully folded by each pilot and they were stored in the trouser pockets of their flying suits. When the pilots needed the maps, they pulled them out and turned them over, which meant that each point automatically followed on from the last. This avoided the prospect of endeavouring to fly an aircraft while trying to make sense of finding a location on a map that was spilling out and covering the windscreen, which in any case would then inevitably have been buffeted away by the strong winds.

It was on one of these solo local cross-country flights that things didn't quite go according to plan for Peter. It took much for a young pilot to use his initiative with speed and a calm manner and get down in one piece, without losing his nerve. He had been airborne for some time on the final leg returning to Gatwick when all of a sudden, quite out of the blue, a carpet of fog descended rapidly over the Surrey and Sussex countryside. Not only was Peter flying through it, which is terrifying enough, but he had to try and land somewhere in the pea-souper, preferably keeping the aircraft, as well as himself, intact. This was his blind-flying test without much of a rehearsal. Magisters were built to be relatively simple aircraft – the only form of communication is a small tube running from the instructor's cockpit to the pupil's. As there were no radio or navigational aids and he was flying solo, the communication tube was somewhat redundant and Peter was very much alone. He flew around the airfield through the fog thinking desperately just how he could get the aircraft down in one piece. The fog seemed to be dissipating in patches, but not enough, he felt, to make a landing. The fog was still blanketing the grass airfield and he didn't want to make a prang.

There was no way in which he could make contact with his instructors, who should have been expecting him back around now. What Peter could not know was that the instructors had heard the drone of the Gipsy Major engine above them and they had calculated from the duration of the exercise that he should have been returning about now in any case. He could not see that they were actually below him, under the carpet of fog, waiting to see what he would do.

Peter made a decision. There was no way in which he could put the Magister down on the airfield at Gatwick. So what were the other options open to him? With amazing calmness for an eighteen-year-old, he began to think of the other airfields where the pupils had landed during their exercises: airfields that were in close proximity to Gatwick. He remembered there was an airstrip at Redhill. Heading due north for roughly three minutes, he made for the grass airfield south of Redhill. The fog was still dissipating . . . much more so than at Gatwick. He was very pleased, and not a little relieved, to see that the fog was now decreasing rapidly. As he approached the strip on final, landing the Magister, the fog cleared altogether, leaving perfect visibility.

Jumping out of the cockpit, Peter made a dash for the nearest telephone, wanting to inform his instructors that he was fine, the Magister was fine, in fact, everything was fine. He managed to get through and spoke to Flt Lt Burnett. 'I was getting a little concerned', Burnett said. 'All right, as soon as this damn fog clears, I'll take off and join you at Redhill. I want to make sure that you haven't damaged the Magister or yourself. Hold on!'

A little later, Peter heard the drone of another Gipsy Major engine as Burnett appeared out of the now-perfect sky. He waited until Burnett had landed and taxied close to his own aircraft. Burnett examined the aircraft carefully. 'Very good', he said after a while. 'You did the wise and sensible thing. We heard you buzzing about above us, but couldn't see you. When we heard your engine head towards Redhill, we thought something might be wrong. You took evasive action and did the next best thing. Well done, Ayerst.'

Burnett highlighted the foresight, decisive execution and level-headed approach Peter had taken when faced with making such an important judgement. The incident may well be another factor in piecing together just how Peter survived the war. Any fighter pilot requires firm resolve, determination and a cool head in the heat of battle. The spirit of the blue skies was developing rapidly.

The pupils were tasked with a number of these cross-country flights (fog-free!), which they had to successfully complete in order to strengthen their skills and pass their navigation examinations.

These examinations came in the form of flights as well as theory in the classroom. On 2 December, Peter was to be graded on a flight to Hamble, south-west of Southampton. He was briefed to land at Hamble, refuel and return to Gatwick. Taking off from the Beehive at 10 a.m. on a cold and chilly winter's morning, the Magister flew in a south-westerly direction. Fifty minutes later, Peter landed on the grass airfield close to the village that was located on a small peninsula jutting out into Southampton Water.

Cross-Country Test – 2 December 1938

The duty pilot for Hamble that day, one Goodfellow, was grading student pilots on their ability to land at the airfield. As far as Goodfellow was concerned, there could be only three types of landing, 'good', 'medium' or 'bad'. Goodfellow lived up to his name when he wrote in Peter's logbook that in his opinion, young Plt Off Ayerst had made a 'good' landing. It may have been the exhilaration of success, the relief of passing the examination or it may have been the cold wind snapping around Peter as he flew back, but it took rather less time to fly to Gatwick, taking the best part of thirty-five minutes. Perhaps he had been assisted by a tailwind.

In December these flights culminated in what was known as the RAF Test. This was it, the real thing. If the students passed the Test, they would be accepted for advanced training. It was the key to joining the RAF in toto; *per ardua ad astra*: through hardship to the stars. If pilots failed, well . . . Of course, the whole point of this Test was to see whether the student pilot could put into practice what he had been taught up to that stage. The Test was administered by regular senior officers, adding a heightened tension to the proceedings. Flt Lt Burnett and the other instructors could only watch and cross their fingers. One of these senior officers, a Flt Lt Lovell-Gregg, monitored the pilots throughout the Test. With his rakish moustache and even shorter clipped tones, Peter thought Lovell-Gregg seemed to exemplify everything a typical officer of the RAF aspired to. That morning, Lovell-Gregg was to be the students' judge and jury, watching them inscrutably for any sign of incompetence. The Test was to last for forty minutes, during which time the pilots were to demonstrate their ability in elementary flying.

That December morning seemed colder and chillier than the rest.

'Good Morning, Gentlemen.' Lovell-Gregg greeted them. 'For your test today, you will perform everything you have been taught by your instructors thus far and have continued in your solo flights. After your take-off, let's see how you're all getting on with climbing turns and steep turns, I want to see some spins and recovery, and put full power on and bring it round. Right, off you go!'

For Peter, those forty minutes literally flew by! He passed, of course. He was going to be a fully fledged member of the Royal Air Force, soon to be posted for advanced training, *per ardua ad astra* . . . Twenty-one of the student pilots passed the course of No. 19 E&RFTS at Gatwick in the autumn of 1938. One pilot had failed. It may be because the course took place sixty-five years ago, it may be Peter's gentlemanly conduct, but the name of the pupil who failed goes unrecalled.

The Royal Air Force continued to expand during the winter of 1938/39. Peace in their time continued for just a few more months. The expansion continued to grow all over the country, including the cold, grey flatlands of Lincolnshire. The modernisation programme took in the countryside around the market-town of Grantham, perching off the A1 trunk road. Grantham was to be the birthplace of No. 12 Flying Training School.

Peter had been on the first training course at Gatwick. He was also on the first advanced training course at Grantham. He was accompanied by the student pilots who had also succeeded in passing No. 19 E&RFTS at Gatwick. The location had changed but the characters Peter had come to know well had not. Charles Green, the Rhodesian, was still there, as was Buchanan from the Irish baronial family and Dalton, who had a dreadful stutter. The boys from Gatwick soon discovered that they were not the only pupils on the course. Other student pilots from a similar elementary flying course had travelled south from Prestwick airfield near Ayr. It was fitting that the pupils from Prestwick and the students from the south merged at an equidistant point in the country. There were forty pilots in total on the Advanced Flying Course at No. 12 FTS. Although the Gatwick group had arrived together, they were soon split up into different Flights, as at Gatwick. Peter, posted into 'A' Flight, soon got to know the pilots from Prestwick. There was MacDonald, who assured everyone that he didn't have a farm, and Tommy Balmforth with whom Peter immediately got on well because they shared a passion for rugby. Balmforth had been an excellent scrum-half, playing rugby for Headingley, and went on to play for the RAF. Others included Blair White, Spoole, Rivington, Johnson and Hook, who was a good laugh; John Hardacre, killed later on in the Battle of Britain; a couple of Canadians, Bill Ward and Walker; Iain Christie, and Johnny Bowring from the shipping family, whose father had been Lord Mayor of Liverpool and a gentleman amateur pilot, Cuffey King-Clarke.

Every one of these pilots had been initially selected to continue training on single-seat aircraft or switch to twin-engine training. Those who switched to twin engines got to grips with the Avro Anson. Peter reckons about two-thirds of the pilots at No. 12 FTS were selected for advanced training on the twin-engined Ansons, while the remaining third were selected for fighter training.

The pilots selected for training on the Ansons were usually posted to Bomber or Coastal Command. The remaining third, who were posted on to single-seaters, were expected to make the grade for Fighter Command. They were also expected to pass by flying brand-new Harvard aircraft that no one in England had actually flown before.

It was young men like Peter, in their late teens and early twenties, who were usually chosen for fighter aircraft. The pilots selected for twin-engine training were normally a little older; they were generally considered to be more stable in terms of character, being in their mid-twenties. Peter and the rest of the pupils selected for single-engine training were thought of as a little more cranky, a little more wayward. Peter was the second pupil on the course to fly a Harvard. Moreover, he was only the second pupil pilot in the entire country to fly a Harvard.

It helped to be a little cranky when it came to flying the North American Harvard. British industry had been totally unable to meet the RAF's requirement for aircraft, in particular training aircraft in 1938, because orders had not been placed in time. Consequently, a great outcry ensued when aircraft from foreign countries were ordered. The first of 400 Harvards arrived at Grantham from the North American company across the Atlantic equipped with British instruments and a radio. They also had bucket seats that were tailored to accommodate seat-pack parachutes. Back in the United States they were known as Texans, but in the UK they underwent a name change. Like the Magisters at Gatwick, their paint scheme was bright yellow, indicating a training aircraft.

Peter was impressed with the Harvard. It was much bigger in size than the petite Magister. It was typically American – brash with an unrefined shape, faster and heavier with a more powerful engine. It had an airscrew with constant pitch control, which came as a novelty to him. Controlling the pitch at take-off allowed a far greater performance from the Harvard. As the pilots climbed into the cockpit preparing for take-off, they were briefed to make sure that the setting had been switched to fine. Once they were airborne at about 500ft, they were supposed to change the setting to coarse. If the pilots forgot, the Harvard soon let them know, clattering incessantly. It was a terribly noisy beast. For such a large plane, the two-bladed propeller didn't seem large enough. One of the other modern features of the Harvard was a retractible undercarriage. The pilot pulled a lever and watched for the undercarriage lights on the instrument panel to turn red when the wheels were up. A flick of the lever when the Harvard came in to land and the lights changed to green. As with the Magisters, the first batch of Harvards presented problems when spinning, with the same fatal consequences. Peter recalls no problems with the Harvards sent to Grantham; if there were any problems, it was with the pilot – not the plane.

Peter took his first flight in one of these Texan beasts on a cold, wet day, 20 January 1939. Advanced training at Grantham continued in a similar vein to that at Gatwick. He went through the same procedures as he had done on the Magisters – but what a difference, what a difference! His first flight on that grey January day was one of familiarisation and the learning of effect when handling the controls. Peter and the other boys marked for fighters learnt precisely the same flying techniques and processes as on the Magister. They discovered how the Harvard behaved. When the instructors thought the students had picked up the basic rudiments of Harvard-flying, it was time to go solo. Peter did the same old things on his solo: taxiing, straight and level flying; taking off into wind; approaches and landings; medium turns with and without engine; and spins. He says that no matter what a pupil flew, or where he flew it, the standard of RAF training was precisely the same, following the student throughout each and every course. January and February were probably not the best times for learning how to fly a new aircraft, even if there was a war looming in the shadows. The lack of daylight and the snow meant that flying on the course had to be postponed for the best part of a month. It took Peter four weeks to get to the point where he could take his solo. The snow fell on the Harvards and blanketed the grass airfield. Landing on the snow would have been at best hazardous, at worst fatal. It meant that, as a result, Peter and the others on the single-engined fighter course had more than their fair share of lectures.

Late February came and the snow had disappeared. The winds from Siberia still howled from the North Sea but the days were getting longer, even if they were still dull and grey.

So it was that on 20 February 1939 Peter finally took his solo flight in the Harvard. The instructor agreed that Peter was more than competent in medium turns with and without engine, climbing turns, precautionary landings, navigation tests, air navigation, side-slipping and spinning. It came as no great surprise to Peter to discover that he had passed.

Meanwhile the training continued, and not just in the air. He remembers that all forty pilots on the course universally abhorred getting up at 6 a.m. 'every bloody morning', to take part in what the Air Force rather euphemistically called PT. To them, it was sheer bloody hell coordinated by a sadist by the name of Sgt Jones. Peter says he was a real bastard of an instructor. A Welshman who wasn't very tall in height but made up for his lack of inches by his incredible fitness and powerful personality, Sgt Jones made his flock go out each morning for about half an hour into the bleak Lincolnshire morning, shouting at them as they performed various exercises under his watchful eye before traipsing back for a bath, breakfast and the start of the day proper. Peter's recollection is that, not content with watching them 'freeze their balls off' in the cold, Jones would continue his vicious streak of sadism with verbal abuse, ripping the pupils off a strip, pretending to treat them as officers. What he was actually doing was reminding them all that they were in fact only acting pilot officers on probation. 'Now, *gentlemen*,' he would say in his sarcastic Welsh lilt, 'you haven't even started yet. You're all bloody lazy this morning.' Then as an afterthought, '– *gentle men!*' In the depths of a January or February winter, when the snow was on the ground and the icy wind came in from the Russian Steppes, it was Sgt Jones's main purpose in life to make sure that all the officers went through their exercises. He was, however, lenient! Concessions were made during this arctic weather. Jones had a hangar where he had them running around incessantly, numbed to the bone with physical jerks and star jumps, trying to loosen up their stiff and frozen muscles. Even so, Peter sums it up by adding, 'God, how we hated PT.'

Learning to fly the Harvard was just one tiny aspect of the course. The relaxed approach to studying that had been present on the elementary training course had long since gone. The lectures at Grantham took on a more serious academic objective. Peter remembers having to study many more subjects which were less to his liking. Administration and Air Force Law among others, all had to be scrutinised. This was now the real thing. Peter and his colleagues were being groomed as officers and all that being an officer in His Majesty's Royal Air Force implied.

The emphasis was on self-discipline. Each pilot was responsible for his own actions. In addition, the pupils were required to study basic drill practice, which took most of their time for the first three months: learning the basics throughout the wet, muddy winter on the parade square on a blanket of snow, marching in line, marching as a squad, saluting with vigour.

After Peter had been there for three months or so, the second course intake, fresh from their elementary training, arrived in Grantham to learn the difference between the two training courses and the high standard required in becoming an officer of the Air Force. Their course trailed by three months, so Peter's intake were now considered to be the senior course, but this still meant practising drill, moving on to senior stages which included saluting to a senior officer with a rifle.

As at Gatwick, the course was split into two flights, where 'A' Flight flew in the morning with lectures in the afternoon, while 'B' Flight carried out the same routine in reverse. And then the following week, 'A' Flight would study in the morning and fly in the afternoon, with vice versa for 'B' Flight. Despite the discipline required, Peter felt it was all rather civilised. At about 4.30, maybe 5 p.m., the officers on the senior course went to the mess and had tea, which was a casual affair served in the anteroom. The officers didn't sit down at a table, as they did at breakfast and lunch, to be served by waiters. Usually there were just a few sandwiches or biscuits that had been laid out along with some tea. Pilots relaxed, reading the papers for a while and seeing what was happening in the world (although most could guess), and would then go to change for dinner.

Like breakfast and lunch, dinner was a formal affair. It was all part of the learning curve for would-be officers. Peter and his colleagues wore lounge suits or dinner jackets, and full mess kit once a week. Once changed, they might have a sherry before the meal in the anteroom. Bars in their present form were unknown, so officers stood around holding a drink or propping up, perched on stools. It was all waiter-service. It was all very urbane. A waiter would come over for their order. 'Half a beer, please.' Back the waiter would come, glass on tray, where each officer signed his drinks-book. There was a limit of £5 per month as to how much pilots could spend on drink. Officers with the constitution of an ox, managing to exceed their limit, were hauled before the Commanding Officer of the RAF station. Peter can testify that, though it may not seem much today, £5 bought a lot of booze back in 1939.

But it wasn't just drinks bills that officers had to keep an eye on. Once a month mess bills would be sent to pilots, which they had to settle before the 10th of each month. The station commander would be very keen to see anyone who hadn't!

'Why haven't you paid your bills? What's wrong?'

'Sorry, Sir. I haven't got any money left this month, it seems to have . . . disappeared.' Seeing the Commanding Officer once was a chastening experience; seeing him because an officer had exceeded his mess bill and hadn't paid by the relevant date meant that that officer's stay at Grantham was going to be a short one. As acting pilot officers, Peter and the others on the advanced course received the princely sum of 11s 10d per day. Once they were promoted to full pilot officers, the sum shot up to 14s 6d. A flying officer received nearly £1 per day. Once a month, the officers had guest nights. Everything was laid out to a very high standard for these events: a candelabra was specifically hung for the purpose; port was laid out on the officers' tables, toasts were made to the King. The purpose of evenings such as these was to demonstrate to Peter's course precisely what the RAF required from its officers. It was teaching young officers just how an officers' mess should be run and how they were expected to behave. Although the food was good and the drink flowed, the purpose was to instil in each of them a sense of formality, standards and proper behaviour.

The flying training was administered on a five-and-a-half day basis. If the weather was good enough, the emphasis tended to concentrate on taking to the air rather than sitting at a desk in a classroom. At weekends, officers would fly until Saturday lunchtime, perhaps have a bite to eat and then have the rest of the afternoon and evening to themselves. The more diligent among them focused on their studies. All the members of the senior course relaxed on Sunday. One of the main activities that seems to have occurred on a Saturday evening was a visit to Nottingham to enjoy the dance-halls and clubs. Whether they were creatures of habit or whether they had found the best venues for miles around, the officers almost always ended up in Grantham or Nottingham city centre, about 25 miles to the west. They began these excursions by piling into each other's cars. Cuffey King-Clarke brought a huge, beautiful open-top 1928 Rolls-Royce. It was much admired by the other pilots. King-Clarke seemed to be financially well disposed, which explained his liking for open-top Rolls-Royces, which he used to good effect in his favourite pastime of motor-racing. He was one of the last gentlemen-racers, a breed of amateurs who drove, and flew, for the sheer sport, for the love of it. It was the taking part that counted. King-Clarke didn't need an impending war to climb into a cockpit; it was in his blood. Peter thinks the open top Rolls was wildly out of place around the fenlands of Grantham or, indeed, for that matter at Prestwick, and it would have caused quite a stir with the locals.

King-Clarke was very accommodating with his Rolls when it came to transport for the boys for a Saturday night on the town: 'Anyone want to come to Nottingham tonight?' he enquired.

'Yup! Thanks, Cuffey.'

'Well, come on then . . . what's the hold-up?'

'Get off my legs!'

'Well, get off my head then!'

'Are you ready in the back? No? Well, tough! We're off.'

Bodies surged forward towards the 1928 Rolls, squeezing

legs, arms and other body parts in where it was possible, filling up the front seat, filling up the back seat, sitting on the floor at the back. In all, Peter thinks about seven or eight managed to pile in. King-Clarke, it seems, didn't worry about the increased weight of the car. He had temporarily forgotten that Rolls-Royce cars were built for comfort and elegance; they were not meant to achieve a place in the Guinness Book of Records! Surprisingly, the car regularly made the journey to Nottingham.

There were two hotels on either side of the main square in the city centre. Both were considered to be rather up-market places; certainly the officers needed a proverbial arm and a leg to drink there but then, as lads in their late teens and early twenties, they walked on clouds; they were RAF officers and all that stood for; they had their wings and consequently they thought they were rather up-market people! Certainly, the boys ended up in both venues in their civilian suits, having a beer or three in each establishment, moving on at about 8.30 or 9.00 p.m. to The Trip to Jerusalem, a pub that was partially submerged in an area of caves, and, as Peter says, 'Boy, did that place jump!' Unsurprisingly, the boys from No. 12 FTS had a few more beers. 'Hey! It's about ten o'clock,' someone would say; 'I'm in the mood for a dance. I reckon the Victoria beckons!'

The Victoria Ballroom had a huge dance floor with various dance bands that Peter thought were extremely tight. More importantly, the Victoria was laden with girls, plenty of girls . . . lots and lots of lovely Nottingham girls. Pilots had no problems picking up girls. Peter soon found he and some young local lovely would get on like a house on fire as they swung out across the ballroom floor, dancing the foxtrot, the slow foxtrot and the waltz. He also found that there was no need to stand 6ft away from his partner, better to hold them close, sometimes very close. He'd have his arms round her, she'd have hers round him. Invariably, the conversation would get round to what he did for a living. Quite naturally, quite nonchalantly, he'd answer that he was an RAF 'fly boy'. To see the look of admiration on her sweet face! The way her eyes grew wider, the way her mouth opened in surprise, then broke into a smile. And the way she pulled him even closer. It did wonders for his ego. It worked wonders on the girl!

The Victoria closed around midnight – no playing into the small hours of Sunday – and the boys, some with girls in tow, returned to King-Clarke's Rolls to pile back in. Most of them, if not all, were the worse for wear. It was subsequently a more subdued journey home to Grantham than the rowdier drive down. Given the odd wrong turning in the dark, combined with the occasional drop of alcohol, King-Clarke managed to get his men back to No. 12 FTS by about one in the morning. Nearly all of them would fall fast asleep in the back.

Attending church parades eight hours later on the same Sunday morning proved particularly challenging. Putting on their uniforms with a head that felt like thunder and eyes that were as red as the lipstick that the girl last night was wearing, they moved heaven and earth to arrive at the service held at the RAF chapel for 9 a.m. How they actually looked, Peter can't seem to quite recall!

Once the pupils from Gatwick and Prestwick had arrived for the advanced course, they were then entitled to purchase – and wear – their RAF uniforms. Tailors from Moss Bros and Hector Powe came to the mess armed with tape measures, doing their best to tout for new business, to measure pilots who had just passed their basic course. Peter bought his uniform from Hector Powe with an allowance of about £100, which at the time seemed a great deal, but he found it soon disappeared on the amounts of various kit that they were expected to acquire. The kit was extensive – a full mess kit, which was quite expensive, complete with service shoes; black ties and blue shirts; peaked caps; forage caps; as well as brown gloves and a greatcoat – £100 was not going to last for long.

All the uniforms were bespoke; nothing was off the peg. Once the tailor had taken Peter's measurements, he returned a few days later with various bits of cloth in various states of dress for fitting. The fitting was shown to and inspected by a senior RAF officer. Peter and the boys had a squadron leader at Grantham who was particularly fastidious about the cut of each uniform worn by each officer on the advanced course. It had to be perfect. None of them was going to look out of place! He took great delight in telling the tailors in no uncertain terms what he thought of them if the fitting didn't quite match his sartorial standards.

In keeping with most young men of their age, the students who transferred from Gatwick to Grantham were looking for excitement and exhilaration; very few were concerned with the danger factor. If anyone was going to kill themselves, each student reasoned, it was going to happen to someone else; never to them. There wasn't a thought in that direction as far as Peter was concerned. However, a number of students did manage to kill themselves either through stupidity or over confidence. As far as Peter can remember, there wasn't a single accident involving the Magisters at Gatwick, but there was one incident at Grantham when a young student forgot to lower his undercarriage. The Harvard was the first training aircraft used by the RAF that had a retractible undercarriage. Students who had been familiar with Miles Magisters or Hawker Harts would not have had to concern themselves with adding a further point to their already-burgeoning checklist. It seems likely that this is what happened to the student on the Harvard as he came in to land. Peter suspects that the student was too busy worrying about throttling back and positioning the aircraft. Remembering to flick the lever that lowered his undercarriage must have slipped his mind. It was probably the first wheels-up landing in a Harvard. The pilot was unharmed, apart from his pride, but the aircraft did not come off so lightly.

The pupils taking the twin-engine course were going through their paces on the Ansons at the same time as Peter was going through his on the Harvards. The Avro Company had delivered their Anson aircraft which had first come off the production line in 1935. These Ansons were meant to be used in a reconnaissance role but, in keeping with the RAF expansion scheme, they were soon pressed into service as trainers for bombing, navigation, gunnery and radio communication. They proved to be surprisingly versatile aeroplanes but always appeared ever so slightly ungainly, with their bulbous, protruding nose. There was a sound and logical reason as to why the nose protruded, providing much-needed room for a bomb aimer. From a pilot's point of view, there was excellent visibility because of extensive fuselage glazing. This glazing was also extremely useful for the navigators on the course.

Every once in a while, Peter did his best to cadge trips in Ansons. And it wasn't purely for the flying. Grantham had one particular pub (the White Hart) which he went to regularly. There was a particularly appealing young lady who frequented the same place: nice pub, nice girl. They got chatting. The airfield was at that time flanked by a public road that ran along one side. Peter saw this girl on occasions, with her camera, taking photos of him climbing into one of these Ansons. How he must have wished he was on the twin-engine course at that time!

As the course reached its conclusion, news was filtering through that Hitler had invaded Czechoslovakia. It is true to say that this news made the boys feel somewhat apprehensive about the likelihood of a forthcoming war. Probably for the very first time, they had actually stopped and thought about the consequences of what they were doing. For most, it was probably the first step to maturity. But the training continued just the same until they had completed their course. From the middle of July 1939, Peter and the other fly-boys were approaching the end of their advanced training, with just one month remaining. The RAF authorities sent the pupils to armament practice camp in the wilds of Penrhos airfield, close to Abersoch in North Wales. Peter found that this involved air-to-air firing from their Harvards towards a drogue-aircraft. They also practised air-to-ground firing and manoeuvres such as dive-bombing with 25lb bombs. The Anson boys were there too. They were dropping the same type of bombs on the bombing range, some distance from Peter's target practice. Air-to-ground firing consisted of trying to hit a flat-topped buoy in the sea at 50yds. Peter came screaming over the green Welsh headland in the Harvard, only to be suddenly confronted by a vast expanse of watery blue with a large, stark white arrow pointing towards the buoy which was placed above the waves. Senior RAF officers safely on land looked on through binoculars, studying the results from each pilot. When the Harvards practised dive-bombing, they began at about 2,000ft before dipping the nose into a relatively shallow angle, levelling out at about 500ft. Peter found that air-to-air firing was even easier. Target drogues were attached to old Westland Wallaces: heavy, ungainly, obsolete biplanes that were a relic from the 1920s. The Wallaces were incredibly slow; they could only manage about 80mph, 90mph tops, so the drogue trailed 300–400yds, way below the Wallace. He approached the Wallaces in a quarter attack, coming in behind and from the side, trying to line up the drogue in his sights at about 120mph, before he pulled up and broke away, releasing the trigger that fired the guns. He would then break off from the attack. Peter found that the best technique was to allow for a deflection shot by actually putting his sights in front of the target. The fact that Peter was analysing what was happening to his shots at a speed of 120mph shows great maturity in the cockpit for an eighteen-year-old. Not content with the results that he had achieved, he began figuring out how to improve his firing results which shows the makings of not just a fighter pilot, but an ace. Of course, it is imperative that successful fighter pilots have a good eye in a combat situation. With just a split-second to line up a target and successfully shoot an enemy aircraft in a dogfight situation, making the most of practices like the one at Camp Penrhos was essential.

The weather in Wales was wonderfully, and rather unusually, warm and sunny. When the pilots had completed their flying and armament practice, they retired to the nearest village of Abersoch, a well-known holiday resort. Peter and the other thirty-nine on the camp certainly gave it their thumbs-up, putting in a lot of swimming at St Tudwals Bay. Abersoch also had a very pleasing pub that the boys enjoyed when they were off duty. They met some very nice people in Wales, including some particularly pleasing ladies. One of these girls, Pat Peaple, was a wonderful artist. She insisted on painting two pictures of the RAF boys around the bar. The first showed suave, well-dressed figures, some with moustaches, laughing, drinking and chatting up ladies. It was entitled *The RAF at Work*. The second showed suave, well-dressed figures, some with moustaches, laughing, drinking and chatting up ladies. It was entitled *The RAF at Play*.

The pilots completed No. 12 Flying Training School in August 1939. It had taken ten long, nerve-wracking months to succeed, but Peter had done it, he had his wings. He was a genuine, qualified pilot of the Royal Air Force. As at the completion of the elementary training course at Gatwick, Peter has a vague idea that just one out of the forty who had been on the first advanced course at No. 12 FTS failed to qualify. Although it must have been wrenching to fail the elementary course at Gatwick or Prestwick, it must have been a crushing experience to go through both courses, only to fall at the final hurdle. The pilot who failed to qualify had been on the twin-engine course with the Ansons, and Peter suspects that, in the words of the senior officers who made the selections, he was probably just a little too stable.

At the end of August, the thirty-nine pilots who had qualified had received their postings. It was the end of the first course at No. 12 FTS. No more close dances with Nottinghamshire girls or drinks with the lady who took photographs of him; it was on to operational flying. The real thing had arrived at last. Tolly Rothwell, Cuffey King-Clarke *et al* all went their separate ways to various fighter, bomber and coastal squadrons around the country. Peter was posted to No. 73 Squadron at Digby, some 25 miles to the north-east between Grantham and Lincoln. His final flight on a Harvard at Grantham was on 11 August 1939. By the 23rd, he was flying a Hurricane.

THREE

Brave Blue World

Peter's training was complete; the time had come to put it all into practice. With the distinct threat of war, it appeared that he and the other pilots would have plenty of opportunities to use it. The pilots were excited at the prospect of flying real operations with squadrons, even if they were a little apprehensive – for Peter and the others, it was a brave blue world.

Three other pilots on the same course at Grantham with Peter were also posted to No. 73 Squadron: John Hardacre, Blair White and Alan Johnson. The four of them set out for a new world full of life and exhilaration in August 1939.

Five years later, Peter was the only one still alive. Hardacre had been shot down during the Battle of Britain. Peter describes him as a lively flamboyant character; a bit of a dandy, a dedicated follower of fashion. Hardacre proved his sartorial flamboyance by making sure his shirt-cuffs were far longer than they needed to be, a vast expanse of cotton proudly hanging from underneath his jacket.

The top of his handkerchief drooped ceremoniously out of his breast pocket. The rest of the squadron thought it would fall out at any moment. White was different to Hardacre; serious, introverted, rather quiet and probably a little shy, Blair preferred to keep his distance. He was killed later in the Middle East. It was surprising that Johnson had made it through the advanced course at all because he came across to the other pilots as very immature, too young to be in the RAF. He seemed a little out of his depth here; an eighteen-year-old boy in a military blue uniform. It wasn't long before Johnson, too, was killed.

Peter's first impressions of operational life with No. 73 Squadron were underwhelming. RAF Digby, he thought, was not a patch on Grantham, especially the mess area. At Grantham the mess had been a comparatively modern brick building, but the single-storey ramshackle 'hut' before his eyes was less than salubrious. The squadron pilots, however, pulled together and made the best of it, instilling a decent atmosphere as best they could. Fortunately, he didn't have to suffer the conditions of RAF Digby for long. He remained there for just four weeks before he and the squadron were posted to France. The posting to France was the real thing and everyone knew it; the brave blue world was waiting.

RAF Digby was home to two squadrons during September 1939. Peter had been posted to No. 73, but No. 46 Squadron was sharing the same facilities on the chilly Lincolnshire airfield. Suddenly and quite out of the blue, he was posted to No. 46 Squadron, spending a week with it from 27 August to 4 September 1939. No. 46 Squadron had originally been commanded by Sqn Ldr Dickie Barwell. His flight commander was a New Zealander by the name of Pat G. 'Jamie' Jameson, who later went on to become an air commodore. Peter's week with the squadron was the beginning of what was to be a great friendship with Pat Jameson during and after the war. Peter thinks it's interesting how we are led through life. Call it fate, destiny or luck, it's as though on certain occasions through our lives there is some force, a spirit that watches over us, nudging us in specific directions, preparing us.

His Spirit of the Blue was certainly watching over him during this particular week, and, in his own words, he had spades of luck. By 4 September he was posted back to No. 73 Squadron. It was to be a decision that made the difference between life and death. He doesn't know why he was recalled to his original squadron – perhaps the commanders thought he was a steadier chap; perhaps they drew straws. Perhaps there is another explanation . . . Because eight months later, disaster overtook No. 46 Squadron.

German forces had captured the Norwegian port of Narvik by April 1940 in a bid to maintain its protection of its shipments of iron ore. It was the intention of the Prime Minister, Winston Churchill, to capture the same port, and the pilots and ground crew of No. 46 Squadron were subsequently dispatched. In early June, they were evacuated, along with ten remaining aircraft, onto the aircraft-carrier HMS *Glorious*. Landing Hurricanes on board a moving vessel was difficult at the best of times, but this was made worse by the fact that the pilots had never landed on a carrier before. In addition, the Hurricanes at this stage of the war did not have arrester hooks; reducing their speed was therefore most important. In the absence of hooks, sandbags were tied to each tail of a Hurricane to act as a weight so that crew members could quickly grab the tail fins when the wheels touched down on the deck. All ten Hurricanes landed on board the *Glorious* and were making for Britain when, without warning, HMS *Glorious* was attacked by the pride of Germany's fleet, the *Scharnhorst* and *Gneisenau*. Within the space of twelve hours, *Glorious* had been sunk.

Later on, Jameson told Peter what had happened after the *Glorious* had been holed. With Sqn Ldr Kenneth 'Ring' Cross and twenty others, he managed to jump overboard and make for a life-raft. During the next few hours, while they were hoping to be rescued, most of the twenty survivors in that life-raft perished through a combination of hunger, thirst and injuries sustained from the attack. Space on the raft was scarce, and Cross, together with Jameson, took the decision that in order to increase the chances of survival for those who were still living, they would heave the corpses of their fellow pilots overboard into the North Sea. It was, of course, a terrible decision to have to make, but there is every chance that had Cross and Jameson not taken the action they did, the death-toll in the raft might well have been much higher. Cross and Pat Jameson survived and were eventually rescued. Moreover, had the posting to No. 73

Squadron not come through, there is also every chance that Peter might well have been in that life-raft . . . Perhaps something was watching over him.

On 3 September 1939 war was officially declared. Once the news had broken that Britain was now at war with Germany, it was understood by the pilots of No. 73 Squadron that they were to leave Digby as part of the Air Force contingent of the British Expeditionary Force (BEF), and their brief at this stage was to proceed to France. In all, just four squadrons were sent as the entire operational fighter air force for the BEF: No. 73 Squadron was not alone in providing air support to the ground forces; three other squadrons had been classed as 'mobile', which meant that when war was officially declared, they too would be required to move to France immediately. No. 1 Squadron was based at Tangmere while Nos 85 and 87 Squadrons were located at Debden; and each squadron was equipped with Hurricanes.

The stakes had been raised by the British Government, and the pilots were fully aware of this.

In Peter's words, they had a pretty good idea that things were looking dicey. They were also aware that life was going to get very tough out there. The authorities took the view that only experienced pilots should be part of the BEF: pilots who could perform well under pressure, pilots who could be trusted to bring back their precious machines. Four operationally inexperienced pilots were no use to the striking air force. The decision was subsequently taken that Peter, Blair, John and Alan were too raw and unproven to fly the Hurricanes to France because Hurricanes were going to be a scarce commodity.

No. 73 Squadron had its fair share of personalities that Peter got to know properly now that he had been posted back. The squadron was commanded by B.W. 'Tiger' Knox, a wild Irishman who personified his nickname: tiger by name, tiger by nature. Peter says he was as wild as they came – 6ft 2ins, big and broad-shouldered with a red face because he used to knock the booze back a bit.

Knox had a loud voice, especially when he'd had a few drinks in the mess bar; you always knew when he was there. The Tiger oversaw two flight commanders: 'A' Flight was commanded by Reggie Lovett, while Ian Scoular oversaw 'B' Flight. Scoular was Peter's flight commander. Peter found that Scoular was calm and measured, not bombastic or pompous, and as a result he thoroughly liked him. Scoular went on to claim eighteen enemy aircraft.

No. 73 Squadron also had the first fighter ace of the Second World War – Edgar 'Cobber' Kain was 'B' Flight's deputy flight commander under Scoular and he was also Peter's section leader.

Peter describes Kain as relaxed, happy-go-lucky and not conceited in any way. His temperament may well have been influenced by his relaxed upbringing in New Zealand, hence the nickname.

To many back home in Britain (and other Commonwealth countries), Cobber Kain was the first of many fighter pilot aces destined to become legendary household names, their faces printed on cigarette cards and fought over in playgrounds by young boys. The press also played their part. According to them, Kain was the first Knight of the Sky of the Second World War, having shot down five enemy aircraft and been awarded the Distinguished Flying Cross. He was thus termed the first fighter ace of the war before the Battle for France had begun on 10 May 1940, when the Germans invaded the Low Countries. He was to receive constant media attention for the remainder of his brief life.

The other pilots in the squadron were about as different and diverse as you could get. They all had one thing in common, however. Their brave blue worlds revolved around exuding an air of confidence and arrogance. 'Smooth' Holliday, as his nickname suggests, was very much a ladies' man. Two months later, Peter recalls that Holliday had left the squadron because he 'didn't quite fit the bill' as a fighter pilot in France, lacking the necessary aggression. Another unfortunate member of the squadron was Ian Brotchie, a little Scot who was killed a year later. There are many tragic and ironic fates in war. Having become squadron leader at Debden in 1941, Brotchie was just preparing to take off when another aircraft literally landed on top of him.

Peter was friendly with Graham Paul, who was also in 'B' Flight, and, in Peter's words, 'Graham was good value'. Paul flew in France, but once back in England, he never returned to operational flying. There were also two sergeant pilots in each flight, Sgt Ken Campbell, a rather fine artist who was shot down in 1941 and ended up in a POW camp, and Sgt Pyne. 'A' Flight consisted of Reggie Lovett, Tub Perry, Dickie Martin, Fanny Orton, Pete Walker and Sgts Stuckey, Speake and Phillips.

The call to arms in France required getting to grips with a new aircraft that pilots newly based at Digby had to master as quickly as possible. Learning how to fly a new aircraft operationally was vastly different from having the relative luxury of time at the Flying Training Schools. Moreover, it was not just a question of getting to grips; in order to ensure survival, pilots had to know precisely what they could – and could not – do in a fighter aircraft. Training aircraft like the Magister and Harvard were relatively simple and straightforward when taking off and landing. Operationally, knowing precisely the limitations and assets of each front-line fighter aircraft could – and often did – mean the difference between life and death. For Peter and the intake from the Flying Training Schools, it was a case of acquiring experience on Hurricanes as soon as possible.

Both No. 46 and No. 73 Squadrons had used the same fighter aircraft at Digby, the Hawker Hurricane. It was a big fighter aircraft for its time, much faster than both the Magister and the Harvard. Peter and the other raw pilots realised that the Hurricane was in another league; it was a vastly superior aeroplane. It reached new heights in terms of engineering, but operationally it was untried and untested in a combat environment. Delivered to squadrons for active service at the beginning of 1939, the only flights pilots had taken with the two-bladed fixed-pitch wooden airscrew were those of familiarisation and tactics. The expedition to France would be the Hurricane's first major test, but Peter's first flight in one had been nine days earlier, back in England, as borne out by his diary entry for that day: 23 *August – Experience on type, one hour.*

The plane was high off the ground. Peter admits to being fairly apprehensive before his first flight in his first fighter aircraft. It was hardly surprising. The flight was to be straightforward; no tricksy stuff – just the basics; purely a familiarisation flight, like those he had flown on his previous solos on the training courses. He found that the controls of the Hurricane seemed remarkably heavy, especially the ailerons. The Harvard seemed very light in comparison. By the time he flew a Hurricane the second time, he had been posted across the Lincolnshire grass at Digby to No. 46 Squadron. After clambering into the cockpit and awaiting further instruction, Jameson told him to concentrate on circuits and landings.

By 2 September, it was all change again as Peter had returned to the fold of No. 73 Squadron, where Scoular told him to take off and do two or three circuits. Peter did so, remembering to bring the wheels up, flying around and familiarising himself with the controls. He decided to come in and try his first landing. The wheels came down . . . the flaps came down . . . WHUMP! The landing had been a little heavy but at least he was back on terra firma. He taxied in, only for Scoular to tell him to take off again. The roar of the Merlin engine increased as Peter opened the throttle and the Hurricane took to the Lincolnshire skies once again. After another circuit, he came in on final, easing the Hurricane on to the runway, nice and light; no heavy landings like last time. He was determined not to make the same mistake again, and this time he brought the Hurricane down without any problems. Scoular gave Peter the thumbs up; his solo had been all right. He had made three flights. So far the Hurricane had behaved itself, but there were times when the ground crew had had to start it with a crank handle, although it was possible to connect the aircraft to a battery and start it that way.

The order had come through – No. 73 Squadron was to leave for France immediately. Experienced pilots were to fly Hurricanes to Octeville airfield, close to Le Havre, while the new pilots were to cross the Channel by special arrangement. This 'special arrangement' meant embarking in a troopship from the British Expeditionary Force. Peter was assigned to arrange logistical procedures for the main party on arrival in France. These procedures were carried out on board the BEF troopship as it was leaving Southampton. The squadron was accompanied on board by Tub Perry from 'A' Flight, as well as the squadron doctor, and they found that, as well as airmen, the ship was full of soldiers and various pieces of equipment, including transport vehicles, which had already been winched on board.

By 18 September Peter had received his first taste of operational flying. Led by Cobber Kain, his section had taken off from Octeville airfield, practising tactics and formation flying, including one-ship and two-ship attacks, formation sector recce and defensive patrols. It was a baptism of fire for the rookie pilots. Peter had been inside a Hurricane cockpit only three times. Two weeks prior to this, he had just completed his first solo, and now here he was – here they *all* were – flying operationally. Enemy aircraft were now a very real threat. The brave blue world had arrived. As Peter says, he had had 'bugger-all experience' – just over two hours to get used to the Hurricane.

To begin with, the flying routines were just the same as at Gatwick and Grantham; 'B' Flight alternated with 'A' Flight as to who stood by in readiness each day. There were occasions when the whole squadron was sitting in cockpits, ground crew at the ready, standing by for training patrols or formation techniques. When one Flight was on Readiness, the other

Flight would either relax or practise formation flying. The weather was very warm and sunny in those early days of September 1939 and when Peter and the rest of 'B' Flight were off duty, they travelled to the coast. Walking along the cliffs, they'd scramble down to the sea and have a swim. There was no need for them to take swimming costumes; a towel was all that was needed, and they soon got into the French custom of bathing *au naturel*.

A few days later, No. 73 Squadron and No. 1 Squadron, also based at Octeville, moved to Norrent-Frontes, a small airfield close to St-Omer. Peter flew one sortie before the squadron was moved on again and the men lived under canvas in ridge tents with a marquee as a mess tent. They constructed a bar from an old wooden box. Peter also remembers that while they were at Norrent-Frontes they were put to work digging trenches, but he can't recall why. The other two mobile squadrons, Nos 85 and 87, were stationed nearby at St-Omer.

The decision was then taken to split the Hurricane squadrons; Nos 1 and 73 would head south as the fighter element of the Advanced Air Striking Force while Nos 85 and 87 remained in the north as the fighter element of the Air Component of the British Expeditionary Force.

Peter came to know the eastern French border of Lorraine and Champagne intimately, especially around Metz and Verdun. Two or three miles outside the town of Etain there was an airfield that adjoined the village of Rouvres. From early October 1939 it was to be their home for the best part of nine months. The airfield was small; one squadron consisting of twelve aircraft was ample, and it was certainly not big enough to take two. As a consequence, No. 1 Squadron was posted 60 miles away to Bar-Le-Duc, which meant that No. 73 was now further forward, closer to the front line. A solitary road ran snake-like along the side of the airfield and there were wonderful views of the village from the airfield, with the church spire and the school rising majestically above the horizon.

Meals were served in the schoolroom, which also acted as a very fine and efficient officers' mess where they rigged up a bar, close to the open fireplace. Drinking in the schoolroom was often accompanied by the sounds from the squadron's gramophone, the strains of Fats Waller playing in the background. Peter remembers that 'Tiger' often had a drink or two at the bar but then mysteriously retired to his billet, armed with a bottle of scotch for company, holing himself up.

Each evening, every officer in the squadron was tasked with censoring letters written by the ground crew. As there were some two hundred airmen in the squadron, it took quite a time to read all the intimate letters to mums, dads, wives, girlfriends. Having read these letters, it was down to Peter and his fellow officers to black anything out that might be classed as sensitive information. They had been briefed previously as to the sort of information that should be censored – military information, mention of locations, etc. The author of the letter would, of course, never know that his letters had been censored. Peter always found this task unpleasant and was only too happy to hand the letters to the NCO, ready for dispatch via the British Forces Post Office.

With the arrival of autumn, the pilots were glad not to be sleeping under canvas. They had been billeted in and around Rouvres with French families. Peter was billeted in a house owned by an old couple who he thought were probably in their seventies. The old man had hunched shoulders and a moustache and beard, and he always wore a typical French cap. Peter was the only pilot billeted with them and was given a nice room with a comfortable bed and a duvet. The winter was very cold and the duvet was not thick enough, so he used to put on extra nightclothes. The washing facilities were basic – a jug filled with cold water and a basin. However, he did have a batman, Ashley, who came into his room each morning with a jugful of hot water for shaving. The couple always left the front door open for him. Eight months later, Ashley was drowned along with others from the squadron on board HMT *Lancastria*. Although his billet was adequate, Peter found it a little lonely. During the spring of 1940, sometime in March, a billet became available in a larger house already occupied by two pilots. Peter was only too happy to have some company, and it was closer to the airfield and a 100yds nearer to the village.

Although there were eighteen aircraft on the airfield, the two Flights were about as far apart as you could get. 'A' Flight was based towards the top of the airfield, nearer the village, while 'B' Flight was situated at the more remote end, about half a mile away. At the bottom of the airfield, 'B' Flight erected and maintained a ridge tent which the men called their 'offices', where they kept their flying gear and parachutes along with a bench. These were less than perfect conditions in which to store flying equipment, but at least it was protected from the elements of a French autumn. In addition to the 'office' there was a dugout surrounded by sandbags which the pilots called their Operations Room. Peter says that things were basic – a couple of telephones on a small desk, together with a few radio sets which were not particularly effective. They were for contacting the Hurricanes as an early warning device, but in reality they provided extremely limited radio contact for the airmen who manned them. Unless the Hurricanes were flying at very close range to the airfield, the Transmitter Receiver-8s (TR8s) could not effectively receive a signal.

No. 73 Squadron was very much left to its own devices. Although under the auspices of the Advanced Air Striking Force, no assistance or support whatsoever was provided for the squadron by the French Air Force, in the shape of either aircraft or personnel. A few soldiers from the French Army were on hand at Rouvres, however, and were used to operating the squadron's early warning system. In fact, they *were* the early warning system! These *poilus*, who wore great fore-and-aft caps with khaki greatcoats, were the squadrons' eyes and ears and their function was to observe and warn the British fighters of any enemy action. The soldiers were stationed on the far side of the rough track that ran alongside the perimeter of the airfield, positioned so that they were equidistant from both 'A' Flight and 'B' Flight. A glance from either position up or down the airfield meant that pilots were able to take off at a moment's notice. Resources were limited. Their base was nothing more than a deepish trench encased with sandbags and a pair of binoculars attached to a stand.

Peter recalls that they peered around the sky with the binoculars and if they thought they saw an aircraft which they couldn't positively identify, they would wave a huge red flag perched on a long stick, which the Flight on readiness would see flapping from half a mile away. 'Christ! The flag's going!' The system wasn't foolproof. Both 'A' and 'B' Flights would see the flag raised aloft, rippling to and fro, but were often not aware of the reason the French were signalling so frantically. As there was a lack of radio contact with these *poilus*, all No. 73 Squadron could be certain about was that the Frenchmen, gazing through the binoculars, had seen *something* in the sky. That something might just as easily be British as German.

There was no real opportunity at Rouvres for Peter and the squadron to practise night-flying. In any case, at this stage of the war neither the Germans nor the British attacked during the night, preferring to make daylight patrols. Certainly the airfield at Rouvres wasn't big enough to withstand night-time landings from Hurricanes whose pilots had difficulty in seeing precisely where the aerodrome was situated. In addition, they didn't have the right night-flying facilities. There were no glim-lamps that could be used as a method of signalling an approach onto the airfield. Subsequently, they stuck to day-flying, from dawn until dusk.

Because their location was in the north-east of France, Peter's squadron was the closest of the four RAF fighter squadrons to the German border. The one barrier that had separated the Germans from the French was the creation of the Maginot Line. It was the pride of France, apparently impregnable. Completed in 1934, the line cost more than £30 million to build. Peter visited this southern section of the line as a guest of the 15 BCC French tank unit. Having explored this part of the Line, he was given a *diplome de caparelle d'honneur*, signed by the unit commandant. Peter thinks it was astounding – a vast underground labyrinth that descended deep into the bowels of the earth, stretching from the Swiss border near Strasbourg, right up to the Western side of the Rhine, then turning westwards to Luxembourg. It was fascinating to see the type of engineering feat that man could achieve by living underground; a subterranean colony with railways, engines and wagons, and living quarters. The only visible sign of defence from the ground was large gun turrets, but even these were operated from underground.

Unfortunately, construction stopped at this part of the line, just south of Luxembourg, close to the borders with Belgium and the Netherlands. French thinking at the time had been that this particular stretch of Allied land reaching to the coast of the Low Countries was protected from any potential invasion threat by the Belgians. They also thought that in any case the Dutch were able to defend their country against the Germans. The Germans invaded the Low Countries on 10 May; instead of attacking it from the north, they merely went round the Line and the turrets were never put to the test. Vastly overrated by the French, the Line contributed heavily to their downfall.

No. 73 Squadron received a number of invitations from other French military units based at the Maginot Line. 'We invite six of your officers to come to dinner on the date enclosed.' Reggie Lovett and Ian Scoular, along with pilots from each flight, took turns to accept each invitation. One immediate benefit was the prospect of some good French cuisine. It also allowed each pilot to take the occasional evening off.

The squadron returned the favour. A dinner was held in the schoolroom at Rouvres, on 16 November 1939, where Peter believes the guests were members of the 15 BCC tank unit. He still retains a menu from that evening. It demonstrates the lack of rationing in the early days of the war:

Le Consommé Royale   Le Pompée
Salade Asparique Chantilly   Le Genoise Verdunoise
Le Jambon d'Alsace Prantannières   Le Coq au Pâté

The location of No. 73 Squadron had an unexpected but very welcome benefit. Rouvres, Metz and Verdun were situated in good wine country: Lorraine, which made well-structured but unknown wines, to the east, and Champagne to the west. The boys found that wines were inexpensive, so they bought what was available: Traminer, Chablis, Nuits St Georges 1933 and Champagne Mumm Cart d'Or.

Being an officer in a squadron meant that Peter and his friends had to confine their activities to the mess. But there were no bathing facilities at the airfield or at their billets. Once a week this was resolved by taking a van holding no more than five people and travelling to Verdun. The purpose for the journey was to visit the Hôtel Vaubonne. Over the ensuing nine months, Peter and company got to know the owner and his wife very well.

The priority at the Hôtel Vaubonne was to have a good bath, for which the owner was well paid. How good it felt to wallow in the water and feel the warmth on their skin after seven dirty, sweaty days. Refreshed and clean for another week, the boys would put on some clean underwear, smarten themselves up and nip down to the bar, ready for the ensuing party. They all found that there was nothing like a bath to put the spring back in their step. At about 8 p.m., the five of them would decide to eat, with the addition of plenty of wine. As they had found in laying on the party for the French tank unit, wines and liqueurs were extremely cheap; it would be rude not to! Some three hours later – depending on how much wine had been consumed – Peter and the group would clamber back into the van, and return to their billets.

There were other incentives in making journeys to Verdun for a long hot soak in the tub. A well-known French ballet troupe entertaining (predominantly) French troops had travelled from Paris to put on a show in the town, and had decided to stay at the Hôtel Vaubonne. Whether it was because Peter was wearing clean underwear he isn't certain, but one of the dancers, Geneviéve Ione, took more than a shine to him. The feeling was reciprocated. She was very attractive with sculpted eyebrows, a flat nose and quite the largest, luscious ruby-red lips. It isn't surprising to discover that Peter took a sudden interest in ballet during his time at the Vaubonne. Unfortunately their time together was all too brief; Geneviéve, along with the others in the troupe, had to move on to entertain more troops, possibly more pilots, around the country. He says it was fun while it lasted and he still has her photograph.

The officers were given periods of leave lasting forty-eight hours on a few occasions. Just as the Vaubonne was favoured in Verdun, the Hôtel Lion d'Or was the preferred choice for many in Reims. Peter recalls that everyone used to head there – situated in the main street, the pilots found it had an excellent atmosphere and it used to buzz. The boys' routine at the Hotel Lion d'Or was very similar to that of Verdun – as soon as they arrived, the first thing to do was to have a bath. Washing away the muck, grime, sweat and stress of patrol-flying appears instrumental in reviving a pilot's spirits. Of course, there were other ways to revive spirits. Feeling part of the human race again, they ambled down to the bar for a drink and a meal. The bar was jam-packed, full of other RAF officers who were recuperating and relaxing from their skirmishes with the enemy fought over the border. In his words, after a skinful at the bar, Peter and the others headed out of the front door, crossed the road and straight into the Palais de Champagne bar on the opposite side of the road. It was an extremely attractive bar where the round wooden tables were fashioned out of old barrel-tops and, to match the seats were made from empty barrels. The town was famous for one thing, and as the name implies, the Palais de Champagne sold it by the bucketload. When in Rome . . . so they did. Their liking for and knowledge of the king of wines increased dramatically during their trips to the Palais. They were paying the equivalent of 2*s* 6*d* for a bottle. As a consequence, Peter adds, they 'didn't half used to slosh it back'.

6 November 1939

Peter had not come across a Messerschmitt Me 109 during his two months' posting to France. That was about to change, and 6 November was going to be his baptism of fire. The Me 109 had a fearsome reputation. It had been used to good effect just three years earlier when it had put the fear of God into the Spanish during their Civil War. Therefore, unlike the Hurricanes, it was – along with its pilots – operationally experienced by the outbreak of the Second World War and Luftwaffe pilots were justifiably proud of its speed and agility. It was certainly faster than a two-bladed Hurricane, and was considered quite simply the best fighter aircraft in the world. With a maximum speed of 359mph at 12,300ft and armed with a 20mm Mauser cannon firing through the propeller hub, along with two 13mm machine-guns, it was no surprise that the Me 109 was treated with respect by the RAF pilots.

All the pilots were on a Wing exercise that particular November day. No. 1 Squadron, based at Bar-Le-Duc, was due to join No. 73 Squadron at Rouvres and the two squadrons were going to put up the first fighter offensive patrol of the war: twenty-four Hurricanes in squadron formations patrolling just into the German border, over the Maginot and Siegfried Lines.

Peter was alone at the airfield, sitting in his Hurricane on what was called aerodrome defence. Similar to a state of readiness, it was a role that required observation, reconnaissance and the possibility of a little combat if an enemy aircraft was spotted in the vicinity. He looked out over the airfield. The sun was warm and there were blue skies everywhere. No one would want to attack on a day like this. He looked at his watch. Not quite 2.30. A voice brought him back from his thoughts. 'Sir! Sir! For Christ's sake, get going; the red flag's waving!' He looked to his right, over to the little road and the early warning post. The *poilus* were waving the flag with enthusiasm.

Then he looked up at the sky . . . and there it was. A little dot travelling in a westerly direction, high up in the azure blue. This was the enemy aircraft he was supposed to chase. But then the aircraft decided to fly over the airfield, high up at about 20,000ft. The Rolls-Royce Merlin engine roared into life and Peter hurtled over the grass. He realised that making a fast take-off with a two-bladed airscrew was never really going to be very feasible because of the lack of power from the engine. The take-off went on and on. Peter increased the throttles, climbing as hard as he could. The Hurricane was inordinately slow. It took him about ten minutes to match the enemy aircraft in height.

'Hang on, what's he doing? Why has he changed direction? Why's he heading east? Perhaps he's seen me take off.'

Time seemed to drag. The throttle was still on maximum. Peter had been chasing him for quite a while. As an operationally inexperienced pilot, he was intent on chasing the enemy raider, determined to have a crack at him. Most pilots with his lack of operational experience would have done precisely the same thing.

'Good, matching his height. Closing in on him . . . still over half a mile away . . . not too long now . . . Keep going . . . Christ! . . . Where the bloody hell am I? . . . Easterly . . . I'm too far east! . . . Jesus! . . . I'm over Germany!'

What Peter had omitted to do in all the excitement was to keep a weather eye on his compass and make a mental note of where he was. He now realised that by flying in an easterly direction for so long, he was well over Germany.

'Hang on . . . what's he doing now? Diving, making for cloud cover . . . Balls, won't get a shot at him . . . right, let's head back.'
He turned back on a reciprocal heading; at least he was now heading back towards France. As the Hurricane turned, he

looked down over his starboard wing. Inside his turn – and below him – there were nine aircraft, in line astern formation, turning in precisely the same direction. Peter hadn't seen any sign of either his squadron or No. 1 Squadron. Surely he could hardly miss twenty-four Hurricanes in the vicinity?

'Good, there they are. The boys want me to join on the formation.' So Peter tacked on the end of the line astern formation with the other aircraft at 18,000ft. But something didn't seem quite right. They looked unfamiliar. *Were* they Hurricanes? No. Perhaps they were French? What the hell were they? Whatever they were, they had black crosses on them. Large, ugly, bloody great black crosses painted on either wing.

'Sweet Christ! Bloody Messerschmitts.'

Peter gave a quick squirt from his guns towards the tail-end Charlie, (the last aircraft in any formation) and shoved the stick forward so that the Hurricane flew into a very steep dive towards some broken cloud 3,000–4,000ft below. He made sure that he kept an eye that the aircraft flew westerly. 'They've seen me.'

Nine Me 109s peeled off and began to chase him. The Hurricane was fitted with a special booster on the throttle called the tit. In order to increase the speed, a tiny wire had to be broken which allowed the pilot to pull the booster, initiating the engine's running on full-bore, giving extra thrust for a limited amount of time. Heart pulsating, throat dry, eyes wide, Peter broke the wire and pulled the booster tit. What he didn't know at that time, but was told by witnesses after his ordeal, was that there were *another eighteen* Me 109s on patrol, scattered all over the November sky. Having seen nine of their comrades peel off after something, they in turn decided to investigate. So, in effect, there were not just nine on Peter's tail, but *twenty-seven*.

How was Peter feeling at this point? Does he recall panicking? No, he replies; he was a pilot in the RAF, but he does admit to being more than a little scared. As he says, at the time he was 'shitting his knickers'. He tucked himself into his pilot's seat, ducking in front of the armour plate that protected the back of his head. Darting and nipping in between the broken cloud, he kept an ever-watchful eye on the direction bearing of the compass. It pointed west.

There were no radio or directional aids to assist Peter. Moreover, he was aware that the tit booster had been on full pelt. He saw one of the landmarks that pilots looked for when evaluating their location: factories which had sunken glass windows painted blue by the French . . . He was back over France but he didn't have the foggiest idea precisely where.

Twenty-seven Me 109s were still chasing one under-powered Hurricane flown by one green, scared, very nervous pilot. Peter prefers to think of it as one Hurricane leading twenty-seven Messerschmitts towards a group of French fighter aircraft. Never had Peter been more relieved to see a bunch of Moraine-Saulnier 406s and Curtiss P-40 Hawks. Salvation had arrived. This was to be the first genuine dogfight of the Second World War, with a total of over thirty aircraft fighting over the French border. Nine Me 109s were shot down by nine French aircraft. He realised that he had been in the air for some time. As if the enemy aircraft weren't enough to contend with, Peter was about to be confronted with another problem. Because of the action, he hadn't seen that his fuel gauge was very low. He had to find somewhere to land – and soon. Far away in the distance he could see some aircraft circling on the horizon. They kept circling and as he flew towards them, they kept on circling.

'Please let them be French. Please let them be French.'
They were.

The needle on the fuel gauge rested on the bottom. Unable to afford the luxury of flying a circuit before he landed, Peter went straight in onto the grass airstrip; it was now or never. Peter selected the lever which automatically lowered the undercarriage. The rubber tyres came closer towards the grass . . . closer . . . closer . . . until they made contact. The roar of the Rolls-Royce Merlin lessened as the throttles decreased. He finished his landing and taxied towards the active side of the airfield. As he was about to turn it off, the engine cut. He had run out of fuel. In analysis, he had flown two-thirds of a rather large triangle. He had taken off from Rouvres, climbed to the south of the Luxembourg border, following the Dornier until he had reached the area around Homburg and Saarbrucken, just west of Kaiserlautern. It was here that he realised he was well over the German border. He thought he had turned on a reciprocal heading back west, but in the mêlée and confusion over the nine Messerschmitts, he had actually flown towards the south-west instead. The airfield he touched down on with literally a drop of petrol to spare was Nancy. It was probably just as well that Peter hadn't returned to his original reciprocal heading, having taken a mis-direction, because there is every possibility that he might not have found an airfield in time. Peter stayed the night at Nancy with good reason, for his Hurricane had been shot up with a number of holes, evidence of his ordeal.

The following morning, after a brief inspection of the Hurricane, Peter left Nancy for the short journey to Rouvres. Damage to the aircraft didn't look too bad and in any case it wasn't very far to Rouvres; all Peter had to do was to keep heading north in order to complete the final piece of the triangle. The greeting he received from the No. 73 Squadron ground crew at Rouvres was less than effusive: 'It was a bit bloody dicey coming back with your aircraft like that, wasn't it?'

His face remained blank. 'What do you mean?'

'Didn't you notice one of the bullets had damaged your tailplane? It could easily have come adrift.'

What had happened on the previous day was the largest air battle of the Second World War to date, and Peter had been right in the centre of it. Because of his skills in evading the twenty-seven Messerschmitts, he was dubbed Decoy by the boys in the squadron. This had been his first real taste of combat. And he had come through it. It had been, in every sense, a baptism of fire. As on the navigational exercise at Gatwick when he flew blind through fog, his survival may well have been due to his extraordinary presence of mind amid the mayhem and chaos of air combat. Moreover, he now had invaluable experience of fighting with the enemy. Experience was to be the key for a fighter pilot; the more you had, the better your chance of survival.

The magnitude of this episode was played upon by the press, not least by the *War Illustrated News*, which covered the event in an article dated 22 November 1939. It was accompanied by a dashingly portrayed double-spread illustration painted by the artist, C.E. Turner.

The brilliant exploit of the French Air Force on the Western Front on November 6th, when nine fighter machines attacked three times their number, bringing down nine enemy aircraft without loss to themselves, is in the real tradition of French valour.

Two stages of midway phase and the end of this epic battle waged in a series of individual combats over a wide area over Forbach and Serreguinines, are in part illustrated by these remarkable interesting pictures.

A fact in which the RAF may feel justifiable pride is that the French success was the outcome of a British pilot finding himself far over the line, after pursuing a German reconnaissance machine and actually joining up with a Messerschmitt formation. The enemy pilots did not recognise the British machine at first. When they did, the pilot was able to escape and led Germans into the arms of the French.

The event was also featured in daily newspapers in Britain, especially the *Daily Mail* and the *Mirror*. It also made the *Southend Standard*:

Westcliff airman's busy day – Chased by 27 planes. Westcliff officer in thrilling escape – an unwitting decoy.

The local paper told the story in true Boys' Own fashion:

> When on a chilly day in November, Plt Off Peter V. Ayerst, whose home is at Southbourne Grove, Westcliff, took off from an aerodrome behind the English lines in France to chase a German plane that had been sighted, he little thought of the exciting adventure that lay ahead!
>
> There was no doubt that Plt Off Ayerst had served as an unwitting decoy and as a result, he was dubbed Decoy by his colleagues.

Peter returned home on leave. Back in Essex, he went to Southend aerodrome, not far from his parents' home at Westcliff. He knew that the civil and light aircraft that droned over the coast at the weekends had been replaced by No. 54 Squadron which had initially been based at Hornchurch but was now relayed at Southend.

Peter met two pilots, Al Deere and Colin Gray, who were to become legends during the Battle of Britain. This was a friendship which lasted until well after the war. The two New Zealanders had much in common with Peter, showing the same determination and resolute character. They were of the same mould, vintage and character, having joined before the outbreak of the war on a short-service commission. The three of them had a lot of fun together, largely revolving around the bar in the station mess.

Peter feels it is fair to say that Deere didn't suffer fools gladly, then, or indeed later on in his distinguished career. He distinctly remembers the twang in their accents. Deere was solid, reliable and an excellent pilot. When they met in 1939 at Southend, Peter was just nineteen, and Deere was twenty-two. He was determined, gritty and resolute, but compared to Colin Gray, Peter thinks Deere was positively introverted. Gray was a real live-wire: extrovert, gregarious and outgoing. In Peter's words, 'they were bloody good chaps'. Peter decided that it would be a good idea to have a party at his home at Newenden and he invited twelve pilots, including Deere, to Southborne Grove. Peter's brother Jack recalls that it was quite a party.

The rest of 1939 was spent back in France on the Rouvres airfield. The patrols and frays with enemy aircraft were increasing. Christmas was held in the school at the airfield, but the only festive observation that the squadron made that year was to hang two sprigs of mistletoe above the fireplace. Peter felt it was a shame that Geneviève wasn't there beneath! At least there was the warmth of the fire and the comfort of a beer or two from the bar. The only Christmas spirit was to be found from the hotels and bars; there wasn't any in the air.

Too many patrols to fly, various formations to practise. The New Year of 1940 provided some respite; pilots at last could catch their breath because the snows were heavy and cold that winter. The Hurricanes stayed where they were, idle and dormant under a blanket of white. It was impossible to get them off the ground in these conditions. The only good piece of news was that the Germans couldn't take their aircraft up over the lines either. The boys in France continued to receive Christmas Greetings from friends and relatives back home and Peter received a card from his old firm, W.A. Sparrow and Sons. It was dated 28 December:

I got a host of greetings in the Christmas mail but none that I valued more than yours. I naturally took it as a greeting to the office and it was therefore passed around immediately. You will have since received a little card from us which bears witness to that effect.

It went on to inform Peter of the company's war effort:

McGregor is in the London Scottish, Mr Raven is in the Royal Defence Corps; S.G. Page with the RAC and Stewart is in the Royal Artillery. May good luck go with you everywhere and may you return safely.

An epidemic of German measles ran wild through the village of Rouvres and the nearby town of Etain that January. It was the general consensus among the pilots that the Germans hadn't managed to bomb them, so they had resorted to other ideas! In fact, only two of the squadron members went down with measles: one was Cobber Kain, the other was Peter. They were packed off to convalesce in nearby Epernay, recuperating in a château that had been requisitioned by the British Army. It was the nearest thing the British Expeditionary Force had had to a hospital, and it was run by British doctors and nurses.

Peter and Cobber were shown into a ward on arrival. They noticed that there were ten young aircrew, all suffering from the same thing. They were hospitalised for a couple of weeks until they were given the all-clear by the doctors. The château-hospital was some 90 miles from Rouvres, so Peter rang their unit at about 11 a.m. one morning.

'Hello. It's Peter. Got any transport for Cobber and me?'

''Here's the situation. We don't have any spare transport at present. Sorry. The only thing we can possibly send for you is an ambulance, but it won't be with you for another five hours.'

He told Cobber. They looked at each other. What were they going to do for the next five hours?

They ambled out of the château-hospital into the avenue. It was the first time they had noticed there were large, elegant, beautiful châteaux in the rue. One particular château lay directly opposite the hospital and the pair noticed three words engraved on a plaque: Moët et Chandon. The same thought struck each patient.

Their French was pretty good, so they went up to one of the staff inside the château. 'We've just come out of hospital, we're waiting for some transport. Could we have a look round?'

Cobber and Peter were taken into the cellars that went on for miles and miles lying deep underneath. Down one wall were wooden racks bearing millions and millions of bottles, the necks of which sloped downwards. They were told that because the sediment gravitated towards the neck, this was a simple and efficient method of removing it. In a process called remuage, someone known as a remueur then came along and gave each bottle a quarter-turn. Word had got around that two RAF airmen were in the building. The managing director heard that they were in his cellars and summoned them to his office, where hands were shaken a little stiffly. 'Have some champagne', said the managing director, and he proceeded to pour some of the finest champagne the boys had tasted – and over the past few months they had tasted some! It was certainly the best medicine they had received over the last two weeks. Cobber and Peter chatted with the MD in his office for a couple of hours or so, then they thanked him for his hospitality and walked, a little unsteadily, outside to wait for some transport. Eventually, the ambulance from Rouvres turned up. It was, in fact, the most suitable transport the unit at Rouvres could have sent because, as Peter says, they were both so drunk. They returned to Rouvres laid out on stretchers in the back of this ambulance!

The cult of the fighter pilot was just beginning. With pilots like Edgar 'Cobber' Kain, the spring of 1940 gave the government publicity machine the perfect opportunity to improve public relations between Britain and the situation in France. People on the home front wanted to read about the dashing knights of the sky; they wanted to see their pictures. Moreover, it gave the Government a golden opportunity for recruitment. Both Nos 1 and 73 Squadrons received an increasingly large interest from reporters, especially the British press, who described the men behind the myth: that is, the men who flew in the vanguard of the British Expeditionary Force. There were visitors from all over the world, and Peter remembers giving an interview to a Greek reporter, although he says that most reporters, who arrived at Rouvres in a little de Havilland Dragon Rapide, went straight to Cobber Kain. A couple of well-established reporters made a particular impression upon Peter. The *Daily Mirror* was represented by Stanley Devon, the only reporter who had been allowed to wear an RAF uniform with the word 'Press' sewn prominently on his shoulder. He was also an excellent photographer, taking various pictures of the squadron in 'classic' fighter pilot poses – pilots 'scrambling' towards their aircraft; pilots astride their mounts; pilots taking whatever the Hun could throw at them. The *Daily Mail* had sent Noel Monks, who had also written *Squadron's Up*.

Peter's first kill came in April 1940. As he says in his logbook, 'I clobbered my first Messerchmitt Me 109 and damaged another.' The squadron was flying so many patrols at this time that he says he had to get one sooner or later, it was merely a matter of time. RAF pilots saw Me 109s either in combat or on patrol and it was a happy-go-lucky kind of scrap:

6 April – Chased a Dornier 17. It dived very steeply and made for home. Machine damaged in fuselage.
7 April – Offensive patrol of six aircraft at 23,000ft. Met six Me 109s. Me 109s immediately turned back for home when they sighted Hurricanes. Several pilots fired their guns at long range. No enemy aircraft confirmed. Self, one damaged, since confirmed.
7 April – Offensive patrol between Thionville and Boulay. Nine aircraft at 26,500ft. Encountered approximately twenty 109s. Shot down one, crashed near Boulay.

For many pilots, getting their first kill was a defining moment, not just in their career, but also in their life. It was almost as if they felt they had been 'blooded' and it was life-changing. Peter doesn't feel that he had any experience like that. The only thing akin to sentiment he felt was, 'got you, you bastard!'. Unlike for many fighter pilots, for him it was not a sentimental event. He says that he never felt sad or unhappy about it; no way, quite the opposite. Three cheers. The incident on 7 April was reported by Noel Monks, Special Correspondent to the *Daily Mail*:

Another Essex man, a young pilot officer from Westcliff, sent an enemy aircraft crashing on the outskirts of Guling-Moselle.

The British authorities were being overrun by the German forces, and it was decided to withdraw the air component. Peter thinks that perhaps they were getting edgy about the possibility of the Germans invading France. By 11 April No. 73 Squadron was posted to Reims for a week, but eight days later it was moved back to Rouvres and back to the usual defensive patrols:

21 April – Patrol at 25,000ft. Squadron Leader More led the nine aircraft ran onto Me 109s and Me 110s, about thirty in all. Three 109s and two 110s shot down. Flying Officer Walker wounded in the shoulder. Self one 109 shot down in Hurricane 'O'.

Peter didn't have time to enjoy his victory, watching his prey crashing to the ground. He says that one of the lessons he had learnt early on was that you couldn't afford to sit around and watch 'your' aircraft because there were other enemy aircraft on your tail, waiting to do precisely the same to you. Even if pilots thought they had damaged one, the ones who had survived didn't hang around. They always had to look round behind them to see if there were other enemy planes on their tail, look behind them three-quarters of the time and in front for the remaining quarter. The proportional difference had been well-worked out; most attacks came from behind.

When pilots found themselves in a dogfight they never really saw where their bullets ended up and therefore could never be absolutely certain that an enemy aircraft had been hit, unless it exploded or flames were licking around the fuselage; they knew that bullets might hit an enemy aircraft but they couldn't tell precisely where. Peter's eight machine-guns, four in each wing, had been calibrated to 250yds. The guns were aligned so that the pilots fired their bullets in an X shape, with the centre of the

X being the fuselage of an enemy aircraft. Peter and the other pilots had just fifteen seconds' worth of firepower, although he says that that is a long time. They kept their thumbs on the firing button for no more than two, perhaps three, seconds. If the pilots picked up an enemy aircraft within a distance of 300yds, their bullets would have long since crossed over, missing the aircraft at the top of the X. As the pilots were closing in to about 250yds, the momentum of speed from the Hurricane meant that the centre of the X was now directly on the fuselage of the enemy aircraft. At 200yds, the pilots had to break off. Tracer bullets were used initially, but Peter and the boys found that they were more of a hindrance than a help because the tracer bullet had a different trajectory path and tended to drop quickly.

All the pilots had come across Me 109s by this time, but the Luftwaffe's new twin-engined fighter-bomber, the Me 110, was still relatively unknown over the green of Rouvres. Unlike many who came across it, Peter thought it was vastly underrated, although he agrees that it didn't have the agility of an Me 109.

It was during the spring of 1940 that the war began to gain momentum in earnest. A direct consequence of this was the need for more RAF recruits to swell the ranks of ever-increasing trades: balloon operators; cooks; pilots aged eighteen to twenty-eight; air observers; wireless operators/air gunners.

To raise awareness of the diverse roles available within the Air Force, the publicity department began producing recruiting pamphlets. The front page bore the title: *On His Majesty's Service, The Commanding Officer, Royal Air Force Recruiting Office*. A photograph of a man from each trade smiled contentedly and the accompanying slogan said that 'The Royal Air Force needs men like these NOW!' Inside the pamphlet, a headline stated where recruits should enrol, followed by a column of recruiting centres all over Britain. And in the centre of the pamphlet, flanked by Swansea to Skegness, Glasgow to Gravesend, was a photograph of Peter in his aircraft, looking towards the photographer. He got quite a shock when he first saw it. 'Bugger me! I was smiling at the camera, complete with Irvin jacket, flying helmet, sitting astride the canopy of my Hurricane.' It was one of many taken by the *Daily Mirror*'s Stanley Devon, a classic image of a fighter pilot. Evidently this was the view shared by the RAF publicity department, who saw this photo as a shot of a nineteen-year-old to whom aspiring pilots could relate. Peter had become the face of the RAF.

No. 73 Squadron found that it was now coming into contact with the Luftwaffe on a daily basis during the spring days of April 1940. Pilots flew along patrol lines, mostly defensive, such as the 30-mile line between Thionville and Metz, patrolling at a height of 25,000ft in a Vic formation. After about an hour, another Vic formation from the same flight took over and this pattern continued for most of the daylight hours.

Peter also remembers flying offensive patrols. Occasionally they were taken further forward, closer to the border around Metz, towards the direction of Saarbrucken. These offensive flights were provocative, deliberate, flown in the hope that the Germans would pick them up, take the bait and have a bang at them. The pilots anticipated that flying over enemy lines all day would eventually entice the Luftwaffe, but Peter says they didn't play very often. Opportunities to shoot at the enemy came seldom because the No. 73 Squadron pilots did not actually meet the Germans all that often.

In addition to the fighters, the Luftwaffe sent over individual bombers, like Dornier 17s, for observation and reconnaissance flights. The bombers used to come over at quite a high altitude. If the RAF pilots were lucky enough to be airborne at the time, Peter recalls that they might be able to 'have a go' at the Dornier. No. 73 Squadron had settled into a routine, accepting it for what it was. Peter feels that they were, more or less, feeling their way in France; testing the aircraft, the flying formations, communications, testing themselves to some degree. In fairness, the Germans were probably doing the same.

As far as Peter was concerned, by late April things were beginning to hot up a bit, but none of the squadron realised that an invasion was imminent. Everyone thought that the Luftwaffe was sending over more planes because of an improvement in the weather, whereas what these aircraft were actually doing was testing equipment, formations, techniques and strategy for the invasion of the Low Countries. On the same day, the Germans came over and bombed Rouvres airfield while ground forces systematically invaded Holland and Belgium and all points in between, from the Channel coast in the north to the south, around Verdun, Metz and Rouvres.

Up until now, both sides had been probing each other, testing each other; searching for a weakness, a chink in the armour that might be breached. It was to prove a lull before the storm. The truth was that the British Expeditionary Force was overwhelmed and under-resourced by the thunder and lightening of the Blitzkrieg which struck on 10 May 1940. The Germans invaded the Low Countries, heralding an intensity in the war. The next month was going to be a rout for the British Expeditionary Force; a sorry and ignominious exit to the aspirations of the senior staff who had planned the operation as well as those who were fighting in France. Allied forces were not to set foot on continental soil for another five years. Hitler had gained the upper hand.

As the German forces were pushing ever westwards, Peter was ill with a very high temperature. He was not alone: another pilot, Derek Kain, had contracted the same virus. It was time to say goodbye to Rouvres. The others in No. 73 Squadron were told by BEF HQ to retreat immediately from Rouvres; they were to be posted forthwith to the relative safety of Reims airfield. Because they were suffering from the virus, Peter and Derek were unable to fly and were subsequently told to make arrangements for the withdrawal of the squadron. Remaining at Rouvres, they organised the evacuation. The school that had been home to the squadron mess for the past nine months had to be emptied; ground crew and vehicles had to be evacuated with speed and safety. Once the withdrawal of the squadron had been completed, Peter and Derek Kain were able to leave.

As they recuperated, the others prepared the aircraft; shouts from ground crew and airmen striking tents and carrying kit, trucks pulling away, the air full of Merlin engines – warming up, idling, taxiing and roaring down the French grass for the last time. The Hurricanes soon disappeared, bound for Reims.

The squadron stayed at Echemines, near Reims, for about a week or so, catching its breath, before being withdrawn once again, this time to an airfield in the south which Derek Kain and Peter had been asked to locate. They found a reasonable grass-strip at Gaye, near the town of Troyes. Driving back, they returned to Reims and informed the authorities, who told them the following day that they were to base themselves at Gaye in preparation (not that they could prepare much!) for the arrival of the rest of the squadron. The authorities then decreed that No. 73 Squadron should retreat to Gaye.

While they were still at Reims, the squadron received details from Advanced Air Striking Force HQ that all pilots, NCOs as well as officers, who had flown in France since September 1939 were to be sent back to Britain. The intention was for all pilot officers, including Peter, to be relieved en masse, but only when replacement officers began to arrive. This was the signal for the mass retreat of the AASF; the rout had begun. It would be fair to say that at this stage the pilots' views on what was currently happening to the squadron had become somewhat wayward. Peter recalls that the general train of thought among them was along the lines of 'Christ, what the hell is going on?'

It was at this point, while the squadron was waiting to be relieved from Echemines, that Edgar Cobber Kain was killed in an unnecessary and pointless flying accident. Kain had been flying one of the older Hurricanes, virtually time-expired. He had completed his tour and had finished his flying with the squadron but had decided to stay on for a few extra days. Peter was not witness to what precisely happened but was told by the others that Cobber had been beating up the airfield. By all accounts, he had been performing a victory roll, but unfortunately his stunt was too low to the ground and he went in. Peter thinks he might well have been flying too low and had actually hit something. There is every likelihood that Kain had been showing off, and a direct result of Kain's death was the immediate banning of victory rolls over airfields. Britain's first fighter ace of the Second World War was dead. It is interesting to speculate how many more kills Kain would have added to his tally if he had survived.

At the end of May Peter left Gaye together with Dickie Martin and Graham Paul, making their way to Paris by train. On reaching the French capital, the trio stayed there for a night during which they had time to relax and get their thoughts together. It also gave them a much-needed opportunity to let their hair down. After recent events, they didn't need much of an excuse. Peter recalls that they had quite a party that night.

The following morning, they decided to split up and go their own way in order to reach the destination port of Cherbourg; it was every man for himself. Transport was minimal: there were no trains and any motor vehicles were severely hampered by the mass evacuation of the French populace. The roads were completely blocked nose-to-tail with refugees, mile, after mile, after mile. Cars were pulled by horses so that every available space inside could be used for personal possessions; mattresses were tied to the roof of each car and their owners walked along beside their cars, matching the slow plodding pace of their horses. Peter managed to hitch a lift on the back of an old open-topped potato lorry to the north of Paris. It was one slow-moving column, blocking the road entirely, and if an oncoming vehicle tried to pass from the opposite direction, pandemonium ensued. It hampered Peter's potato lorry and it was a rough ride, sitting on the sacks of potatoes with just one small bag of kit. He swears that that vehicle had square wheels.

The lorry made it to Cherbourg, however. Having negotiated the arduous roads from Paris rather the worse for wear, Peter arrived at the port only to discover that mayhem and turmoil, which he thought he had left behind, had followed; confusion, chaos and disorder reigned supreme as the members of the once-proud Expeditionary Force shouted, pushed and jostled one another, clambering to get aboard the ships that were being bombed by the Junkers Ju 87 Stukas.

Peter discovered that safe passage to Britain was at a premium; very few ships had made the journey to Cherbourg and, as a result, equally few spaces were available. A similar pattern was emerging away to the north-east, at Dunkirk. One ship had already berthed in the harbour, full of soldiers and airmen, and the crew was preparing to leave with haste. Peter was told by the officer organising the boarding that if he did not manage to secure a position on this particular ship, he would have just one last opportunity of leaving France; there was only one other ship prepared to pick up troops from Cherbourg, because the harbour was still being heavily bombed. Peter says the ship was packed and he had a hard time fighting his way on board, but he was not prepared to spend much time on the harbour. His gain was someone else's loss but it was every man for himself. He was determined to leave France.

Cherbourg and Dunkirk were not alone in the mass withdrawal of the British Expeditionary Force.

All along the north-west coast of France, every port and harbour was being pressed into service, coping with the tide of British evacuation that was now increasing at a rate of knots.

Sixty ground crew from No. 73 Squadron had boarded HMT

Lancastria from the port of St Nazaire. The ship had just left the harbour on 17 June, making for home, when it took a direct hit. As a result of the bombing, thirty-five souls from the sixty on board were lost, including Peter's batman, Ashley. In total it is estimated that 2,500 lives were lost. This was one of the worst maritime disasters of the entire war involving a British merchant vessel.

Peter travelled across the Channel by night, eliminating the chances of being bombed during the 120 miles to Britain. It was with some relief for the passengers that the ship reached the safe berth in Southampton docks early the following Saturday morning.

Stepping onto English soil, Peter was told to report to the Railway Transport Officer (RTO), an Army officer who was briefing soldiers disembarking from ships on exactly where they should go. He was, however, less competent with pilots. His behaviour may have been in response to the ill-feeling and resentment that had materialised between the Army and the Air Force. Because the Army had been bombed incessantly at the ports, they felt, quite wrongly, that the RAF had not provided sufficient air cover. The RTO advised Peter that he should head back to his original RAF station, Digby.

He caught the Waterloo train from Southampton station. That Saturday morning was a particularly lovely day, bright and sunny. As the train travelled through the pleasant Hampshire countryside, he looked out of the window and couldn't quite believe what he saw; white clad figures playing cricket on immaculate village greens. It was if nothing had changed, almost as if England had been oblivious to what was happening on the other side of the channel. As he says, 'There we were, buggering around France for the past three weeks going without sleep (when we did, it was in some very strange places), hardly eating; having an incredibly rough time.' When the train arrived at Waterloo, they were stopped by an admin officer who informed Peter that he was to be given 48 hours' leave, reporting to RAF Digby on the following Monday.

Peter rolled through the gates of RAF Digby on the Monday and met three other survivors from France. All were shattered and were longing for a decent spell of leave.

The survivors were told that the AOC of 12 Group wanted to see them forthwith. AVM Trafford Leigh-Mallory was about to come to prominence during the Battle of Britain. His brother George had ascended Everest in a tweed jacket and hobnail boots. Extremely ambitious, Leigh-Mallory was regarded by many as 'an upper-class twit', a man who was not up to the job. He was to clash in the summer of 1940 with the Commander-in-Chief of Fighter Command, Hugh Dowding, but especially with Dowding's right-hand man, the AOC of 11 Group, AVM Keith Park.

Leigh-Mallory met them in a small room in the officers' mess at Digby. He told them that things were crucial at present in regard to the invasion and they were going to find themselves in a very acute position in the future. The survivors had been in France for nine months, they had been through hell. Not surprisingly, they thought that leave might be granted and asked him. According to Peter his terse reply was: 'You can have four days. Then I want you to report to some new units which we are forming.' 'They are to be called Fighter Operational Training Units, OTUs. We have two at the moment: one at Sutton Bridge where Hurricanes are being used, and Aston Down where they have both Spitfires and Hurricanes. As far as you chaps are concerned, I want you to go to Sutton Bridge.' The only time that Peter met Trafford Leigh-Mallory was short and to the point.

The BEF and the Air Component had proved to be a disaster. Valuable resources – men and machines – had been lost. Few lessons had been learnt from No. 73 Squadron's time in France, and what little had been learnt was incorporated hastily throughout the summer, during the Battle of Britain. In terms of battle tactics and combat, Fighter Command still had much to organise.

What had been gathered so far had been due to the pilots of Nos 1 and 73 Squadrons. In many ways, Peter and the rest of the pilots had been guinea-pigs during the Battle for France.

FOUR

Instructor!

Operational Training Units (OTUs) were a new concept in the Royal Air Force in the spring of 1940. In keeping with the RAF modernisation programme, the philosophy behind the training units was to develop and impart the practical knowledge of pilots with operational experience to pupil pilots who had completed their advanced courses and were to be posted to their squadrons.

In June, there were two fighter OTUs that had been established in Britain: No. 5 based at Aston Down in Gloucestershire, and No. 6 located at the Lincolnshire airfield of Sutton Bridge. The survivors from No. 1 Squadron were posted to Aston Down. After four days' leave, as commanded by Trafford Leigh-Mallory, Ian Scoular, Dickie Martin, Graham Paul and Peter found themselves at Sutton Bridge on 14 June 1940. Peter went into Hurricanes in the same flight led by his old flight commander, but he wasn't there for long: after three weeks, Peter was to be posted to No. 7 OTU at Hawarden, a recently formed operational training unit, on 6 July.

During his time at Sutton Bridge, Peter acquired invaluable flying time on other types of fighter aircraft that were now considered obsolete and were being used as training aircraft. He managed to get his hands on a Gloster Gladiator on 19 June. Small and agile, the Gladiator was the last biplane fighter of the RAF and had been at Digby with No. 73 Squadron before it was equipped with Hurricanes. He says that he found it light and responsive compared to the Hurricane; he was airborne before he knew where he was. Scoular, his flight commander, had never flown the Harvard, and Peter took him in one once for a familiarisation flight. He also flew the Fairey Battle, a three-seater, single-engined light bomber designed for a crew of pilot, navigator and gunner. It was not a success. More than 100 Fairey Battles had been delivered by the outbreak of the war, and most had been sent as part of the Advanced Air Striking Force. The aircraft's poor defence and lack of power came to light. After 10 May the aircraft suffered heavy losses, losing thirteen to anti-aircraft fire on one operation alone. The following day a further seven out of eight were lost. It was soon realised that the Battle was anything but formidable! Although it was equipped with the same Merlin engine as the Spitfire and Hurricane, it was underpowered and heavy, with a massive wingspan, and Peter's thoughts on the aircraft emphasise its failings. How did he find it? He found it bloody useless! Nevertheless he was asked to chauffeur one of his instructors to Swinderby in a Battle. Peter Powell-Sheddon was known as a forceful character. He explained to Peter: 'You see, I'm getting married on Saturday and the ceremony is taking place at a church nearby. Just be a little careful when you approach finals; they're doing a little building work.'

Expansion had begun at the airfield and construction of suitable buildings was now growing apace.

Peter agreed to fly him; it was for a good cause and should take only thirty minutes to fly from Sutton Bridge to Swinderby. As the Battle approached the airfield, Peter could see what Powell-Sheddon meant about the building work – a significant amount was taking place. The undercarriage from the slow, clumsy aircraft was lowered and the rubber tyres found the grass. Peter threaded the Battle through the maze of new structures springing up on the Lincolnshire flatlands, taxing to a halt. As Powell-Sheddon clambered out of the cockpit he turned back, with a grin on his face:

'Cheers Pete!' he said.

'Have a good wedding!' replied Peter. Some two weeks later, Peter was called before the Commanding Officer at

Sutton Bridge: 'Do you know why you are here, Ayerst?' asked the officer.

'No Sir.'

'Did you land a Battle at Swinderby recently?'

'Yes Sir.'

'You do realise, Ayerst, that aircraft are not supposed to land at Swinderby because the airfield is being developed? And who gave you permission to land?'

The feet shuffled. 'Well, no one Sir. We just landed there.'

'I see. Why did you take a Battle in the first place?'

'I was taking Powell-Sheddon to his wedding, Sir.'

In his own words, Peter received nothing more than a mild dressing down. Powell-Sheddon saw the Commanding Officer and explained that it had been his idea all along.

June was warm, hot and sunny in the fenland base of Sutton Bridge. Everyone was well aware that the Luftwaffe was beginning to penetrate over the skies of southern England with increasing regularity. What was later to be termed the Battle of Britain was just beginning.

The numbers of pupil pilots entering through the gates of Sutton Bridge also increased. Peter, Dickie, Graham and the others were briefed that the training they gave to these pupils should be as comprehensive as possible. Much of these techniques were 'hot off the press', stemming from the instructors' recent experience in France. The sort of training that pupils received included attacks on single aircraft, dogfighting, blind-flying instruction and formation-flying in cloud.

Blind flying into cloud was a particular technique that Peter favoured, leading the rookies into formation and heading into a bank of cloud. Trusting their nerve in cloud was extremely difficult for pupil pilots. As a technique it was somewhat rudimentary when compared to today's blind-flying techniques. In addition to flying into cloud, the instructors would place a hood over their pupils' heads and get them to sit in the back seat of the Harvard to become accustomed, while the instructor sat in the front.

It was becoming increasingly clear that fighter squadrons were losing their pilots. They needed replacements with the utmost speed. The decision had been taken by the RAF that fighter pilots who had just completed their advanced course were required to join operational squadrons as soon as possible. In order to push these pilots through to the squadrons, the authorities realised that there were not enough operational training units at present and that the two existing units at Aston Down and Sutton Bridge were not going to be able to cope with the ensuing flood. The decision was taken therefore to establish a third operational training unit, No. 7 at Hawarden, Cheshire. A handful of instructors were picked from Sutton Bridge in tandem with a handful from Aston Down, and together these instructors formed the nucleus for the new OTU at Hawarden.

Three weeks later, after his arrival at Sutton Bridge, Peter was told that he was to be sent to this new training unit at Hawarden. In order to bridge the gap between advanced flying and operational flying, the unit was given Spitfires as well as Hurricanes. The basis of instruction at Hawarden comprised about a third of the instructors from Sutton Bridge, together with a third from those at Aston Down. Peter reported to Hawarden along with Ken Campbell, the sergeant pilot who was a particularly good artist, the diminutive Scot, Ian Brotchie, and Sgt Pilkington. He discovered that his close friends, Graham Paul and Dickie Martin, were to remain at Sutton Bridge. Those instructors who came from Aston Down included Cam Malfroy from New Zealand – Malfroy had played tennis in the championships at Wimbledon.

Peter was one of the first instructors to reach the new airfield, which crept over the Welsh border. Hawarden was some 5 miles to the west of Chester, and Wrexham was 10 miles due south. RAF Sealand was a stone's throw away. From the airfield, the instructors could see the mountains away in the distance to the south-west, while the River Dee flowed through Chester, running in a channel to the estuary, and then out and away into the Irish Sea. Unlike Swinderby, no expansion scheme was taking place at Hawarden – just a large grass field with a small semi-detached building.

The instructors initially lived under canvas. It took Peter back to his days in France, but the difference was that this time he had a bell tent of his own. In time-honoured tradition, a large marquee was established with the obligatory bar as the officers' mess. One half of the semi-detached building was given over to a base for unit headquarters; the other half was employed as offices for Gp Capt O'Neill, the unit's Commanding Officer.

The purpose of operational training units was to draw on the operational experience of pilots like Peter so that they had instructors who could teach pupils precisely what they had learned in France, such as new ways to evade an enemy, new formation tactics or different shooting practices. This was rather ironic in Peter's case because he was still only nineteen. The instructors at Hawarden began by giving new pilots some dual-instruction on the Miles Master, a two-seater advanced trainer. It was an ideal aircraft to get to grips with because it was a high-performance trainer, filling the gap which led to flying high-performance operational aircraft.

The Master bore a likeness to the Hurricane and had similar characteristics to both the Hurricane and Spitfire. In terms of performance, the Master was only about 15mph slower than the Hurricane.

Of course, these pilots could already fly – the objective was to familiarise and gain competence on approaches and landings when they flew the Spitfire. Peter climbed into a Spitfire for the first time at Hawarden on 6 July 1940, spending 30 minutes on a familiarisation flight. Thereafter, having flown his first trip, he was then instructing pilots on it. Five days later on 11 July, he was carrying out a defensive operational patrol in one of these Spitfires!

Pilots, especially pupils, found landing a Spitfire extremely difficult due to the nose; Peter realised that he couldn't just approach and land on finals in the same way that he did in a Hurricane, because he couldn't see what lay ahead. Peter discovered and instructed student pilots accordingly that the answer was to approach the airfield at an angle, then, at the last minute, straighten out ready for landing. The Spitfire was considerably different from the Hurricane, particularly on take-off and landing. On take-off, Peter found he had to keep checking that his line was clear. On finals, he could easily make a square approach in a Hurricane, losing height crosswind and turning at about 500ft, landing on the angle he had chosen. In the Spitfire, he had to learn a different method of approach – curving the Spitfire round before he made his final approach.

Instructors gave their student pilots about two or three solo flights to get the feel of the Spitfire. As they gained confidence, gradually becoming familiar with the controls, the instructors started to take the students up, giving them a taste of what it was like to fly in a formation. Although some experience had been gained on their advanced flying courses, Peter says that flying in formations could be a little dicey at first, because while he instructed them over the R/T that they should stick together, keeping line and length, in reality he saw them flying all over the place. At times, he says, 'it could be bloody hairy!'.

Although the pressure was on these pilots to join the fighter squadrons at the earliest available opportunity, they had a short period to acclimatise on the Spitfire. What Peter and the other instructors would have given for such training. They, of course, had had to learn the hard way; their training had been on the job.

Having managed to shape his students into some reasonable standard of formation flying, Peter then set about instructing new tactics that he had picked up during his time at No. 73 Squadron. There was no time for gentle regularity in the heat of the moment; aircraft had become much faster and tactics used during the Battle of France were dispensed with. Three strategies in particular were rejected – No. 1 Fighter Attack, where a section of fighters attacked a lone enemy bomber by flying and attacking line astern; No. 2 Fighter Attack, where fighters climbed astern and individually attacked an enemy bomber before breaking away; and No. 3 Fighter Attack, where a flight of six fighters individually concentrated on attacking their opposite number in an enemy formation.

As well as the instruction of tactics, pupils also gained experience on firing the Browning 0.303 machine-guns. No. 7 OTU possessed a firing range at Hawarden by the River Dee where the students calibrated their sights and harnessed their guns. Unlike Peter's air-to-air training on his advanced course at Abersoch, there was no target-tug aircraft available to pull a drogue.

Students trained at Hawarden for a period of about three weeks before they were posted onto operational flying. They were urgently required by the fighter squadrons which were so desperately short of fighter pilots. Peter says that their total flying time was minimal. The pilots left Hawarden with just fifteen to twenty hours on Spitfires. It was, quite frankly, not enough.

It must have been a little strange for a nineteen-year-old instructor to be training pupil pilots who were much older than him. Part of the role of an instructor included aircrew selection, and Peter remembers that he and his colleagues had to cut certain pilots who just couldn't cope with the training for a Spitfire because they lacked the necessary ability and feel. Unable to deal with what was required from a fighter pilot, these students were then posted onto bombers or went into a training role; they just didn't have the touch to fly a Spitfire in operational conditions. Flying a Spitfire was vastly different from a trainer, and successful fighter pilots needed a special sense of awareness during their training period.

The instructors and pupils were flying Spitfire Mk Is during Peter's time at Hawarden. It was faster than the Hurricane and Peter enjoyed the Mk I, but the one drawback was the lack of an automatic system for raising and lowering the undercarriage; the only way to raise the wheels was manually, with a hand pump. The process was rather hard work, especially for a novice pilot. He would select the switch to 'up' on the wheels-up lever, then would have to reach for the long pump tucked away to the right of his right leg. As it was situated so close to the side of the metal fuselage, Peter says that instructors could always tell novice pilots who had just taken their first solos because the backs of their hands were rubbed raw from the pumping. If they wore gloves, the back of the leather would be blanched. Pupils – and instructors – soon learnt to place their hand ON TOP of the pump.

The other telltale sign that novice pilots had only just taken their solo was the sight of a Spitfire porpoising up and down into the air. Once they had taken off, pilots had to change hands rapidly, swapping the right hand gripping the joystick with the left. The right was employed to pump while the left gripped the joystick, and this aerial seesawing was caused by the novices pumping away at the undercarriage. Peter says that it happened to pilots almost every time, without fail. In the end, the instructors advised the pupils on how to remedy the situation: 'Now look, when you're holding the joystick in your left hand, dig your left arm into your ribs so that you, and the Spit, will have more stability.' Peter certainly felt that the Spitfire was a sharper aircraft than the Hurricane. The aileron controls, in particular, were more sensitive. The controls on a Hurricane became excessively heavy, especially in a dive, and he says it was a joy not to have to fight them.

Because of the regular influx of new and novice pilots, Peter came across a number of students who were to epitomise what being a fighter pilot was all about. They became legends. Two such notable students whom Peter instructed at Hawarden in July 1940 were Paddy Finucane and Paddy Barthrop. Both pilots had some, albeit limited, flying experience prior to arriving at No. 7 OTU. Barthropp had flown Westland Lysanders in France. Westland had produced Lysanders to fulfil an army cooperation role, but the aircraft did not fair well in France. Indeed, it suffered drastic losses, and as a direct consequence Lysander pilots were recalled and assigned to other duties. Barthrop was one such pilot who had been transferred to the Spitfire. It may have been his Irish roots, but Peter thinks it is fair to say that he was a bit of a wild one; he was, however, very amusing and extremely likeable. Barthrop had joined the RAF before the outbreak of war, and therefore had much in common with many of the instructors at Hawarden. It was not unusual to see Peter and Barthrop enjoying several beers in the mess: a rare occasion of pupil socalising with instructor. Barthrop became a POW during the war, and established a Rolls-Royce chauffeuring service to the entertainment business and aristocracy afterwards.

In contrast, Paddy Finucane was far more serious-minded than Barthrop. Peter described him as more steady and reliable. It took him less than a year to become a fighter ace, but by 1941 he was shot down over the Channel and failed to bale out. Peter was also responsible for training the RAF's highest-scoring fighter ace by the end of the war. This was James Edgar 'Johnnie' Johnson, who had just completed his training course at No. 5 FTS, 5 miles down the road at RAF Sealand. In keeping with the personality of a fighter pilot, Peter says that Johnson was a lively character who liked a drink. Many pilots had a particular passion for life's pleasures at that time. Most young people do in any case, but fighter pilots, living daily with the constant threat of death, found that drink alleviated the stress. No one knew if they would return the next day. Johnson was older than many at Hawarden, certainly older than Peter, and he went on to become an air vice-marshal.

It is interesting to speculate how much these fighter pilot legends owe much of their high-scoring tallies and survival to the instruction, advice and experience imparted by Peter. Although a pupil had to have an awareness, a feel which cannot be taught, to make it as a fighter pilot, this innate awareness in a pilot's personality had to be channelled correctly – it had to be used properly at 25,000ft if the pilot was to survive. Peter and his fellow instructors took this raw material, honing it and instilling vital discipline in the air over an incredibly short timeframe. It was this instilling of discipline that contributed significantly to a pilot's survival, and certainly to the likes of Barthrop and Johnson.

Peter was also responsible for instructing three pilots who were among the first to arrive from the United States and went on to fight in the Battle of Britain. Much was made by the media of the importance of bringing America into the war, since she was at this point still neutral. Focusing on American pilots was one way in which the American people could see the vital difference their boys were making. Later on, many flyers from the States came over to Britain to fly and fight against Germany.

The Americans whom Peter instructed were dubbed the 'Three Musketeers' by the press.

Peter recalls that all three had different characters but they were great fun. Andy Mamedoff was of medium build and fairly solid in terms of physicality, swarthy in complexion with black hair. Red Tobin was tall and slimly built. His nickname was given to him at an early age because of his red hair. The third 'Musketeer' was Vernon 'Shorty' Keough, no more than 4ft 10in in stature and easily the shortest pilot in the RAF. He also had a slightly humped back, which Peter believes may have been sustained from a parachute injury. Keough had been a professional parachutist at air shows all over America during the barnstorming days, making something like 400–500 jumps before he left for England. In fact, like many American pilots after the First World War, all three had taken up barnstorming, touring rural towns and villages from one coast to the other, to display breathtaking aerial performances. By the time they reached Hawarden, it was certainly true that they knew how to fly an aeroplane. The Three Musketeers were posted to No. 71 (Eagle) Squadron after their instruction and they were killed before the end of the war.

Peter took Shorty Keough for a familiarisation flight on 18 July 1940, taking Mamedoff the following day for some dual flying. A couple of days later, he took the Three Musketeers up in formation. Peter has kept a newspaper cutting of Shorty Keough's death in his logbook, but there is no date.

Pilot Officer Vernon Charles Keough, who was one of the best known professional stunt parachutists in America, was lost while on patrol on Saturday off the East coast as a member of the Eagle Squadron, the all-American fighter unit of the RAF. Known in the Squadron as Shorty, Keough was under five foot and claimed to be the shortest pilot officer in Fighter Command, but he was great in defensive spirit and a fighter pilot of outstanding ability.

After their disastrous combat record, Fairey Battles were now used as hack aircraft, with instructors managing to transport their 'crew' in them; they were far more effective as an aerial taxi. Peter used a Battle to good effect when he went on a jolly, piling six bodies into the back: one pilot and five in the back, flying down to Hendon airfield for a night out on the town. They frequented the Liaison Club in the Prince's Arcade between Piccadilly and Jermyn Street. It was during the autumn of 1940 when London had to 'take it', suffering under Luftwaffe bombs in what was the beginning of the Blitz. Peter and his colleagues were in the Liaison Club when the first of these bombing raids struck. As the bombs dropped all around them, Peter and the others slept on the sofas, covering themselves with tablecloths.

The Battle of Britain continued to rage in the skies over Kent, Surrey and Sussex for more than four months. New tactics and formations had been devised to repel the intended German invasion.

This meant that much of Peter's and his colleagues' experience from their days in France was fast becoming out of date; tactics had moved on. The squadrons in south-eastern

England were devising the best and quickest methods of combat with the German Me 109s, much as Peter had done a year before. The instructors realised that relying on obsolete strategies was useless; the information they gave had to be contemporary and up to date so that pupils received the best-possible instruction. It could make the difference between life and death. By the autumn of 1940 the decision was taken by Gp Capt Seward, the Commanding Officer at Hawarden, along with the Officer in Charge of Flying, Wg Cdr Hallings-Pott, to post instructors to operational squadrons in order to keep pace with any changes. Peter was attached to No. 54 Squadron at Catterick. It was while he was in the bleak flat wilds of North Yorkshire that Peter met the New Zealanders, Al Deere and Colin Gray. Things had changed since they had last seen each other at Southend; Deere was now promoted to flight commander, but Colin Gray was as irrepressible as ever.

Accommodation and the matter of billeting at Hawarden was an issue that the CO, Gp Capt O'Neill, was keen to settle as soon as possible. It was unrealistic for instructors and pupils to sleep in tents with the onset of winter. Eventually, the training unit managed to requisition Hawarden Castle. For the first two weeks of the requisition, pilots shared the castle with the Gladstone family, who still lived there; the owner at the time was the grandson of William Gladstone, Prime Minister to Queen Victoria. Peter met him briefly and recalls he was in his sixties and accompanied by his sister.

Peter was the first member of the training unit to be billeted in the castle. He was given a marvellous room that was fully carpeted and had a very comfortable bed with a deep mattress. He had his own wash-basin and the bathroom was just down the corridor. It was sheer luxury after sleeping under canvas in the bell tent, but the euphoria was short-lived. When Wg Cdr Hallings-Pott saw the room, he pulled rank and commandeered it for himself. 'Peter Ayerst, out of there! I want that room.' So, Peter Ayerst went to share another room, equally luxurious, with a fellow instructor named Colin Brett. Like Peter, Flt Lt Brett had started flying before the war, but was a few years older. Peter says he used to drink pink gin as if it were water. In the evening, as the two prepared for bed, Brett would meticulously place a gin on the wash-basin shelf. There was a very good reason for this, he told Peter. As he began to clean his teeth, he would periodically reach for the glass, rinsing his mouth out with the gin. As Peter says, sometimes he would get incredibly blotto. The two received frequent visits from old friends, in particular from Harold Bird-Wilson, known as Birdie, who went on to become an air vice-marshal. 'Come on in, Birdy,' Peter said, reaching for Brett's bottle, 'have yourself a gin!' Brett was to leave Hawarden shortly afterwards for the creation of a new training unit, which was established at Pembrey, South Wales.

All the instructors were real characters, and Brett was not the only one at Hawarden. Among their ranks was a highly decorated fighter pilot ace who had flown Sopwith Camels during the First World War. Peter recalls 'Taffy' Jones as a Welshman with a huge, black, bushy moustache and a stutter.

Once flying was over for the day, it was customary for both student pilots and instructors to make the short trip to Chester. Peter remembers that one of their favourite haunts was the bar at the Blossoms Hotel. It was especially nicely furnished and well-to-do and they had to be extremely respectable. Old habits die hard, and a bottle of champagne would be purchased and split between the group. One evening, Taffy got hold of a swizzle-stick and placed it in his glass. As he began to rub the stick with his hands, backwards and forwards, the cry of 'Cheers!' went round the table. Old Taffy was still there, concentrating on the swizzle-stick between his hands.

'Why are you taking those bubbles out that have been so expensively put in?'

'Well,' he replied in earnest, 'it's the only f-f-form of exercise I get these days!'

Not content with spending the rest of the evening at the Blossoms, the instructors moved on a little later to another bar nearer the town centre where they became 'unrespectable'. Peter recalls many girls visiting the bar, which may be one of the reasons why he thinks it used to jump!

His flight commander at Hawarden, Peter Powell, was well known for having one drink too many, and Peter describes him as 'getting a bit boozed up' during the Chester trips. Peter used to have an old Morris Ten which served as the OTU taxi service to Chester.

'Come on Pete,' Powell would say, 'let's have a drink in town.' They did and Powell would have quite a few drinks. There was one particular occasion when Powell got quite drunk. After the trip to Chester, Powell and the others scrambled into Peter's Morris, as usual. The instructors were at that time billeted in the castle, and in the entrance on a pedestal stood a large bust of William Gladstone, proudly keeping guard over his family house and eyeing guests as they set foot in the castle. Peter thinks it was quite a valuable piece. On their return from the trip, they pulled up and all piled out of the car, opening the door of the castle as quietly as their inebriated state would allow. Powell stepped inside the entrance hall, whereupon the eyes of Gladstone met his. The flight commander swung his arms about, left hooks, right hooks, upper-cuts; staggering towards the bust, staring at the statuette, sizing him up. As Peter entered the hall, his eyes opened wide and his jaw nearly hit the floor, in his words, as Powell's fist made contact with Gladstone's bust, knocking it off its perch. Both of them stood frozen to the spot as the bust toppled, wobbling furiously on its pedestal, about to crash to the ground. Peter shook himself out of his trance, just catching the bust in time before it smashed on the floor. Peter ruefully adds he cannot bear to imagine the trouble he and Powell would have been in if the bust had shattered.

Although petrol was strictly rationed, the instructors (and probably a few students) never bothered with authority, driving straight up to the petrol-bowser and filling the tanks of their cars; everyone was doing it. Peter admits it was a bit daft really because they were fuelling their cars with high-octane petrol which has a tendency to blow the engine up. Having thought this over, they mixed oil to lower the temperature and thereby cooled the engine. The authorities decided that this had to stop; it was not a good example to the students. Moreover, petrol was rationed for a good reason. They devised a scheme, for those still determined to beat the system, by colouring the fuel. If a 'smuggler' was stopped and asked to open his bonnet and the carburettor was a pink colour instead of black, it could only mean one thing, and he was caught.

All the instructors benefited from their time at Hawarden, away from the stresses of operational flying. For Peter, it was a way of letting off steam, a welcome opportunity for relaxation after the trials, rigours and ultimate débâcle of France. Hawarden provided them with an opportunity to recharge their batteries, to catch their breath before they themselves were posted onto other operational squadrons. Away from the frenetic action of the Battle of Britain taking place along the south coast during the summer of 1940, the instructors at No. 7 OTU regained their mental awareness and composure: a vital element for survival for a young fighter pilot.

Against all odds, the RAF had defeated the daylight raids and the aerial might of the Luftwaffe; the Battle of Britain had officially ended. But in November 1940 the Luftwaffe were to begin their night-bombing campaigns on cities and major towns all over the country. The Blitz had begun.

During the latter part of the Battle of Britain, casualties in the fighter squadrons were becoming severe and the demand on instructors to rush pilots through the operational course was therefore extreme. Peter flew fifty-six flying hours in August, the average flight being just under an hour's duration. In addition to their instructing, instructor pilots still had to carry out patrols on a regular defensive pattern.

One of the unique aspects of Peter's record is that he flew combat missions for the entire duration of the war, even when his posting to Hawarden was considered non-operational. This is precisely what happened on 14 August. Although officially an instructor, Peter recorded a kill in his logbook on an operational patrol. There were also periods when he was called to Readiness, patrolling over Liverpool. During the summer of 1940 Britain had adjusted its clocks to what was termed Double British Summer Time, that is two hours ahead of Greenwich Mean Time. The clocks had been put forward not one hour, but two. This gave factories, volunteer forces and other contributors to the war effort more daylight hours to work, thereby increasing productivity. On one notable occasion at about half-past seven during the evening of 14 August, the instructors had packed up flying for the day and sat in the marquee, by the bar, with a beer in hand. It was a pleasant evening and this was a welcome chance to relax. Suddenly, they heard loud bangs, followed by firing which seemed to be getting louder. They looked at each other, then made for the flap of the marquee. Someone said, 'What the hell's that?' Away in the direction of RAF Sealand, they saw an aircraft flying in the distance about 5 miles away. The bangs were bombs dropped by the aircraft over the Training School. Three of the instructors, Wg Cdr Hallings-Pott, Sqn Ldr McLean and Peter started to run towards the Spitfires nearest to them, one of them shouting, 'Get three aircraft started. Get them going! NOW!'

It was an unintentional scramble. The ground crew had just begun to put covers over the Spitfires but whipped them off immediately they heard the call, turning the Merlin engines so that the aircraft burst into life. The three dashed towards the aircraft, pulling on their parachutes as they ran, jumped into the purring Spitfires and tore off over the airfield in pursuit of the lone bomber.

They picked up the Heinkel He 111 at about 2,000ft over Sealand, just as it began a second bombing run. Hallings-Pott and McLean lined the Heinkel up in their sights, pressing the button on their D-ring. Both instructors scored direct hits but it pressed on. It was Peter's turn. He went in at about 200yds astern of the Heinkel, carefully choosing his moment. He could see some bullet holes in the German's tailplane but nothing more; no fire nor flames. He could also see the rear gunner firing back and missing. Peter pressed the gun button, firing directly into the fuselage. He must have hit the engines as the bomber rapidly lost height in the dusk. The other two Spitfires had broken away and had returned to Hawarden but Peter stayed with the stricken Heinkel, watching it sink lower and lower until it crash-landed.

A sixteen-year-old boy had been playing the cornet in the Alhambra Theatre, Shotton. At about 9 p.m., he stood at the top of Salisbury Street, chatting to a friend. Suddenly the Heinkel shot across the bottom of the street, 20ft above the ground, closely followed by Peter's Spitfire. It was quite a sight for them. The sixteen-year-old was to become the well-known orchestra leader, Syd Lawrence.

The pilot made a wonderful job of landing the plane, flying *under* electric pylons (quite a feat for a bomber!), wheels up, stopping 50yds short of a farmhouse. The four crew members had survived the attack and were taken prisoner, but before they left the wrecked Heinkel one of the crew had placed detonators in the fuel tank. As they surrendered, the aircraft exploded, cockpit and wings ablaze. Only the tail unit and half of the fuselage remained. The following day, Peter, McLean, Hallings-Pott and others travelled the 5 miles from Hawarden to see the wreckage. The Heinkel crew remained in Britain as POWs for two months before being shipped to Canada.

Some forty-eight years later, Peter met them again in less confrontational circumstances. They thanked him for shooting them down because they had been given better food in Canada than in Britain! During his time as a POW, the navigator and bomb-aimer, Heinrich Rodder, had studied medicine, something he had wanted to pursue before the war. By the time he got back to Germany he was virtually a fully qualified doctor. It was at Rodder's home in Troisdorf, nestling between Bonn and Cologne, that Peter stayed during subsequent reunions to mark the anniversary of their initial contact. He found Rodder to be a keen gardener who had a swimming pool in the garden. Peter says that Rodder was the one who rounded up the rest of the crew, and the former enemies had some good times together. Until recently, Peter exchanged Christmas cards with Rodder, Artur Wiesemann (pilot), Walter Schaum (flight mechanic) and Heinz Kochy (radio operator).

They told him exactly what happened on 14 August 1940 – from their point of view. Their Heinkel had been one of three bombers taking off from their base in northern France. One of their comrades turned back fairly soon after take-off, while the other was pounced upon by Spitfires based at Warmwell in Dorset, and shot down. Wiesemann's aircraft was now flying alone, but the decision was taken to press on. He found that there was quite a fair amount of cloud about and the pilot decided to use this as cover, limping in and out, hiding from the presence of any fighters that might have been lurking.

One of the crew said to Peter that he thought he saw a shadow reflected in the clouds. It turned out to be the reflection of the Heinkel.

There is no doubt that Artur Wiesemann was a skilful and brave pilot. Indeed, he had received the Iron Cross for his part in the Spanish Civil War, so he knew what he was doing.

Wiesemann's crew had carried out two successful bombing runs on RAF Sealand, resulting in a serious amount of damage. The main guardroom, sergeants' mess and airmen's blocks were all badly damaged. They thought it was a piece of cake because there were no defences to prevent them, no anti-aircraft fire – nothing. 'Let's go round again,' one of the crew had said to Wiesemann, 'this is an absolute doddle. We've never had such an easy time!' By deciding to turn round a third time, Wiesemann and the crew had given Peter, McLean and Hallings-Pott enough time to rush from the bar, clamber into the Spitfires and fly the short distance to Sealand. It is hard to speculate, but if that third run had not been carried out, there is every likelihood that the Heinkel crew would have made it back to France.

Hawarden was not just about instructing, however. Peter had to attend a parachute course at Weeton, close to Blackpool, where he lived in the officers' mess. There was no time to admire the illuminations; having travelled north in his old black square Morris Ten, the first thing he did when he arrived in Blackpool was to find a hotel and have a drink. It was in a hotel, having a drink, that he came across a fellow student pilot from his elementary flying course two years earlier at Gatwick. Wickham had been on a different course from Peter because he had entered the RAF as a Volunteer Reserve, not on a short-service commission. None the less, that didn't stop them from talking about old times, catching up with each other's news. 'Peter! Good Lord, what are you doing here?' Peter told him, over quite a few drinks. Wickham glanced at his watch; it said 9.30 p.m. 'Come on,' he said, jumping to his feet, 'let's go to a club.' Wickham had been posted to Blackpool and consequently had discovered the hot-spots of the north-west. There was music. There was dancing. There was more drink. Peter looked at his watch, it was midnight. 'It's time I made a move back. Big day tomorrow. Great to see you again', Peter said.

He was driving along the Blackpool seafront when he saw headlights flashing behind him in his mirror. Strange, he thought; why would anyone want to flash him? But he slowed down and stopped. It was only when he stopped that Peter recognised it was a police car. The police officer opened his car door and stepped out, walking slowly towards Peter, who wound down the window.

'Do you realise, sir,' said the policeman in a thick, authoritative Lancashire accent, 'that you were doing 60 miles an hour in a blackout?'

'No I didn't', replied Peter. 'Quite honestly, I didn't think my car would do 60 miles an hour!'

The officer opened the door of Peter's car. Peter rather wished he hadn't because he half-fell out, lurching towards the pavement. He thinks that it was at this point that the officer charged him, not because he was drunk (fortunately there were no drink-drive laws at that time), but because he was speeding!

Two or three weeks later, he was required to go to court. One of the ground officers at Hawarden, Griffith Williams, had been a barrister before the war and he agreed to defend Peter. On the day of the hearing, they flew from Hawarden to Blackpool aerodrome, 'borrowing' a Miles Master. The pair travelled into town, making court on time. Evidently, things must have been quiet. News that particular day must have been rather scarce as the editor of the local paper seems to have printed the court's findings in its entirety.

60mph did not seem fast to 250mph airman who shot down Nazi in northwest.

Said to have brought down a plane in the northwest, Flying Officer Peter Vigne Ayerst arrived at Blackpool Police court today for exceeding twenty miles an hour in a blackout. He was fined £3.

It was stated that he was travelling at sixty miles an hour along South Promenade in the early morning. Later, Ayerst and another RAF officer, Mr Griffith Williams who is a barrister, arrived in the court and Mr Williams said that they had had to fly to Blackpool. He admitted the offence, but submitted that Ayerst's car was of ancient vintage – a defendant in other circumstances would be only too pleased with the recommendation that it could do sixty miles an hour!

Accused had been piloting aircraft in France, in this country flying at 250mph, and did not realise that he was travelling at an excessive speed. After hearing the explanation given, the bench agreed the fine as stated.

Unfortunately, Peter's little Morris Ten was not to last the course. During the spring of 1941 he and she parted company in dramatic style late one night. Because black-out requirements were still being enforced, cars were driven with covered headlights, which meant there was just a slit providing a minimal amount of light so that the driver could see where he was going. Peter still doesn't really know what happened that evening. One minute he had been driving along; the next he was lying upsidedown in the car. He was to discover later that he had hit another car head-on, the force of the collision rolling Peter's car by 180° over onto the roof. He must have hit his head on the top of the car as it rolled over. Having escaped and survived dogfights in France (along with a few shaky moments with one or two pupil pilots while formation flying), it was ironic that he had come unstuck near his base of Hawarden.

After the accident, although he felt fine physically, he was suffering from dizzy spells. He was taken to hospital, where the doctors confirmed that Peter had concussion. They told him that until he was 100 per cent fit and until the spells had dissipated completely, there was absolutely no way that he would be allowed to continue his instructing. Most of the students flew as if they had dizzy spells; the last thing the RAF needed was an instructor-pilot who actually had them for real! So, for the first time in two and a half years of flying, Peter was grounded for his own safety.

It may have been just the accident, but when looking at what happened objectively, another explanation for the cause would seem to be the accumulation of fatigue combined with stress. Because of the rapidity with which the pupil pilots needed to be put through the operational training system, while at the same time maintaining a high standard of flying, undoubtedly instructors were placed under undue pressure. All this, of course, had followed what was in Peter's case a harrowing period in France. He needed a rest.

He was sent to convalesce in an RAF hospital at Babbacombe near Torquay for a month. The building used as a hospital had been a big hotel before it was requisitioned, and with wonderful grounds overlooking the sea it was an ideal location for patients to relax, far away from the routine and rigours of flying. Recuperation involved gentle physical exercise as part of the patients' treatment, and while some played croquet on the lawns, others, including Peter, preferred – and were allowed – to swim in the hospital's own pool.

Every Saturday night the hospital laid on a bus in which the patients would be taken to a beautiful hotel on the cliffs of nearby Torquay for a social evening – it was the closest thing to a mess that they were allowed: dancing, with the odd glass of beer for refreshment. Some of the Babbacombe patients were guinea pigs (pilots who had been badly burnt and disfigured, unable to escape from their burning aircraft, and who had been given ground-breaking plastic surgery by Archibald McIndoe at the Royal Victoria Hospital, East Grinstead) who had been sent to Devon to convalesce.

The Saturday nights in Torquay were, of course, all part of the rehabilitation process and were a very gentle form of social integration with the public. The technique followed a path similar to that McIndoe employed with his guinea pigs at East Grinstead, taking them to the nearest pub so that those with horrific injuries could feel relatively comfortable in a public setting. It took as much time for them to feel accepted amid the public glare as it did for the public to recover from the initial shock of seeing such injuries, but the technique had proved results; it worked.

Peter remembers that there were some fairly ugly sights, and most of the patients stayed by the hotel bar and drank. It was as difficult for the non-burnt patients not to gape and gawk at their fellow patients as it was for the public. Peter did all he could not to stare at them, but found it wasn't easy. Misshapen, disfigured faces with burnt, discoloured skin looked back at you; you could see their mouths working but it was difficult to concentrate on what was being said because you were so struck by their appearance.

There was dancing. Some patients shuffled around the floor as best they could, hobbling awkwardly on crutches out of time with the music, though the shuffling and hobbling seemed to improve after the intake of a few beers. It was quite a pitiful sight for the other patients watching the guinea pigs board the bus from Babbacombe, shambling and shuffling pathetically, but it was a different story on the return journey; try and stop them – the wonder of alcohol had transformed them. Crutches were flung about with wild and gay abandon and nothing and nobody could get in their way. Laughing and singing and shouting filled the bus back to Babbacombe.

During his recuperation, Peter was not allowed to drink in quantity – a couple of pints at the most. The doctors had told him that too much alcohol would trigger the dizzy spells again. Wisely, he listened to what they said, but it must have been undeniably hard for a young man of twenty to forego the pleasure of a few drinks. Once again, his resolve, tenacity and determination in adhering to the doctor's advice came to the fore.

He had been posted to Tangmere Wing, near Chichester, where Nos 145, 610 and 616 Squadrons were based. He met up with Johnnie Johnson who had been posted to No. 616 Squadron along with Nip Hepple. Another pilot in a similar situation to Peter, Billy Wicht, was there too. Wicht was a Catholic and knew the Padre. He borrowed the Padre's car, a Hillman Ten, when the four of them decided to go into Brighton. They had a few drinks, they danced and met a couple of girls, who were particularly friendly and invited them back to their flat. It was a happy evening. At midnight, they decided to head back. It would take them an hour to get to Tangmere, it was pitch dark and there were no road signs to help them. Wicht drove back with Peter in the front while the other two passengers went to sleep against the windows.

Suddenly Wicht heard a crack. 'Christ!' he said, and slammed on the brakes. He had taken a wrong turning where Welsh

Guards were on duty. He explained that he was lost and was given directions to the main road. Fifteen minutes later, the car seemed to overheat. They got out, unscrewed the radiator cap and found the radiator was empty. They knocked on the door of a nearby house for some water. With the radiator topped up, they set off again. After twenty minutes, it overheated again and again the radiator was empty. They scratched their heads and came to the conclusion that the hose pipe must have had a serious leak. It was by this time 12.40 a.m., but fortunately a house was close by. Although they didn't want to bother the occupants, their need for water was imperative. Understandably they were not well received. With the car topped up again, they managed to reach the officers' mess. Just as they got back, the car boiled over a third time.

The next morning they went back to the car to see what was wrong and immediately saw what had happened. A bullet hole was seen entering the car from beneath the rear window, through the middle of the car – straight past Johnson and Hepple who were asleep leaning against the windows, past Peter and Wicht – through the dashboard and into the header tank. What Wicht had heard was the bullet crack as it entered the car. It is intriguing to speculate what would have happened if the three passengers had been sleeping towards the centre of the car! Perhaps the spirit was looking after Peter again?

Peter's month of convalescence came to an end on 20 August 1941. He was told the news that he had been dreading. It had firmly been decided that he was not going back to operational duties with a fighter squadron in the light of his recent condition, at least for the moment. He might be over the worst, but the doctors could not be certain that he was totally cured. They did not want to be responsible for the loss of a valuable pilot having a dizzy spell at 20,000ft, blacking out and killing himself in the process. More time was needed to see how he fared. Before he could sit in the cockpit of a Spitfire or Hurricane again, placing him on a senior navigation course suited everyone: Peter would be working towards a vital aspect of fighter pilot training and the RAF could still monitor his progress. As a result, in early September he was placed on a senior navigation instructor's course located at Cranage, near Knutsford in Cheshire.

Peter began his course at No. 2 School of Air Navigation, virtually two years to the day since war had been in full force. The grass airstrip at Cranage was littered with Avro Ansons, scattered in all directions. The course consisted of theory and a great deal of practice which took place in one of the numerous Ansons. Peter was a student again, plotting various navigational exercises in the back of the aircraft. The course lasted five weeks and Peter passed to become a qualified senior instructor in navigation. Much of the theory involved working out figures and degrees – an integral part of navigation – and his resilience and determination to get to grips with the theoretical aspect of the course had paid dividends.

The requirements for navigational skills differ vastly between fighters and bombers. It is fair to say that the skills needed by a navigator in Bomber Command are far more complex than those needed by a fighter pilot. The difference lies in the workloads; a navigator in a bomber concentrates solely on getting his crew from base to destination and back. A fighter pilot has to be able to focus on myriad skills – pilot, navigator, gunner, wireless operator – he is a complete bomber crew rolled into one. Moreover, these skills have to be fully mastered if a fighter pilot is to survive because he is the only member of the crew.

The dizzy spells had not returned. By 1 November 1941 Peter was back as a senior instructor in an operational training unit, No. 58 OTU Grangemouth, on the banks of the River Forth. Although this unit had been established after Hawarden, the authorities had taken the step of prefixing each operational training unit with a number 5. As a senior instructor, Peter was accountable for lecturing pupils on the role of navigation. After the classes, it was time for some flying practice. A de Havilland Dominie lay among the army of aircraft, and Peter piloted the biplane while six of his pupils were in the back, busy working out where they were, where they should be and how they were going to get there. He placed a special emphasis on local navigation.

After being in the back of a cramped and slightly obsolete biplane, the pupils were itching to climb into one of the many Spitfires at Grangemouth. They were to find that navigation in single-seat fighters was a different experience. As he had done at Gatwick, Peter set his pupils compass courses to fly for a certain period of time which changed after ten minutes or so. In addition to concentrating on these courses, they also had to look for certain landmarks on the ground, which required vast amounts of map-reading. It was not an easy thing to master at 330mph.

Peter kept his hand in at flying fighters. As often as he could, he took the Spitfires into the air – to test out the re-emergence of any dizzy spells – and his flying gained in confidence as time wore on. By Christmas 1941 it had been more than eight months since the accident and he had been flying on and off for almost five months without a relapse. He was as sure as he could be that the dizziness had gone for good.

The New Year of 1942 arrived and he remained at Grangemouth as a senior instructor for the next five months. The posting finally came through on 6 June; he was back on operational work – it was the moment he had been waiting for. He – or rather the authorities – had bided their time, waiting, seeing how Peter's health fared. With hindsight, though it must have been incredibly frustrating for a young fighter pilot champing at the bit to fly with a squadron, this enforced 'rest' at Cranage and Grangemouth meant that Peter really was fighting fit by the time he was posted to Ouston.

He was now one of three pilots who were to be instrumental in establishing a new squadron, No. 243 at Ouston near Newcastle. Ouston was situated in the North-East, considered to be a fairly quiet part of Britain because of the lack of heavy daylight bombing. It was therefore a good location for the training of pilots; the chances of being called to stand by at Readiness were minimal; there was little chance of having to sit around waiting for a scramble, which would have taken up valuable time for training. In addition, No. 243 would not have to be called away flying defensive patrols. It gave the three enough time to establish a good training schedule.

At that point, No. 243 Squadron comprised the Squadron Leader, Peter as Senior Flight Commander in charge of 'B' Flight and Butch Lyons as 'A' Flight Commander. Peter had known Lyons since he was a pupil at Hawarden, and they were great friends. Lyons was known as Butch in the RAF because his family owned a kosher butcher's shop in Petticoat Lane, reputedly the biggest kosher butcher in the country. Butch was a great chap with fair hair and a red face. Peter says he had an immense zest for life.

Throughout the summer of 1942 the squadron grew as more pilots were gradually posted. Part of Peter's remit as Senior Flight Commander was to make sure that these pilots could fly the new Spitfire VB individually, as well as in formation. By now, many pilots had had some form of operational experience, and most who arrived at Ouston could fly Spitfires. There were a few, however, who were still coming fresh from their advanced training courses.

Although new pilots were continually swelling the ranks of the squadron, after just two weeks Peter was moved on to yet another course, albeit for five days. The RAF Instructors' Beach Course was held at Inveraray on the banks of Loch Fyne, and Peter enjoyed his brief sojourn in Scotland before returning to Ouston.

Training continued apace, and the original three were pleased with the direction in which No. 243 Squadron was heading. By 25 July, however, that had come to a halt, at least for Peter. The situation for the Allied armed forces stationed in North Africa was looking bleak. They had now reached an *impasse*. The German Army, with its formidable tank divisions, was now pressing on the Allied troops and forcing to them to defend rather than attack. They could not defend for ever.

The RAF had been asked by the Commander-in-Chief, General Sir Bernard Montgomery, to provide aerial cover and protection for the ground forces, and the decision was taken to send twenty experienced fighter pilots to the desert. The operational experience in France combined with his understanding and skills as an instructor meant that Peter was a very experienced pilot, and consequently he was chosen to go to the North African desert.

The route was long and arduous by ship. A large convoy of forty troop- and supply-ships took their necessary diversionary route, avoiding the stealth and deadly accuracy of German U-boats that had wreaked so much havoc during the Battle of the Atlantic the previous year. Destroyers flanked the convoy on either side, acting as escort. The fleet set off from Scotland on 27 July 1942, heading north towards Iceland, then west to America, turning south-easterly for their destination on the western coast of Africa. Peter's ship, a P&O liner called the SS *Narkunda*, was full of pilots. As he says, things were intimate – there were eight to a cabin. Six took the bunks while the other two slept on the floor. A roster was rigidly applied as to who slept in relative luxury away from the cold floor. He recalls that, apart from applying the roster, there really wasn't much else to do – except prop up the bar!

The convoy was in transit for three weeks. By the time it reached Freetown, Sierra Leone, in mid-August, Peter had gone halfway round the world. This, at least for the pilots, was their destination; the ships in the convoy were left to continue their journey round South Africa and then north, on to Suez.

The pilots were put on a small coastal boat manned by a local crew, hugging the coast, until they reached the Nigerian coast at Lagos. Once again, cabin room was at a premium and the boat was riddled with fleas and vermin. For Peter it was a distinctly unpleasant experience, whereas the crew couldn't have cared less.

The transit camp at Lagos was to be their home for two weeks as they waited for a DC-3 Dakota to take them eastwards to the edge of the desert at Cairo. Lagos was packed with expatriates who were representatives from various businesses and trading companies, maintaining an affluent lifestyle and living in very large houses. They were pleased to see the pilots and invited them to stay, one invitation coming from a director working for Barclays Bank. The pilots had reached paradise: plenty of food and loads of alcohol to hand as they sat on the verandah, high up, looking down upon the city of Lagos. It was the last time for a long while that many were to experience such a comfortable lifestyle.

The Dakota came for them, making a number of night stops from Nigeria to Egypt. It stopped at Maidugrai – dungheap of the earth, in Peter's opinion – and at El Geneina as well as Khartoum. Five of them ended up on the rooftop above a nightclub in Khartoum that night; the night was pleasantly warm and some Egyptian girls stood by the balcony. They noticed the pilots, smiled and waved to them. The next thing Peter knew was that each girl was sitting on a pilot's knee with her arms firmly planted around his neck. It took the Dakota 6hr 10min to fly from Khartoum to Cairo. In all, it took nearly twenty-one hours flying time to make the journey from Lagos to Cairo. His introduction to Egypt was staying in another transit area, in a block of flats in Cairo. The adjutant was Flt Lt Arthur Howard, who insisted on running the camp along the lines of a hotel. He appeared with Jimmy Edwards after the war in the popular radio and TV series 'Whacko!'. His brother, Trevor Howard, became well known as an actor. HQ base at Cairo told Peter that he was to join No. 33 Squadron as a supernumerary. Although officially an indirect member of the squadron, he was posted as a substitute because he had yet to gain experience in desert flying. His desert war had begun.

FIVE

Hell Alamein

The Libyan desert is beautiful yet terrifying. It's a forbidding place, a world of violent extremes: harsh sandstorms and raging heat; glimmering hazes and shivering bitter cold; intense blinding light and pitch dark. It connects Africa to the Middle East and, in many ways, it provides the link between two beautiful and remote cultures. Towards the south and west, the Egyptian desert leads impenetrably to the Libyan desert across most of Libya and Algeria, and to the east it crosses Egypt. This area is also known as the Western Desert. It stretches from the busy Egyptian coastal town of Port Said and the Suez Canal in the east to green swaths of hills straddling the Libyan and Tunisian border in the north, and it covers a distance of nearly 1,500 miles. The area includes the sand-ridden Qattara Depression in the south. From tentative sandy streams on the northern coast, the Libyan desert flows majestically into the flood of the Sahara, covering 700 miles. From time immemorial, the Qattara Depression has acted as a natural defence, a barrier to any invading forces.

The main force of Allied troops had been posted to the Western Desert in 1941 to protect and defend British interests. Early in the twentieth century, few politicians were waking up to the significance of the location of the Western Desert in relation to Britain's Empire. Twenty years later, everyone had realised the importance but by then it was too late. Winston Churchill had described Egypt and the Middle East as 'the centre of our Empire which should be defended at all costs' back in 1922, no doubt to cries of laughter from some of his colleagues. But Churchill had the last laugh. Writing in his memoirs after the war, he says that the sum of events that took place in autumn 1942 'was the hinge of fate on which our ultimate victory turned'. One of the most important events that autumn happened in the coastal town of El Alamein.

Early in the campaign, the Supreme Commander of the Desert Forces, General Bernard Montgomery, had declared that 'whatever the military plan, it is vital that the air (force) should be brought in from the start'. It was paramount that the Army and the RAF should operate jointly in order to bring about an Allied success. Peter flew one of just 250 fighter aircraft at the disposal of the RAF.

As far as Peter was concerned, his immediate 'hinge of fate' was the fact that he had been posted as only a supernumerary to 243 Wing in northern Egypt. The Wing consisted of a total of four Hurricane squadrons, three from the RAF and the other from the South African Air Force. Peter joined No. 33 Squadron on 30 September 1942. The other British squadrons included Nos 213 and 238, while No. 1 Squadron came from the SAAF.

All four squadrons shared the same strip of compacted sand known as Landing Ground 154. There were no airfields, merely firm sand-strips called landing grounds, which had been numbered, offering a temporary base among the dunes.

Living conditions were spartan, to say the least. The luxury of a billet with a decent bed and a good supply of water to wash and shave in was a distant memory. Peter was living in tents that had been placed in square holes about 4–5ft deep, specifically dug so that only the roof could be seen. There was a very good reason for this, the logic being that because the tent was 'underground', the pilots were protected from German strafing; bullets would have whistled through the exposed section of the tent. These sunken tents were also a useful shelter in case of sandstorms.

There was a period of two days when No. 33 Squadron

suffered what Peter describes as the most fantastic sandstorm. It was impossible to see more than about 10ft ahead and he had to lower his head in order to walk through it, the sand covering him from head to foot.

All four squadrons in the Wing were flying Hurricane Mk IICs in the desert. These Hurricanes were similar to the aircraft he had flown in France, except that they were fitted with tropical filters beneath the engine to prevent the sand and dust from entering the carburettor. The ground crew cursed the filters because they were constantly clogging up. Peter had just two hours of flying to familiarise himself with the Mk IIC in the desert.

Flying in the desert required a completely different mindset from that required for the defensive patrols of Eastern France. Apart from the sun, there were no landmarks, just an ocean of sand. There were no buildings or structures, and landing grounds and tents were hard to distinguish. As there were no landmarks, it was impossible for the pilots to map-read. There was, therefore, little point in taking a map. The only successful method was to fly following compass courses, keeping an eye on the position of the sun as a reference point. Visibility was usually fine; Peter could see for miles unless the glimmering haze played tricks in the midday heat. The only other real indication the squadron had was the coastline and the blue of the sea, which made a welcome change from the continuous golden sand.

There was one other difference flying in the desert. Peter and the others always flew with their cockpit hoods open as a precautionary measure. He says that as the squadron was operating anywhere between 5,000 and 10,000ft, there wasn't the time or the height to muck about with a troublesome canopy if they found themselves in a sticky situation. A quick exit from an open canopy bought the pilot a few extra vital seconds that made the difference between life or death.

The squadron patrolled over the El Alamein line in the early days of October, operating at low altitude. The members of the squadron were, in Peter's words, a good crowd; like most squadrons it was a blend of pilots from Commonwealth countries. Commanded by Jack Finnis, No. 33 Squadron consisted of a number of Canadians, New Zealanders and a few Brits thrown in for good measure.

5 Oct – Tactical Recco. Nothing seen at all but 3 109s were reported.

Peter's first operational flight in the desert was on 5 October 1942 when No. 33 Squadron took part in a tactical reconnaissance over the El Alamein line. Four days later, he was involved in a Wing strafe over an airbase at Dhaba near the coastal town of Mersa Matruh, 80 miles due west from the Alamein line. There were, in fact, two airfields at Dhaba, adjacent to each other on an escarpment rising to a height of 200–300ft. Because of their height, both airfields were rather exposed. These airfields were known to the British as LG 104 and LG 121.

Contrary to popular conception, it can rain in the desert, certainly in the north – another example of extreme climatic conditions. A monsoon had swept over the Dhaba base, waterlogging the ground and turning it to quicksand. The Wing had been tipped off by the Long Range Desert Group (LRDG) that this aerodrome was full of Me 109s that were unable to fly because both landing grounds were waterlogged; the German fighters were glued to the sand. Flying out of the mire was impossible because of the narrow undercarriage and heavy nose, a similar problem to that suffered by the Spitfire. The LRDG sent intelligence reports saying that now would be a good time to operate, strafing the aerodrome while the fighters were on the ground. Forty-eight Hurricanes from 243 Wing took off on 9 October 1942.

No. 33 Squadron led and headed north out over the sea for 10 miles, skimming the water at about 30ft, then turned due west for 80 miles. It was a bright sunny day and visibility was very good. They could see the escarpment from a distance. As soon as they spotted it, they turned in due south, towards it. The base loomed bigger and bigger as the four squadrons flew on.

They had been briefed that all forty-eight Hurricanes were to stay in formation, and as such, there was no real room to turn left or right because there were too many fighters. They just had to fly straight, each pilot taking his chance on what he saw in front of him and hoping that something would come up. They were not to be disappointed.

As they were about to pull up over the ridge, they noticed a handful of scattered tents inclining gradually up the side of the escarpment. A ridge tent fell before Peter. Suddenly the tent flaps were pulled aside and he saw a face right in front of him, shaving cream all over his chin, wondering where all the noise was coming from. Peter says he couldn't help but give the tent a quick squirt. What happened to the shaver and his tent, he says, God only knows, but he received a pretty severe raking.

The Wing pulled up very quickly and just in time, for they were now on top of the ridge. Right in front of Peter was a Fieseler Storch aircraft. Ungainly in character, Storches were exceptional multi-role machines. Ideal for the desert, they landed or flew out of anything, having an incredible ability for short take-off and landings (STOLs); tests against fighters proved that by flying at 34mph it was an extremely difficult target to hit. Peter says that because it was positioned exactly in front of him, he couldn't miss. On and over the escarpment lay airfield LG 104. The German ground crew were on their anti-aircraft guns by this time, pounding the air with flak. No. 33 Squadron went in at zero feet and were intercepted by about fifteen Me 109s that came from out of the blue. Peter has no idea where they materialised from, but because the Hurricanes flew so close to the ground, there was little risk of sustainable damage. In order to attack the Wing effectively, the Me 109s had to fly at the same height. As it was, their current angle of attack was far too steep, and had they attacked, the Luftwaffe pilots realised that there would not have been enough height to pull out and they would have ploughed straight into the deck.

The spirit of youth – Peter,
6 September 1924.

The Ayerst family, January 1940. From left to right: Tom, Hazel, Jack, Peg,
Samuel, Peter.

Rugby at Westcliff High School, September 1936. Peter is in front row, second from left. Alan Byfield is on his right.

Peter's commission into the RAF, summer 1938.

Peter at Gatwick,
October 1938.

Miles Magisters – new RAF training aircraft, October 1938.

Gatwick Airport – the Beehive, 1938.

Gatwick taken from about 2,000 feet, 1938.

No. 12 FTS, Grantham – December 1938.

Another new training aircraft – Peter in a Harvard, Grantham 1938. No. 12 FTS were the first RAF training unit to receive Harvards.

No. 73 Squadron outside the officers' mess – Le Havre. September 1939. From left to right: Peter, Derek Kain, Tub Perry, Graham Paul, Peter Walker, Fanny Orton, Claude Wright, 'Cobber' Kain.

Christmas 1939 at Rouvres. From left to right: 'Doc' Outfin, Fanny Orton, Ian Brotchie, 'Smooth' Holliday, Tommy Tucker (with armband), Reggie Lovett, 'Cobber Kain'. Peter drinking in the background

Peter in Hurricane 'S' landing at Rouvres, early 1940. Note the two-bladed airscrew and the BEF tail markings.

Scrambling at Reims, 1940. Peter is third from left.

Media interest from a Greek reporter, France, March 1940. From left to right: Sgt Speake, -?-, Reggie Lovett, Ian Brotchie, Peter, Sgt Campbell, 'Smooth' Holliday, Sgt Humphrey, Sgt Stuckey, 'Cobber' Kain, Tub Perry and Fanny Orton.

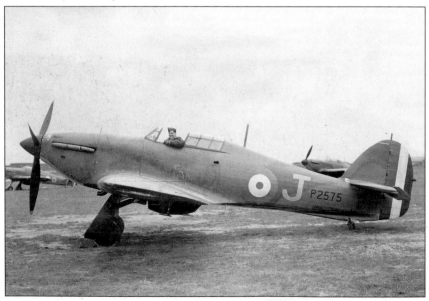

Peter in Hurricane P2575, France, March 1940.

Spirit of the Blue – photograph of Peter at Rouvres and subsequently used in a recruitment pamphlet, France, March 1940.

Fighter Pilot Decoy Ayerst, France, March 1940.

Peter with the Heinkel crew on one of their many reunions at Troisdorf, summer 1990. From left to right: Gustav Ullmann, Dr Heinrich Rodder, Artur Wiesemann, Walter Schaum, Heinz Kochy.

Desert Air Force, November 1942 – Peter with Tom Phillips who had been seconded from No. 1 (South African Air Force) Squadron.

No. 238 Squadron at El Adem, November 1942. Tom Phillips (in white), Roy Marples and Peter.

Peter in his Hurricane, KC-G, en route to LG 125, 400 miles behind enemy lines, formates on a Hudson supply aircraft, November 1942.

Peter's prang at Tebessa airfield, Algeria, Boxing Day 1942.

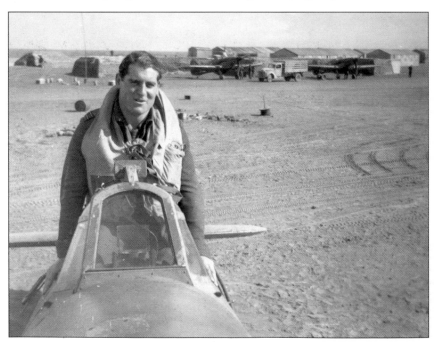

Peter and KC-G at Port Said, March 1943.

Very much in love with a Greek dancer, Peter painted her name on the side of his aircraft, Port Said, March 1943.

Peter and Betty's marriage at Canterbury, 5 June 1945.

Dunflyin – behind the bar of the Three Compasses, Canterbury, summer 1947.

Peter, Betty and Jane in Tankerton, 1948.

Back in RAF uniform, Germany 1954.

Peter (first aircraft from left in front row) leading No. 5 Squadron, Germany 1954.

The Presentation of the No. 5 Squadron Standard, April 1954. From left to right: Derek Gathercole. Nicky Varanand, Peter, Tommy Dawkins, Keith Sturt.

The Man With No Trousers – No. 5 Squadron Fancy Dress Ball, New Years Eve 1956.

The Hurricanes flew on, strafing the airstrip at LG 121, and the Me 109s stuck fast in the sand. They pulled back on the joystick, gaining a little height in order to gain a better angle of fire.

In Peter's words, whatever happened to appear in front of them, they shot at: it was a shooting gallery. The German guns continued to pound the desert air with flak, letting loose everything they had in a torrent of anti-aircraft fire. In return, the RAF pilots gave the German gun crews everything they had, raking the far side of the airstrip.

They had flown over both bases at Dhaba and had reached the far end of the second strip. The Wing had been briefed to stay in formation, and it was difficult to turn back because of the oncoming squadrons bringing up the rear. To overcome this, 243 Wing had worked out in advance that they would continue ahead across the Qatarra Depression – where there were no German troops – keeping low to the deck all the way and turning east to return to their base at LG 154. Just as they were making for the Depression, Peter felt a thud in his Hurricane: the fuselage and controls shook. His Hurricane had been hit but the aircraft was still responding to the controls. The German ground crew had come perilously close to claiming a direct hit.

However, luck was on his side. Three other Hurricanes crash-landed in the Qatarra Depression because of anti-aircraft fire, but fortunately the pilots managed to get back. Peter thinks another two who were hit were captured by the Axis forces and were interned as POWs. In total, nine pilots were missing after the operation. He recorded the day's operation later in his logbook.

9 Oct – Very intense light flak and some heavy. Fifteen plus Me 109s jumped us as we went in at zero feet. Bags of panic. I was hit in the fuselage behind the cockpit. I personally destroyed one 109 and a Fieseler Storch and one tent which was on the side of the escarpment. Regrettable: had 48 Hurricanes on that operation but nine pilots were missing.

The following day, No. 33 Squadron set off early to search for the other missing pilots.

10 Oct – We found two Hurricanes, both pilots OK. Also saw two 109s and a Kittyhawk and a burnt out Wellington.

Peter flew a tactical reconnaissance patrol over the northern sector on 14 October. Thereafter, the scrambles continued apace for the squadron. The Hurricanes operated these patrols at a height of 17,000ft.

14 Oct – Flak was extremely heavy and accurate. Some 109s were seen and attacked. 1 SAAF who destroyed one.

The Desert Air Force's primary role was to support the British Army, which had retreated to the Egyptian coastal town of El Alamein in mid-1942. For over a year, the Allied forces had remained there, pinned down by large German forces. Rommel's Afrika Korps was pushing ever closer, knocking at the door. The British Eighth Army could not hold out for ever; it required ground support but it also needed aerial protection from Luftwaffe aircraft dive-bombing its positions.

For Peter, the past three weeks had been a hectic introduction to the art of desert flying. Now, 23 October was to mark the beginning of an intense bout of combat fighting for him. He was asked by Jack Finnis, his commanding officer, to carry out a reconnaissance of the northern sector area on this date, reporting back with a suitable landing ground for the entire Wing that was closer to the Axis lines. It was a measure of his maturity and experience – despite the fact that he had flown in the desert for no more than twenty-one days – that he was tasked with finding, and found, an airstrip that he thought might be appropriate. This airstrip became known as LG 172. In the afternoon of that day, 243 Wing moved to LG 172, further towards the Axis line, in anticipation of the intended drive by the Allied land forces. The first British shells were fired at half-past eight in the evening, and thereafter the British artillery unleashed a barrage of incredible intensity. Peter believes that this strike was probably the most ferocious and concentrated artillery barrage in the entire war. Never had he witnessed the sight and deafening sound of hundreds of guns pounding the Axis lines. The barrage started just as the light faded, continuing overnight and well into the following day.

At the crack of dawn on 24 October, 243 Wing patrolled the line, providing aerial cover for the British ground forces from the German dive-bombers. The four squadrons were positioned at different height intervals, the top and middle flights providing cover by engaging fighters, while the bottom flight protected the ground forces by attacking dive-bombers.

On that particular day, No. 33 Squadron had been designated 'bottom squadron', and as such was the closest to the activity on the ground. Later in the afternoon, the Wing was in action again when Peter claimed a direct hit.

He called these events 'The Putsch' in his logbook.

24 Oct – Patrol of the line – protecting army, push in the North. 4 Me 109s were seen above but they did not attempt to attack. A small amount of accurate flak.
24 Oct – Patrol of the line – intercepted by 15 Me 109s and 202s [Macchi 202] on reaching Alamein.
Terrific dogfight ensued. Self one 109 damaged. Everybody OK. Bags of activity on the ground.

Peter says that the techniques for aerial combat, or dogfights, were very much the same in the desert as they were in France. The one difference he noted was that they fought at a lower altitude. In France, most of the action took place above 20,000ft; in the desert it could be anywhere between 10,000 and 15,000ft, sometimes lower. A dogfight was usually a head-to-head affair between one aircraft and another. If a fighter was attacked by two or more aircraft, it was not considered to be a dogfight. Peter knew he had to be careful in these situations because the first place the Luftwaffe (and the RAF) attacked was from the rear, which is why he and the other fighter pilots wore silk scarves round their necks. The Sutton Harness straps running over the shoulders were in close proximity to the neck and were pulled very tightly, and because a good fighter pilot like Peter looked behind 75 per cent of the time, before long these straps bit into his neck, rubbing it raw. The bomber boys often pulled the fighter pilots' legs, calling them silk-wearing sissies.

The tactic of approaching an enemy aircraft by coming out from the sun was favoured on both sides and had been learnt over the trenches in the Somme. During the early part of the day, the RAF was to reap the benefit of the sun behind them in the east, but as the day wore on, this advantage was negated as the sun moved directly overhead and later sank in the west, favouring the Germans. Peter and the other pilots tried to get on the tail of the enemy in a one-to-one dogfight scenario, but often there were a number of aircraft at close quarters. When he saw there was more than one, he'd fire his guns briefly, hoping fervently the bullets had struck the fuselage, and then would pull round after another Messerschmitt closing in his sights. With a short glance behind him, making sure there was no one on his tail, he'd have another go. This was why pilots found it so difficult to be specific about their claims; unless they had seen the aircraft diving into the ground, which they could only follow for a brief snatch of time if they wanted to live, it was difficult to be definite. Peter adds that he couldn't even afford to look down for more than half a second because he had to keep looking around for the enemy on his tail. As in France, he didn't really ever know whether they had been successful or not. These decisions were made in split seconds; there was no time to think when pilots and planes were mixed together. As Peter puts it, dogfighting was 'a hell of a schmozzle'. He had now claimed his fifth kill since his first on 7 April 1940, and was officially designated an Ace.

One of the Royal Air Force's objectives in the desert was to protect the British land forces from being dive-bombed by German Junkers Ju 87 Stukas. These had been used with great effect as early as 1936 by the Luftwaffe in the Spanish Civil War. The Germans had also used them during the Battle of Britain but had discovered that they were no match for Spitfires and they rapidly withdrew them. Those on the ground were well aware that a Stuka was about to begin its attack because of the terrifying scream that accompanied its dive. To the land forces it had the desired effect. Now in the desert it had a new lease of life. The Stukas came over the line at El Alamein in a Geschwader (squadron) of either twelve or twenty-four, with a very substantial escort of Me 109Gs.

On the afternoon of 27 October, the Luftwaffe began its major offensive of the afternoon, in conjunction with the Axis land forces, dive-bombing targets, landing grounds and artillery units. The Luftwaffe was determined to show its aerial might and aggression in this offensive, putting up twenty Stuka dive-bombers, twenty Italian Fiat CR-42 and Macchi, together with MC.202 Folgore fighters an escort of some twenty Me 109s. It was a formidable array. Peter and the others from No. 33 Squadron, along with the Hurricanes from No. 1 Squadron (SAAF), provided top cover.

27 Oct – Four 202s seen above. They didn't come down. A small amount of heavy flak. Plenty of activity on the ground.

Not surprisingly, such interceptions had a strong effect on the morale in the RAF squadrons; the Luftwaffe vanguard had been exposed and the favoured German approach, to spearhead an attack by dive-bombing, was becoming unstuck.

Four weeks after joining No. 33 Squadron as a supernumerary, Peter was now leading it on an escort flight:

29 Oct – Scramble and patrol of line with 238 squadron as top cover. Twenty Kittyhawks dive-bombed in Northern Sector. Good bombing!

He had now flown enough flights and had accumulated enough experience in the desert, because on 1 November he was posted to No. 238 Squadron as Senior Flight Commander, where he commanded 'A' Flight. Although it was a moment for celebration, it was also tempered with the sobering thought that he was filling dead men's shoes, because the squadron's previous incumbent was missing in action. He controlled the pilots in his flight, liaised with flight mechanics from the ground crew and maintained the motivation and spirit within the support staff, briefed pilots thoroughly before missions and discussed the trip once they had landed. Administration was virtually non-existent during wartime. As far as the pilots were concerned, Peter had to select those whom he thought would make useful section leaders, depending on their experience, as well as arrange and coordinate operational formations. Peter's opposite Flight Commander in 'B' Flight was a South African captain, Tom Philips with whom Peter got on well. He also got on very well with the Commanding Officer of No. 238 Squadron, Roy Marples, whom Peter had known before in 1941, and it is more than likely that Marples had specifically asked that Peter should join his squadron.

There were few pleasures to be had in the desert, but a mess tent was open to both officers and sergeants alike. It was not practical to uphold the strict rules and regulations of segregation that the RAF normally upheld and so the mess tent was known colloquially as the pilots' tent. Not surprisingly, the focal point of the tent became the bar. Supplies of beer came in the form of cans from the United States, and although they would have preferred pints to 'tinnies', the pilots were grateful for the few cases they got their hands on from time to time. Like everything else in the Libyan desert, it was in short supply.

Peter was responsible for transporting extra supplies of beer by some very ingenious methods.

'Come on, Pete. I'm pissed off with drinking tea all the time,' Marples shouted one morning in early November; 'I need some alcohol. Let's go and grab some beer.'

'Ah, do I feel a trip to Alexandria coming on?'

'Got it in one! Follow me!'

Peter and Marples and a third pilot knew where they could obtain some supplies. It was a brief easterly flight from LG 172; the trio decided to fly three Hurricanes to a large RAF base at nearby Aboukir where the large brick-built mess played a central part in the lives of the service personnel there and consequently was well stocked. Moreover, Roy and Peter knew that, with a smile and a bit of charm, supplies of American beer would be winging their way back to the boys in No. 238 Squadron. Supply was therefore not a problem, but how did they transport it back to base? The solution was ingenious: the wings of a Hurricane Mk IIC are thick; they have to be in order to accommodate the twin cannon in each wing. In keeping with these cannon, the drum containers holding the rounds of 20mm ammunition are also large. Roy and Peter would unscrew the ammunition panels from both port and starboard wings before leaving LG 172 and dispose of any ammunition before placing the cases of tinned beer in the ammunition pans. Without any further interruptions, the trio would hurriedly fly back – three operational aircraft in flight loaded with an armament of beer. They discovered that the Hurricane not only fulfilled its role as a fighter aircraft, it also adopted the temporary role of a heavy transport aircraft.

Food, however, was another matter. It was thought by the pilots to be so bad that alcohol was needed to take away the awful taste. Peter and the others lived on a staple diet of bully beef that seemed to manifest itself in various guises throughout the duration of the week: bully beef fritters, bully beef stew, cold bully beef – several thinly disguised methods in serving up bully beef. Sometimes, Peter says that the cooks became creative with their limited resources, conjuring up a delightful curried bully beef! The only other regular ration to accompany this bully beef extravaganza was the supplement of hard tack biscuits which he found a rather tasteless substitute for bread.

November saw a large amount of dogfighting for No. 238 Squadron. Throughout that month, Peter flew a total of thirty-eight hours, an unusually large number of operational hours to fly in a single-engined fighter. He found during this time that he, along with other pilots, was exhausted owing to the tremendous amount of concentration, focus and exhilaration required from the entire squadron, including the ground crew. The Eighth Army had only partially broken through the line at El Alamein, and the Hurricanes flying above the troops on the ground continued to provide intense and invaluable air cover from the Stukas. Although Allied tanks were slowly edging forward into German territory, the dive-bombers were reaching the targets.

> 1 Nov – Patrol of the line with 1 SAAF. No enemy aircraft seen. Slight amount of Breda flak near the coast.
> 3 Nov – patrol of the line. Met thirty plus Stukas and 20+ 109G escorts. Very heavy ack-ack followed by the Stuka party. Damaged two Me 109s. Sgt Cordwell got a Ju 87.

The German forces on the ground had increased the number of anti-aircraft batteries, trying to scatter the squadron with the ack-ack, allowing the Stukas freedom of action. Peter was not the only one to find this higher proportion of flak distinctly unnerving. But he says that they didn't quite fall for it; although the sky was a real mish-mash of black shell-bursts, the Hurricanes stuck rigidly to their task.

> 3 Nov – Patrol of the line. Several 109s around. 109s attack 33 squadron who were top cover. Useless attacks. Plenty of activity on the ground.

The following day, Peter became embroiled in a dogfight that had disastrous consequences. And he remembers 4 November 1942 particularly well. The squadron had been scrambled for a Stuka party but had missed them, only to get caught up with their Me 109 escort, of which there were about twelve plus in the Alamein area.

> 4 Nov – Got one 109 destroyed and one 109 damaged. Got shot up three times by heavy ack-ack and numerous times by light ack-ack.

And then it happened. He was probably at about 7,000–8,000ft when he got hit by flak, his Hurricane being hit in the tail and in the starboard wing, as well as in the engine. The damage in the wing didn't prevent him from using the ailerons but he had problems controlling the plane fore-and-aft because of the damage to the tail. He wasn't aware that the engine had been hit until he saw plumes of white smoke streaming out of the exhaust manifolds on both sides of the fuselage. The white smoke was glycol, necessary for cooling and lowering the temperature of an overworked engine. The engine coughed and spluttered, time was running out and Peter knew he had to put the aircraft down soon. But where? He was well over the enemy lines at this time and he knew that he was flying in the right direction. He needed to travel eastwards, putting as much distance as possible between him and the Germans, maintaining some height if he was to escape. If he lost height, then he lost distance. All he could do was to fly straight in an easterly direction. It dawned on him that he was not going to make the British lines; the Hurricane was losing too much height and the Germans were firing at him with everything they had. He tried to manoeuvre the aircraft with what little power was left but it proved unresponsive. A track appeared on the sandy ground ahead of him, part of the great Qattara track. There was nothing for it – he had to land on that track and make a wheels-up crash-landing. He came in, the engine whining as the light sandy track came up to meet him. The landing was a trifle heavy as the Hurricane hit the ground, wheels up, slewing along the sandy track until it came to a dusty halt.

Peter was down; his gamble had paid off. But he couldn't afford to relax. As soon as the aircraft had come to a halt and the engine had died, he was aware of a sharp metallic sound. Bullets and shells were pinging against the body of the Hurricane. Leaping out of the cockpit, he lay flat on the ground, sheltering along the fuselage as the Germans continued to fire in his direction. With his radio broken, there was nothing he could do but remain there.

The bright intensity of day turned into a heady richness of red twilight. The glaring heat of the day cooled to a pleasing temperature. Peter thought that the time must have been somewhere about half-past five because the period of twilight in the desert was very short; daylight turns into darkness in less than half an hour. Ill-prepared for an evening in the desert, he weighed up what he should do – stay by the Hurricane in case his colleagues came looking for him, or walk across the desert, making for the Allied lines. 'I'll stay here,' he thought furiously, 'wait until it gets dark – then I'll decide what the hell to do.' He had already come to a conclusion that to head west towards the German lines was foolhardy. The twilight came and passed into darkness. Peter sighed and stood up. 'There's only one thing for it,' he thought, 'continue to walk in an easterly direction. That's all I can do.' He was just about to set off when he thought he heard the drone of a motor vehicle coming towards him. He thought about the possibilities of escape. Could it be Allied? More likely to be a German lorry, and the chance of him being interned in a prisoner-of-war camp for the rest of the war. He was thus very surprised and pleased to hear a voice and a language he understood. It had a twang to it and it was slightly nasal. At that moment, it was the best slightly nasal twang he could ever wish to hear. 'Anybody there?'

'Yes', he replied.

'Hurry. Jump in!'

Peter jumped in quickly and the engine of the jeep rose to a crescendo, tearing off and away, following the track as best it could in the dark. When they were in a safe area, he discovered that the twang belonged to an Australian major, who told him what had happened. The Australian and his driver had watched Peter's aircraft being hit by flak and followed it down but they had to wait until the cover of darkness before they could rescue him; they hadn't dared come out sooner, otherwise the Germans would have picked them off.

The Australian left him with a final sobering thought.

'Of course, you know that track you landed on was the only place you could have landed.'

'Sorry, what do you mean?'

'That track . . . the one you landed on. It is the only piece of land that you could have attempted a landing; the surrounding sand on either side is heavily mined for miles!'

Peter recalls this well – it happened on his birthday! A case, perhaps, of some force – his spirit of the blue – watching out for him again?

4 Nov – Force landed 5 miles inside the 'bomb line' near the Australians.

He had been rescued but he was still in the front line for the following two days because it was not possible to contact his squadron. By this time, No. 238 Squadron had no idea what had happened to him and had consequently posted him as missing. He suspects that the squadron thought by this time that he had been killed by flak, or by the landing. It took him another three days to finally reach his squadron base at LG 172, hitching various lifts with Army vehicles. When he reached base, the boys were a little surprised – and delighted – to see him in one, dusty and dishevelled, piece. As he had been posted missing by the squadron, they awarded Peter a certificate – he was now a member of a select band of brothers, the Late Arrivals Club. Their motto was straightforward – it is never too late to come back. The club had been founded in the Western Desert in June 1941:

> In as much as Peter Vigne Ayerst, in Middle East on 4th November 1942, when obliged to abandon his Aircraft, on the ground or in the Air, as a result of unfriendly action by the enemy. Succeeded in returning to his Squadron, on foot or by other means, long after his Estimated time of Arrival. This member is permitted to wear the Emblem of the Winged Boot on the left breast of his Flying Suit.

In the unfortunate event of being shot down, pilots were given a few resources which it was hoped would prove valuable in getting them home. Maps made of rice paper were hidden, sewn into the lining of flying jackets; compasses made from a small piece of magnetised metal dangling from a thread of cotton were sewn into jacket lapels. The idea was to hold the cotton and wait for the compass to swing round, showing north or south. It was fortunate that Peter did not have to bother with his. One of the more intriguing pieces of paperwork that pilots were given by the British Government were Arabic language sheets containing basic phrases for use in the event of their being lost or stranded. There was also a letter of passage that officers kept with them, which was meant to offer safe conduct. The top half of the sheet was in Arabic, the bottom half in English:

> To All Arab Peoples – Greetings and Peace be upon you.
> The bearer of this letter is an Officer of the British Government and a friend to all Arabs. Treat him well, guard him from harm, give him food and drink, help him to return to the nearest British soldiers and you will be rewarded. Peace and the mercy of god upon you.

There were also some handy points of conduct when meeting Arabs:

Remove footwear on entering their tents. Completely ignore their women. If thirsty, drink the water they offer, but DO NOT fill your water bottle from their personal supply. Go to their well and fetch what you want. Never neglect any puddle or any other water supply for topping up your bottle. Use the Halazone included in your Aid Box. Do not expect breakfast if you sleep the night. Arabs will give you a mid-day or evening meal.
Remember, never try and hurry in the desert, slow and sure does it.

A few helpful phrases translated from English into Arabic were included:

Take me to the English and you will be rewarded. How far? English Flying Officer and enemy.

Finally, there were three lines of information on distance and time.

The older Arabs cannot read, write or tell the time. They measure distance by the number of days in a journey. 'Near' may mean 10 minutes or 10 hours. Far probably means over a day's journey. A day's journey is probably about 30 miles. The younger Arabs are more accurate. GOOD LUCK.

Roy Marples was a tremendous character and Peter had a great deal of respect for his flying skills. Marples also knew how to have a good time when he was off duty; this passion for life may well be why he and Peter got on so well. He and the rest of the squadron used to go to Alexandria, visiting one of the many fleshpots and nightclubs that flourished during the war. Occasionally, two or three members of the squadron borrowed vehicles, driving into Alexandria where they stayed for a night. It provided an excellent opportunity to have a bath because there were no resources for washing in the desert. The only water resource was for drinking, though sometimes there might be barely enough to have a shave.

On one such trip to Alexandria, Roy, Peter and a couple of others had freshened up, put on some clean clothes and gone out for the evening. They never drank spirits during their time in the desert, only beer. This particular night had seen quite a few beers consumed. As they were finishing their meal, Marples suddenly stood up and declared, 'Let's go on to the Monseigneur club. Who's up for that, boys?' On arrival at their favoured Alexandrian nightclub, they found that an Egyptian band was playing music which, to put it mildly, didn't agree with them. They stood and had a drink at the bar and the 'entertainment' continued as an Egyptian went up to the raised podium and sang with accompaniment. The singing didn't get any better. He was terrible. Roy turned to Peter. 'Ah, we can't stand this any longer, Pete. I'm going up.' He strode up to the podium, pushed the Egyptian crooner away from the microphone, grabbed hold of it and declared in his best impression of Winston Churchill: 'We will fight on the land, we will fight on the sea; we will fight in the air and what's more, we will fight in the Monseigneur!' Whereupon the Egyptian crashed to the floor as Marples let loose with a right hook. Suddenly, all hell broke loose. 'Jesus! Come on Roy, let's get out of here!' shouted Peter, grabbing hold of his arm and pulling him away. They got out just in time; the Military Police – not known for their leniency – arrived soon after, intent on finding the instigators. Peter describes Marples as a 'one-off'; whether it was in the air or in the Monseigneur, life, according to Peter, was never dull when he was around. Although he got on with the others in the squadron, Marples was irrepressible; he had a spontaneous streak that particularly struck a chord with Peter. Perhaps it was the same irrepressible streak that he had possessed himself during his days at Westcliff, and now he had found a kindred spirit in Marples. Roy Marples was killed later on in the war.

The El Alamein line had been broken and the Allied forces were pushing forward, forcing the Germans to retreat. It was the turning of the tide and the beginning of the end for German supremacy. Troops were making gradual, steady progress. While the Germans were retreating westwards through Libya, they took the opportunity to supply their forces with lorries and trucks containing personnel, logistical supplies, food, etc. so that another line could be established. The only possibility of withdrawal with such a convoy of vehicles was by road, the Via Balbia, hugging the northern coast towards Benghazi and on to Tunisia. It followed the outline of the Mediterranean coast, the only form of communication running from the east of Tunisia, through Libya and Egypt before reaching Israel in the west; there was absolutely no possibility of travelling south through the desert. The German retreat had to travel along the Via Balbia, and as there was nowhere else for them to travel, they were vulnerable.

The Allied authorities had decided to base a task force 400 miles to the west, which meant this operation was taking place behind enemy lines. The Long Range Desert Group had been out beforehand on a reconnaissance mission, looking for suitable strips of desert ground that were relatively flat and hard, capable of holding aircraft. Eventually one was located and assigned to Nos 238 and 213 Squadrons, designated LG 125. Both squadrons took the bare minimum of ground crew – just enough to look after twelve Hurricanes. American Lockheed Lodestar aircraft and Bristol Bombay freighters transported precious resources of fuel and water. There were no tents for the squadrons; pilots slept in cells that were built with spent petrol tins. Two 5-gallon tins arrived in a light wooden box and pilots placed the empty tins and wooden boxes together, surrounding themselves in little cells, sleeping on inflatable li-los.

The Hurricanes flew at about 10ft, avoiding radar, heading for the stretch of road full of German transport between Benghazi (Agedabia) and El Aghela. The squadrons repeated the flight for four days, duplicating the same attack – twelve Hurricanes strafing the road in line-abreast formation, flying on for a short while before turning 180° on a reciprocal heading in the same formation, each pilot turning his Hurricane in a tight semicircle – '180 Port!' – returning to strafe the road again. Once ammunition had been spent, the twenty-four Hurricanes returned to base, some 200 miles to the east. The pilots had no radio aids whatsoever and therefore Peter adds that navigation proved to be a little tricky.

There was one geographical landmark close to LG 125 that proved to be of great assistance as a navigational aid: a small sandy hillock rising out of the flatlands which the pilots noticed when flying at very low levels. If they had flown at higher altitudes, the hillock would have been lost, blending into the scenery. Taking a bearing from the hillock, the pilots could easily locate LG 125.

For the purpose of strafing, the Via Balbia road was divided into two sections. No. 238 Squadron might initially take the stretch from Benghazi to Agedabia termed the northern sector; No. 213 Squadron might then take the southern sector, between Agedabia and El Aghela, each flight lasting about two hours. The squadrons alternated sectors the following day. It was a mass exodus; so many vehicles were retreating that it became a shooting gallery. As Peter says, 'We destroyed a hell of a lot of vehicles.'

14 Nov – Strafing of road between Benghazi and Agedabia. Two six-ton lorries destroyed. Two six-ton lorries damaged. Approximately six men killed.
14 Nov – Strafing of road between Agedabia and Aghela. One six-ton lorry destroyed and men inside written off.

The Hurricanes took off in the dark from LG 125 the following day without any runway guidance lights. In addition to strafing the road, they also found a sand aerodrome close to El Aghela.

Peter destroyed a Ju 52 transport aircraft and a six-ton lorry. The German forces on the retreat had pulled off the road nearby and had stopped for the night. Mobile kitchens were now set up and serving breakfast with hundreds of men lining up.

15 Nov – Many men killed on parade area. One of our chaps (Sgt Caldwell) was shot down by flak.
16 Nov – Strafing of road between Agedabia and El Aghela. One Ju88 and 3 Me109s seen, also a small amount of light flak encountered. One petrol bowser destroyed. One 6 ton lorry destroyed. Three 3 ton lorries damaged.

The Italians had got wind of the squadrons' base. Although the Italians had an idea of the general proximity of the base, the Axis forces were no nearer in ascertaining from which direction the squadrons had come. To counteract this, reconnaissance planes were ordered up to locate the base. The pilots had initially seen them during the course of their flying and it wasn't long before they tracked the Hurricanes to LG 125. Fortunately, the reconnaissance aircraft could only radio back to their base because ground troops were fully dispatched. Peter got a bullet hole in his rudder that day. Nos 213 and 238 Squadrons just got out in time, the transport and freighter aircraft had arrived, packed up and had left; the Hurricanes were refuelled and were flown back to their original landing ground of LG 101 near the town of Sidi Hanish. It took the pilots two hours to cover the 400 miles back to Allied ground.

16 Nov – LG 125 to LG 101. End of the trip!!

On 17 November, the squadron was moved forward to El Adem. Three days later, Peter escorted Lodestar transport aircraft to Msus, where they delivered petrol supplies for the Army. On the 23rd, Peter flew back to RAF Aboukir from El Adem for more

well-earned beer supplies to toast a farewell to their boss, Roy
Marples. It took over two hours to fly there, covering the best
part of 1,000 miles. The journey was so long that he officially
flew twenty minutes of night-flying!

The Germans were now in retreat, leaving towns, houses and
vehicles with their supplies.

Peter recalls an incident with Neil Cameron of No. 213
Squadron when he, Peter and Roy Marples decided to visit
Tobruk. Cameron, who later became Lord Cameron of
Balhousie, took his squadron Jeep with three others, and
Marples and Peter took theirs. They drove round the harbour
and came across a bar which was fully stocked with drink. The
pièce de résistance was a massive tonneau of wine, 6ft tall and
about the same across. It was full of Chianti, with a wooden tap
at the bottom. It was too good to be true! Should they?
Shouldn't they? Of course, they should! Each took a turn, lying
on the floor of the bar with mouths open wide while another
turned the tap full on.

Peter recalls that fighter pilots in the desert were generally pretty
light-hearted. 'We always thought that the bomber boys were a
little bit dour and I think it goes with the job they were doing. We
were on our own in the aircraft – if anything went wrong, it was
down to us – navigation wise, armament-wise, radio-wise. I think
the type of flying we were doing made chaps more light-hearted;
it was shit-or-bust – there was no point in being down-hearted.
We weren't going back to an officers' mess in the UK each night;
we had to make do with what little resources were available to us.
You made the best of each job you found yourself in. I always
found that the fighter pilots had a bit more *joie de vivre*; they were
living for the moment a little bit more. Our flights were more
intense; three hours was a long time for us.'

Progress was being made by the Allied troops. By 26
November, No. 238 Squadron had advanced to a base at

Martuba, not far from the Libyan port of Derna, 200 miles east of Benghazi. Marples had been posted from No. 238 Squadron, to be replaced by Sqn Ldr Homer Cochrane. At this time Peter was suffering from in-growing toenails and the pain was becoming intolerable. It was arranged that he should have an operation at the nearest hospital at Benghazi. On 11 December, he flew the 200 miles from Martuba to Benina airfield, close to Benghazi. He spent the night in hospital and flew back the next morning. His big toes were covered in bandages and it was a problem trying to pull his flying boots on over the bandages, and managing to hobble into the cockpit of his Hurricane. It must have been equally painful flying back to Martuba with sore feet, but the operation worked.

A week later, on 18 December, Peter became involved with ferrying duties. He was appointed leader of a formation of twelve Hurricanes fitted with long-range tanks, which had to be ferried from Benina to Algeria, with an overnight stop in Malta where it was necessary to refuel the aircraft.

Two Lockheed Hudsons picked up the twelve Hurricane pilots at Martuba and took them to Benina. After an overnight stay, the twelve Hurricanes took off, formatting on the Hudsons which were responsible for navigation. The flight from Benina to Takali, Malta, took two and a half hours. During the flight, they noticed a large German formation of Ju 52 transport aircraft complete with fighter escort, flying south to Tripoli with supplies. The enemies saw each other at 5 miles. In a case of live and let live, the Luftwaffe flew south as the RAF flew north. Peter knew an attack was out of the question because it was vital to deliver the Hurricanes to Algeria, where they were badly needed. It was also unlikely that the German fighters would have left the Ju 52 formation. The Hurricanes and Hudsons landed at Takali and the pilots prepared for an overnight stop before proceeding to Algeria the following day. The next day, however, proved to be awkward. The weather clamped down completely; there had been a torrential downpour in the Malta area and the take-off had to be postponed. The bad weather continued for a week, which made it impossible for the pilots to leave the island. Peter was contacted by Air Officer Commanding Malta, AVM Keith Park, who had been AOC of 11 Group during the Battle of Britain. 'I want you to get these aircraft away as soon as you can.' Park went on to say, 'I realise you cannot fly at present, but you must leave as soon as possible.'

'Certainly sir, we will.'

Because of the weather, the pilots spent the week up to and including Christmas Day 1942 in an RAF rest-house at St Paul's Bay on the north side of the island. It was run by Flt Lt Arthur Howard, the same officer who oversaw the transit camp in Cairo. The meals were meagre: a couple of slices of bully beef and two hard tack biscuits. To add insult to injury, although there was hardly any food on the island, there were plentiful supplies of scotch and Peter says they had nothing else to drink! He left Malta on Boxing Day 1942, bound for Algeria. When the weather cleared, the Hudsons took off, navigating the course for Peter's Hurricane, while the rest of the squadron followed. Their flight plan to Algeria was to ferry these Hurricanes with long-range tanks to Constantine, then fly due south for 50 miles avoiding Focke Wulf Fw 190 fighters that were based nearby on the islands of Pantelleria and Lambedusa.

Flying at zero feet over the sea and then changing course due west, they hit the Tunisian coast between Sousse and Sfax, climbing to avoid the foothills of the Saharan Atlas mountains. But soon after crossing the coast, they ran into solid low cloud. 'Right, close in. We'll formate to get though this cloud', Peter said over the radio. Unfortunately, the Hudsons had now lost them. They were stranded, not knowing where they were, heading in a formation in thick cloud, and the onus fell on Peter to lead them to safety.

To make matters worse, the radio only worked between Hurricane and Hurricane; there was no communication with ground control. With heart pumping and throat dry, he climbed to 10,000ft to avoid the mountains. After about an hour, he decided to descend, breaking cloud at 1,500ft and gauging his direction using his watch and compass. It did the trick. Eventually, he felt the formation must by now be over the mountain range. There was no sign of the Hudsons that had been assigned to navigate, and they saw strange land below them, so Peter wisely decided that there was nothing for it but to find an airfield. He noticed what looked to be a number of large construction diggers preparing a grass airfield; the grass, such as it was, had been stripped away, leaving the rich brown earth visible. He hoped this was Tebessa. The formation was low on fuel by this time – it had been airborne for over three and a quarter hours – and things were getting tight. 'We've got to get in there, come what may', Peter radioed to the others. Leading the group he went in for a landing on the brown strip . . . the wheels touched the rich soil of . . . crump! His Hurricane had come to a direct halt; the soil was in fact heavy thick mud churned up by the diggers and was pulling him down very quickly. He was aware that the other Hurricanes were following him in and he knew he had to leave the muddy strip urgently. He opened the throttle of the engine slowly, very slowly. Equally slowly, the nose sank down, pulling the rest of the plane with it. Peter cut the engine immediately and left the Hurricane where it was, climbing out of the cockpit, the only damage done was to his pride. At least he had found an airfield and it was Tebessa. The diggers had been preparing the strip for the imminent arrival of the US Army Air Force.

The flight from Malta to Tebessa shows once again the strength, resilience and skill in blind flying that Peter displayed in leading the formation of Hurricanes without full radio aids or navigation through thick cloud. In spite of the dreadful conditions, he had the ability to stay calm under pressure, taking responsibility for the pilots and machines in the formation, and leading them to safety. Unfortunately, on the flight to Tebessa one of the Hudsons crashed into the mountains with the loss of the crew. The squadron had four days in Algeria, which they made the most of, exploring the heady delights in Constantine. Peter went into one of the hotels, throbbing with RAF pilots. There, in the middle of Algeria, he bumped into Butch Lyons, who had been sent to the North African invasion with No. 243 Squadron.

'I've been here too long, Pete. I'm getting too stale. Let's take a Jeep, see some of the sights', said Lyons.

'Right . . . when you say 'take' a vehicle, what do you mean exactly?' Peter replied.

'Well . . . borrow then.'

'Borrow?'

And 'borrow' a Jeep is precisely what Lyons did. A good time must have ensued as Peter cannot recall anything about the journey, but he met a friend from Westcliff High School, George Goode, who was navigating Blenheims. It was, for Peter, a small world, and he says that Constantine was interesting in the New Year of 1943.

Four days in Constantine soon came to an end, though, and it was back on operations. They returned from Canrobert airfield in Algeria to Benina in a Hudson on New Year's Day. The Hudson travelled well south avoiding any activity, turning east towards Benina. The flight covered most of the Western Desert, taking 7hr 10min. The next day, the Hudson flew the pilots from Benina to Martuba. Once they had arrived at Martuba, the squadron became aware that their base was being moved once more, this time further east to an airfield called Gamil, very close to Port Said. The authorities had decreed that as No. 238 Squadron had taken a pasting over the past three months, it was to be rested from operational duties and was due to be swapped with No. 94 Squadron. Cochrane asked Peter to fly to recce the town of Gamil so that the squadron would have an idea of what to expect.

The flight was made in stages, the first stop at Heliopolis, the main airport at Cairo. On his way there, a tremendous sandstorm whipped up. There was nothing that Peter could do except fly through it; another case of utilising his skills in blind flying. He was to find out later that this sandstorm stretched across the desert for 80 miles, from Dhaba to the Suez delta. It was an extraordinary experience; absolutely nothing to be seen but a brown sheet in front of you. After various stops, it took him three days to reach the airfield at Gamil. Martuba resounded to the roar of No. 238 Squadron's Merlin engines for the final time as Hurricanes and transport aircraft flew to Gamil. None of the pilots was particularly sorry to leave Libya; for most it had been extremely trying and desperately exhausting.

It was all change at Gamil: a new year at a new base with new operational duties. No. 238 Squadron was responsible for carrying out close escort duties to cover shipping patrols leaving Port Said from the Suez Canal and heading north for Malta or reaching the Allied troops further west along the Libyan coast.

Gradually, a new routine emerged in the squadron. In many respects, it was back to basics. The hit-and-run strafing raids in the desert were replaced with re-establishing simple techniques and exercises that each pilot had mastered on his original advanced flying course. It was supposed to give the squadron a new-found confidence as they practised formations, interceptions, local flying practice, night-flying and even aluminium bomb tests. But things were not very successful. It wasn't all practice. They were still called upon to scramble:

15 Feb – Spitfires tally-hoed – couldn't catch Ju 88.

After their withdrawal from the desert, Peter's days with No. 238 Squadron and the Middle East were drawing to a close. Their evenings were spent in Port Said. As Senior Flight Commander, Peter was given a truck, strictly for business use. He made it his business to drive the truck to the city, taking the rest of the squadron along with him. The boys became familiar with various bars but always finished up at the Eastern Exchange Hotel, which put on a particularly fine cabaret. Like all good cabarets, the Eastern Exchange had fantastic dancing girls. There was one particular girl in the cabaret with whom

Peter fell head over heels in love. She was Greek and her name was Marina. She worked her charms on Peter and he became smitten with her. She also became smitten with him and meant a great deal to him; so much so that back at Gamil airfield he picked up a pot of white paint and a brush and painted her name on his Hurricane.

Peter is not one for reflecting particularly in life; if it happens, so be it . . . but he says that with Marina things could have been different. He felt something heartfelt and earnest for her and she felt something deep and sincere for him. It is more than possible that together they could have settled down and raised a family. As it was, his marriage started with a salad sandwich . . .

He continued seeing Marina until one day in early April 1943 when he was posted to No. 73 OTU as an instructor at Abu Sueir. It is commonplace for instructor and pupil pilot to speak the same language, even if they come from different countries. However, Peter had to instruct five particular pupils from Turkey who couldn't speak a word of English. Needless to say, his Turkish was non-existent, yet it was imperative that he instruct these five Turkish pilots in combat fighting because these particular Turkish officers had been given special priority and authority direct from Churchill himself. It is Peter's belief that the Turkish government at the time wanted to establish a similar operational training unit, and though there were pilots who were competent enough to fly, they lacked operational experience in combat. So, together with Gordon Troke, his Canadian deputy, Peter began instructing the Terrible Turks, as they became known, in combat skills necessary for fighter pilots. If anyone was well versed in that role, it was Peter.

The Turkish authorities saw fit to send an interpreter who spoke a modicum of English. Each morning, Gordon and Peter briefed him as to their plans. He in turn, translated each stage of flying duties to the Turks, who nodded their understanding. Of course, all this was carried out on the ground before the pilots had donned their flying helmets. Once airborne, the 'famous five' flew what they thought Peter wanted. Although he was flying alongside, there was little point in communication and precious little he could do when one of them flew out of formation.

Once they had landed, the interpreter gave a debriefing, explaining just what Peter had felt about the flight. His assessment, either good or downright appalling, was relayed to them. The Turkish pilots were all relatively experienced and all seemed to pass the course.

In addition, Peter used Harvards for dual practice, though of course there were limitations. Most of their battle formation practice was on Kittyhawks and Tomahawks. Produced by the Curtiss aircraft company, Peter found that the Kittyhawks weren't bad to fly but they weren't much good at high level. A later – and performance-refined – version of the Tomahawk, the Kittyhawk was also used by the Turks for air-to-ground firing. It is fair to say that it was not in the same class as the Spitfire. The earlier version, the Tomahawk, was in Peter's words, 'bloody awful'.

Another instructor based at No. 73 OTU at the same time as Peter became a household name later on. Sqn Ldr Neville Duke instructed pilots flying Spitfires in the desert. Occasionally, he and Peter grabbed time for a brief chat over a beer in the mess. After the war, Duke returned to Britain, where he became Chief Test Pilot for Hawkers, responsible for testing and flying the Hunter. It was in an all-red Hunter that Duke succeeded in breaking the World Absolute Air Speed Record at a speed of 727.63mph on 7 September 1953.

The Western Desert operation was finally over for Peter, and he was posted to South Africa on a Central Flying School (CFS) course. It was seen by the authorities as a rest and by Peter as a welcome break from operations. However, there was a period of six weeks to wait before he could join the CFS. To fill the interim, HQ instructed Peter to fly to Heliopolis, where he was to join No. 1 Air Delivery Unit. He was to be flown across the African continent to the air base at Takoradi, in what was the Gold Coast, now Ghana. The base at Takoradi had been the supply depot for aircraft, including Spitfires, as reinforcements for the Middle East. Engineers assembled the aircraft, which were then test-flown.

As part of No. 1 Air Delivery Unit, Peter's role was to fly the Spitfires, leading them in groups of six. Navigation was provided by a Maryland that flew ahead of the flight.

The route to Takoradi was epic, covering 3,000 miles in a BOAC Airspeed Ensign. Taking twenty-five hours, it followed a set of courses from Cairo to Takoradi. The first course of the flight was relatively straightforward, heading south from Cairo to Wadi Halfa, a town at the southern edge of Lake Nasser. The Ensign continued to head south, reaching Khartoum. Having reached Sudan, the Ensign turned west, setting a third course for El Fasher, then on to El Geneina, flying south of Lake Chad and on to Maidugari, Peter's 'dungheap of the earth.' The next leg was to a well-established Nigerian airport at Kano. Finally, the Ensign flew to an airfield outside Lagos, Appapa, where they boarded a Lockheed 14 which flew them to Accra and their destination of Takoradi.

Three days later, a Spitfire was ready for testing. The role to test it fell to Peter, and he found that things seemed to be fine. After six days, Peter, together with the other six Spitfires, was ready to fly the 3,000 miles back to Cairo, breaking their journey at various stages. Peter's first stop was at Ikeja, a new airstrip being built outside Lagos. As the strip at Appapa was too small for Spitfires, thousands of trees from the forest had to be cut in order to make the strip, which has since been developed and is now the foremost civilian airport for Nigeria. From there they flew on to Kano and then Maidugari, situated in the north-east of Nigeria. 'Christ, what a place. I don't know how the maintenance crews managed to get on; I feel sorry for the poor blokes who had to work in this place.'

Why did he dislike it so much? 'I have never been to

anywhere where the flies are so thick. There was wire mesh over the windows of the buildings. The officers' mess was only 50yds from the officers' quarters, yet in order to get from one to the other, you had to put your head down in order to get through the flies.'

The Spitfires were delayed for three days owing to bad weather. Peter was glad to escape from the flies when the epic flight continued to El Geneina and El Fasher, where they stayed for a night before stopping at Khartoum and Wadi Halfa, finally reaching Helwan, Cairo.

The flight is remarkable considering the type of single-seat aircraft Peter was flying. The distances of the flights between stops is also impressive. Perhaps what is most extraordinary is the pilots' courage and skill in flying over incredibly rough and inhospitable terrain. And Peter had to lead the six Spitfires; he was responsible for navigation. He was also accountable if one of the aircraft developed engine trouble. There would be little opportunity for a safe landing over much of the terrain and even less opportunity for survival. It must have been a mental strain as much as a physical one.

Having spent more than a year in Africa, Peter's flying knowledge and experience was widespread and extensive. He had flown to, and stopped at, seven different countries since 1942. Mercifully, the six weeks were up. By 19 September 1943, Peter finally received the call to leave for South Africa, and, unlike the Ensign, he was going to fly in style courtesy of a Shorts Empire flying-boat. During the inter-war years, travelling in one of these had been the height of elegance and luxury. The flying-boat stopped in Khartoum before flying to Kenya, stopping first at Kisumu on the northern shores of Lake Victoria, before heading south-east along the Yatta Plateau for Mombasa. Hugging the eastern coast of Tanzania over the Indian Ocean, they flew to Mozambique, stopping for a night, then on to Beira, Lourenço-Marques.

Drink supplies were scarce on the flying-boat, and they found the only place they could get one in Mozambique was the local railway station. Station is perhaps, too grandiose a word; Peter says it was more of a shed with a train service once a week! The station master who worked in this shed of a station also happened to be the bartender. He was 5ft 2in in height and just the same across, 'built like a brick shithouse', as Peter says. The pilots got talking with him after a drink or two when the conversation turned to party tricks.

'I'll show you a trick', the station master/bartender said. With that, he picked up a six-inch nail and a piece of cardboard. He folded the cardboard into quarters and pushed it against the palm of his right hand. Placing the head of the nail against the cardboard with the other hand, he put a board in front of him. The nail was driven through the board; he had managed to push the nail clean through the board with just his hand. Peter wasn't wholly surprised because his arms were so huge and so wide that he bore more than a passing resemblance to Popeye.

The Empire flying-boat flew on to Durban, stopping there for two days. Captains came and captains went. The final leg of the journey was to the Vaalbank Dam, south of Johannesburg, where flying-boats like the Empire could arrive inland. The whole route took thirty-six hours to fly over a period of five days.

Peter and the instructors arrived in Johannesburg on 27 September 1943 before reporting to CFS at No. 62 Air School, Bloemfontein. The instructing was considered something of a picnic, not only because they were a world away from combat missions but also because the aircraft they flew were gentle and sedate; de Havilland Tiger Moths were already becoming obsolete in the days of 1939 when Peter had been a green pilot. Bloemfontein is 300 miles further south from Johannesburg and about 5,000ft above sea level. A constant breeze is often noticeable at this height, but there are occasions when the breeze whips up into strong and very high winds. Because of the difference in altitude, these winds were much stronger at 5,000ft than they were at sea level, gusting at about 50mph. The stalling point on a Tiger Moth wasn't much beyond that.

Peter had a lot of fun as the morning sun shone brightly when these breezes picked up. Up in the air, he kept the nose of the Tiger Moth right up, cutting the throttles right back, keeping the airspeed just above the stalling point. It was virtually hovering; the Tiger Moth almost became the first vertical and short take-off and landing (VSTOL) aircraft!

He enjoyed the course and it made a break for him. But after a while he wanted a change; things had become too sedentary and it was all too routine. That restless drive and boundless energy he possessed throughout his life was just as strong and it was time to move on. The wind was blowing in a different direction.

Word had got to South Africa that the whole of southern England was swarming with British and American troops, preparing for something. Something was happening – and when it did, Peter wanted to be on the winning side. He says that he had joined the RAF when pilots and planes had reached their lowest ebb. He had witnessed events from the outset of the war, through the most challenging and demanding operations. Things were now looking very much more positive for the Allied forces. He went to see the Chief Flying Instructor about a move, stating his position.

'Is there any possibility of me getting back to England onto a squadron again, just for the final fling?' he asked.

'Well, I don't know, I'll see what I can do.' The Chief Flying Instructor got on the telephone to HQ. He put forward the case that Peter was far more useful to the Air Force as an operational squadron pilot with his experience. The upshot was that Peter returned to England in April 1944, taking two months in transit.

South Africa provided Peter with a number of excellent opportunities for socialising. Towards the end of his tour in the desert with No. 238 Squadron, one South African lieutenant suggested some contacts. 'Peter, you're bound to be in Johannesburg when you get to my country. Go and contact my parents.' Peter duly did so. His parents had a very nice flat in Dunkeld and Leslie worked for the South African Press. The couple asked him to stay with them for a while, to which he agreed. They also introduced him to a number of parties and people and he became well acquainted with their daughter, Pippa, who was about twenty-three. She was currently dating a South African pilot called Dawson Squibb. Pippa and Dawson Squibb were often invited to parties, and Peter, too, was continually invited. Having a chance to let his hair down in a non-military environment was a welcome break. Many of these parties were held by doctors who were specialists in their chosen field and one had a bar rigged up in the style of an English pub known as The George.

On one occasion, Peter became involved in a dogfight of a different kind. Wearing his uniform, Peter and his hosts were invited to a farewell cocktail party one Friday evening for a press contact who was moving on to another post, and Peter knew some of the guests by this time. There were many representatives from the press, including many from the Dutch community, who had their own paper, *Der Faderland*. The party took place at six-thirty in a big room on the first floor of the Carlton Hotel, the main hotel in Johannesburg. In order to reach the room, guests had to pass down a long corridor. Peter left at about 8 p.m. Strolling down the corridor, they became aware of voices speaking in a guttural accent about 6ft behind them. It sounded like Afrikaans.

'Look at that guy in front. Call that a uniform? I'd rather be wearing a German outfit than the one that guy in front of us is wearing.' It was like a red rag to a bull. Heart pumping, Peter spun round and landed a well-aimed right-hand on one of the Afrikaaners, who collapsed on the floor. In his words, 'Never kick a man when he's down – unless he's pissed you off.' As the Afrikaaner lay sprawled on the floor, Peter kicked him firmly up the backside, just to make sure. His hosts looked at each other. 'Come on, quick,' they said hastily, 'we must leave – now! Dusty, hail a cab!' And off they went. Peter's response was one of nonchalance – 'What's the bloody hurry?' he thought.

The next morning, he attended a lunch-time party full of British ex-pats. He was swamped by well-wishers who patted him on the back and were only too eager to shake his hand.

'Bloody marvellous!' they cried. 'We couldn't do that, but it was bloody marvellous to see. You know, you only just got out in time.'

'What do you mean?' Peter replied.

'The Afrikaner's friends had signalled for the entire Dutch element to join them. They were waiting for you outside the hotel with bicycle chains!'

Peter also had a lively time in Durban. One of the many faces Peter came across was an elderly Norwegian gentleman known as Pop Grinaker. Although he had spent his childhood in Norway, his family had moved to South Africa, where he had established a wealthy career as a building contractor for hotels and other large commercial businesses. He had a beautiful house, a beautiful swimming pool and four very beautiful daughters. As Peter says, 'they were all crackers; typically Scandinavian, typically blonde.' He was spoilt there 'something rotten'. While in Johannesburg, Peter had mentioned to Grinaker that he was leaving for England but had to travel to Durban in order to catch a ship that would take him home. When he reached Durban, he'd stay in an RAF transit camp, three or four miles to the north of the city.

'I'll tell you one thing, Peter; you do not want to stay in that place – the accommodation isn't at all good. I am building some flats in Durban at the moment. I have a flat which I stay in when I am there. I'm due to be there shortly – let me know when you reach the station and you can have my flat.'

The train journey seemed long, even for an overnight service, along the 400 miles to Durban. Sure enough, at the station, Grinaker was waiting for him with a servant and a van, ready for Peter's luggage – which consisted of two rather small suitcases. 'Ah, there you are!' He seemed apologetic. 'It seems I've made a mistake! I promised you that you could have the flat but I'd forgotten that I'd agreed that a friend of mine and her son could have it. Don't worry, though. I've booked you into the Marine hotel. It's right on the seafront.'

'Good Lord! I can't afford to stay there', Peter had exclaimed.

'Oh no, no; I'll cover that.'

'Well, I don't know how long I'm likely to be there – I could be there for a few days; but it might be three weeks. It all depends on when a boat arrives for the UK.'

'I insist! It's my mistake. I'm covering it.'

Peter became known as the Uncrowned King of Durban by his pilot colleagues from the transit camp who came to see him at the Edward Hotel. It was the five-star touch: wonderful food and waiter service all the time at every meal and there was a snooker room. Alan Byfield remembers meeting him in the bar of the hotel and Peter insisted he should stay for the night. Alan was Lieutenant-Observer in the Fleet Air Arm and his ship had docked in Durban. 'Porter!' Peter asked. 'Do you have a bed for the night for my friend?' The porter took them to a billiard room where Peter had been sleeping underneath the billiard table.

Alan was told he could sleep on the top. Eventually he got a room. Alan remembers that after a night of drinking on one occasion, he woke up the next morning in bed with Peter and three girls but neither of them can recall anything about it!

During his 'reign' in Durban, in the hotel bar Peter got talking to a Dutch crew who worked on a vessel moored in the harbour. The drinks flowed and sailors and pilot got on well. In the course of conversation, Peter mentioned he had been allocated a boat back to England. They replied that they were due to leave Durban in the next week or so and, as it happened, were bound for Britain.

'You never know, come and see us on the bridge if you're on our ship. What's the name of the ship you're going on?' they asked him.

'The *New Amsterdam*', he replied.

'Well, well; that's ours!'

Peter left Durban on 19 February and was in transit for three weeks until mid-March 1944.

Unlike the journey down, there was no protection from destroyers or company from transport ships. The ship went flat out at about thirty knots to evade U-boats.

The route back was a reversal of the one by which they had arrived. From Durban, the *New Amsterdam* sailed across to the coast of South America, hugging the coast as it headed north, then east towards Iceland and south-east to Scotland. For some the trip was arduous, but although Peter had to sleep in a cabin with five others he was reunited with one of the officers in the hotel bar and spent his days in his cabin. Unlike the other Allied pilots, he was at liberty to do what he wanted within reason: have the odd drink from the cabinet or take meals on his own in the cabin. By late March, he was back in the land of his birth, having spent nearly two years away. Fully rested from the exhausting operations in the desert, he was preparing for the final stage of the war.

SIX

The Boys of Baroda

Almost two years after he had left Britain, Peter set foot on English soil on 24 April 1944.

The desert had now moulded and shaped his character as well as his flying and yet he was still only twenty-three; he had gained formidable experience in his second major operational tour.

The next day, he was posted to No. 124 (Baroda) Squadron. He nodded with satisfaction for No. 124 Squadron was based at Bradwell-on-Sea and he knew the area well. The village was half a mile from the shores of the River Blackwater, on the northern side of the Thames estuary, as it ran inland to Maldon. Bradwell was his home ground, his patch. His new squadron was just forty-five minutes from Westcliff and flying to Southend would take a matter of minutes. He was pleased to be back. Out in South Africa, the English papers had been full of news that things were hotting up back home. There was talk of one last push: an invasion that signalled the beginning of the end of the war. Reports were full of the Americans piling into England and, as a result, something was bound to happen. Peter was now a part of it.

Like many squadrons, No. 124 Squadron had a suffix attached – Baroda. He discovered that it was in gratitude to the Maharajah of Baroda who had financed the squadron as his contribution to the war effort. A basic Spitfire without armament and radio equipment cost around £5,000 per aircraft, and the Maharajah had donated a significant sum of money in order to purchase a number of Spitfires. By way of thanks, No. 124 Squadron acknowledged his gesture, and thus a tiny piece of India was found on an airfield in a corner of Essex. The Maharajah was invited by the squadron to a special dinner at the Savoy Hotel after the war.

In addition to the newly acquired Spitfires, the Maharajah contributed to the pilots' benefit. Every now and again, food parcels arrived from him, containing goodies and packets of sweets which made a welcome break from the rationing endured by Britain for the past five years. Every squadron had an emblem and a motto. Peter's new squadron had a mongoose as its emblem with the motto 'Danger is our Opportunity'. It was to prove appropriate. He found that the breadth of pilots' experience in Baroda Squadron seemed to be far greater than with a normal fighter squadron. As in the desert, he had been posted to Bradwell as a supernumerary, though this time it was not because of his experience; the authorities had posted him to the Baroda Boys because they were flying a new type of Spitfire.

There was one old face he recognised at Bradwell. Hadn't the Squadron CO been at Grantham? The Commanding Officer at Bradwell had indeed been a student pilot with Peter at No. 12 FTU course just before the outbreak of war – Tommy Balmforth. Both men were also interested in rugby, and, perhaps more importantly, both were still alive to tell the tale. Peter had been a squadron supernumerary for just three weeks when Balmforth asked him to step in as Senior Flight Commander of 'B' Flight.

No. 124 (Baroda) Squadron had been the first in Britain to be equipped with the new Spitfire Mk VII and Peter had his first familiarisation flight two days after he joined the squadron.

Although the airframe was similar to the Marks I, II and V which he had flown regularly, the Mk VII was used specifically for interception flights at high altitude. It had elongated wing tips which gave the plane additional wingspan, along with a pressurised cockpit. The Mk VII canopy was shut just like any other, with a seal running round the canopy edge, keeping a constant pressure at high altitudes, and pilots were most appreciative! It was superior to the Mk VIs, of which there were still one or two examples at Bradwell, whose canopies had to be screwed down in order to keep the pressure constant once the pilots had been strapped into their cockpits: time-consuming for pilots and ground crew alike. It was agreed by all that the Mk VII was a big improvement.

Once in the cockpit, Peter and 'B' Flight took their Spitfires to a ceiling of between 30,000 and 35,000ft, their brief being to intercept high-level Fw 190s or Ju 88s that were on photo-reconnaissance missions. The Germans were well aware of the increase in activity in England. Peter says that the whole of the south was one huge military camp, jammed up with Army units, masses of American Jeeps blocking roads, and that the Germans were conscious of the massive American invasion. They knew that something big was going to happen but at this stage their Intelligence failed to find out precisely where or when. The Fw 190s and Ju 88s were sent out to photograph the build-up of men and machines on the ground, and No. 124 (Baroda) Squadron had to stop these photographs being taken.

The Luftwaffe aircraft were a good match for the new Spitfires. The Fw 190 had a reputation for destroying Allied planes in the European theatre; not for nothing was it known as the 'Butcher Bird'. Although the Junkers Ju 88 had been around since the days of the Battle of Britain, it too could still pack a punch. Designed as a medium bomber, it had been the Luftwaffe's most effective resource because of its speed and performance.

Up at 30,000ft, Peter was enjoying flying the Spitfire at altitude. The designers had given it a new engine, a Merlin 64 with a two-speed, two-stage supercharger, enabling the pilots to achieve a far better performance at height, especially when they opened up their throttles, but the honeymoon period was over. Although they were exhilarated by the new Spitfires, Peter and the boys of Baroda found the spring of 1944 exhausting, incessantly patrolling over the Channel. In order to intercept successfully, the patrols were frequent and relentless. In many ways, what he was doing now bore a striking similarity to the defensive lines he had flown over the French border as a raw, green, rookie pilot in 1939. The patrols were flown in pairs – one pair took off, climbing to altitude and radioing to the pair currently on patrol, determining their exact location. Once this information was passed over the intercom and the new pair had rendezvoused, the other brace returned to base.

This method of interception patrols was still found to be the most reliable; an interception would have been ineffective if a lone invader had been picked up by radar, with the Spitfires still preparing to scramble   Peter says it takes a long time to get to 30,000ft! By the time the pilots had scrambled, the enemy would have taken enough pictures and turned back for home.

Patrol implies maintaining a defensive role but the squadron's role was equally offensive. Peter also flew many offensive strikes over the Channel. Many offensive patrols followed the same flight path: over the Straits of Dover, into German territory at Calais, over Boulogne as far south as Le Tréport and back again. These sorties took place virtually on a daily basis, flying for a period of an hour and a half. It was intense work and Peter was often glad to get back to Bradwell.

A local farmer approached the squadron, wishing to sell an old Ford Eight. Did any of them want it? In need of a car, Peter went to have a look at it. First impressions were not favourable; it was in a state of disrepair. He looked under the bonnet. Mechanically, the engine and brakes seemed to be fine, but as he says, 'When I looked inside, the interior was full of pigshit.' Apparently, in the absence of a trailer, the farmer had carried pigs to and from market in the back of the car and Peter recalls that it stank to high heaven. After a great deal of cleaning, with a few invectives thrown in for good measure, he found that the car went like a bomb. It was still going strong in February 1945 when he was posted from the squadron to Castle Bromwich near Birmingham, speeding up and down the main roads from Birmingham to Canterbury.

The photographs that Peter took during the squadron's posting to Manston demonstrate fighter pilots at work and play: characters caught in many moods and gestures – faces grinning, scowling, glancing shyly at the camera: Max Charlesworth, who displayed a special and regular knack for intimate friendships with women and formed a close friendship with Peter; Peter's opposite number in 'A' Flight, Cliff Grey, who had lost his hair at the beginning of the war; Slim Kilburn, who became a test pilot with de Havilland; Johnny Melia, one of the first pilots to be killed in Britain's first jet aircraft, the Meteor – amiable, funny and easy-going, Peter always found Johnny good for a laugh; Canadians, Australians and New Zealanders using a small table in the pilots' dispersal hut to gamble on. There was also a young and strikingly attractive WAAF driver, who drove Peter and the other pilots from the officers' mess to the dispersal hut.

High-altitude flying was demanding, but even so, the boys (and girls) of Baroda Squadron knew that they had been formed because of their flying abilities. There were times when pilots didn't return, their book or pack of cards lying unused on the table or chair they had set two hours ago. This was nothing new, of course; it was an occupational hazard, but No. 124 Squadron had an unquenchable spirit. They all knew they were there because, in Peter's words, they were a cut above the average pilot; chosen to fly new aircraft at higher altitudes. In a sense, their squadron was an elite corps of fighter pilots.

By May 1944 the Germans had good reason to think that the Allies were planning an invasion, given the amount of troop movements in southern England. However, their Intelligence was still unaware of the precise location of the landings and the sheer scale of the operation being planned.

19 May 1944 – Patrolled Dover, fluid six formation. Patrolled North Foreland & Boulogne.

The squadron found that their patrols were getting longer towards early June. And then, on 6 June 1944, came the news. D-Day was announced; the Allied invasion of France had begun. As far as Peter was concerned, D-Day was just another typical day, patrolling the line from Gravelines near Dunkirk in the north to Le Tréport in the south. It was very much business as usual for him while all hell was breaking out on the beaches of Normandy. He summarised his findings of D-Day later in his logbook:

6 June – D-Day; very quiet.

It must be remembered that the Allied invasion took place well away to the west around the Baie de la Seine, while Peter was patrolling over the Straits of Dover, easily 150 miles distant.

In a sense, Baroda Squadron was used as a decoy, lulling the Luftwaffe into thinking that the Allied forces would make an invasion of the Pas de Calais, at the shortest route across the Channel. Axis Intelligence did not suspect that an Allied invasion would take place across a longer stretch of water, towards the beaches in Lower Normandy.

12 June – Patrol Cap-Gris-Nez – North Foreland. Destroyed an Me 109G during a patrol from Calais to North Foreland.
15 June – Patrol Calais – North Foreland. Search for a PRU pilot who baled out between Manston and Gravelines.
17 June – Close escort of 15 Dakotas to landing strip on the beach head. Plenty of activity on the ground.

It seems probable that the Dakotas Peter escorted were full of supplies for the ground troops.

28 June – Sweep behind Lilles. Escorted Lancasters bombing. No balls.

No balls was the Allied codename for attacks on the launch sites for V1 flying bombs in northern France. The bombs themselves were stored in large underground complexes, but the most noticeable landmark for pilots was the massive adjustable 'ski' ramps, an easy target for bombers.

> 30 June – Close escort of 250 Halifaxes and Lancasters bombing Villers-Bocage.

The town of Villers-Bocage south of the invasion beach-head was surrounded by a forest.

Allied troops found that their advance was being held up when they discovered that masses of German troops and armour were hidden deep in the forest. An *impasse* was emerging. The Allied invasion, which had been swift and decisive, was fast becoming a stalemate. To rectify this, Allied commanders decided that the forest around the town should be bombed.

> 30 June – Very intensive heavy flak was put up against the bombers. Bombing was most impressive but three bombers down in flames.

Peter found that escorting bombers in a flight like this was just as intensive, just as frightening, as dogfighting; in fact more so. Understandably, since his Hurricane had been shot down in the desert by flak, Peter had been justifiably uneasy and unnerved about the prospect of anti-aircraft fire.

On close escorts, fighters escorted bombers to the target, waited for each aircraft during the actual bombing and escorted them on the return flight home. It was draining on the nerves; Peter found he had to keep an eye out for enemy fighters as well as the flak, which was heavier, more intense than he had experienced before, and he saw at first hand how it picked off fighters just as easily as it picked off bombers.

By mid-July, the Spitfire Mk VII that the Baroda boys had

come to know and enjoy was being phased out in favour of the Mk IX. Each type of Spitfire had different handling characteristics, which had to be borne in mind by pilots flying in a formation. The handling characteristics became more important to master, the larger the formation. Consequently, each pilot found that flying in a flight was different from flying solo; flying in a squadron was something else altogether. It was essential that all twelve pilots knew precisely what to expect from their mount. Peter says those who were overly cocky were most liable to be caught out. Being caught out by a new aircraft could, at best, be embarrassing, at worst, fatal.

He took his flight up in the new Mk IXs on low-flying Balbo formations which were aimed at getting the pilots used to flying the aircraft in a configuration. Peter's first flight in a Mk IX was on 15 July, as ever, purely for familiarisation purposes. Taking off from the Bradwell strip, he found no problems in flying and adapting to the type. His introduction to the Mk IX, however, was short-lived. The following day saw him back on operations in a Mk VII where his flight had been scrambled over the Dutch islands, their brief being to escort a damaged Liberator back to base. On 26 July, No. 124 (Baroda) Squadron moved to Detling.

Seven weeks after the D-Day invasion, the Allied advance in France quickened dramatically. As the troops swept further east, it was imperative that a chain of radar units covering northern France and the Channel was established in France. A mobile radar station, known as A15, had already been established at Maupertus in the Cherbourg peninsula, but regrettably the radar signal had not yet been programmed to receive enemy aircraft. The location and testing of these radar sites were carried out in relative secrecy; programming, or calibrating, the stations was seen as something of an urgent priority. In order to calibrate the radar effectively, an aircraft had to fly straight and true, setting exact courses and accurate heights. The flight had to be precise; there was no latitude for inaccuracy. A foot above or below the given height or deviation from the flight path meant that the calibration tests were useless.

In order to carry out these tests, a certain type of pilot was required: one with tremendous analytical skill and strength of character. Much of the flying depended on having excellent awareness in and around the cockpit. The authorities automatically went to No. 124 (Baroda) Squadron and selected Peter because of his flying record. He was also the most experienced pilot in the squadron.

On 27 July, he was detached from the squadron and sent to 21 Sector for calibration tests. That morning, he flew from Detling airfield to the A15 site at Maupertus. Unfortunately, the runs were postponed the following day when Peter discovered there was a fault with his aircraft and so flew back to Detling in order to have the fault rectified. On 29 July, the tests began in earnest and continued for the next four days. Each test began with Peter taking off from the A15 site at Maupertus, flying south to St Malo, then out to sea some 75 miles north-east of Barfleur, reaching as far north as the Isle of Wight before heading back to the base at Maupertus.

There was no special transmitter in Peter's Spitfire; every yard that Peter flew on his set course was being picked up and plotted on the screens by the radar team at Maupertus. Each test was calibrated at different heights – 2,000ft, 5,000ft and 10,000ft respectively. The route took Peter directly over occupied Jersey and he must have been a wonderful target, especially at 2,000ft, as the Germans lined up their anti-aircraft guns on him. No matter how bad the flak, Peter had to fly straight and true on his set course; he was unable to escape from it. Understandably, this was the worst stage of the flight for him, and even now, fifty-nine years later, he shudders at the thought of it. It was undoubtedly nerve-wracking and one wonders how he managed to evade the path of the anti-aircraft gun crews, especially over four days. By early August, the tests had been completed and the A15 site at Maupertus had been calibrated.

The Boys of Baroda

What Peter had carried out was no small achievement; it says much for his strength, courage and resolve in participating in a mission like this with complete success. It is highly likely that other pilots would have been less fortunate over Jersey.

On 10 August, the boys of No. 124 (Baroda) Squadron were moved from Detling to Westhampnett, a satellite airfield to Tangmere in West Sussex. Peter was very pleasantly surprised to see his old Kiwi chum, Al Deere, in the Westhampnett mess at Shopwkye House. During the period at Westhampnett, the squadron was very active and escorted Mitchells, Bostons, Marauders, Lancasters and Halifaxes on bombing raids. Five weeks later, on 25 September, the squadron was posted to Manston. As the Allies pushed deeper into France and the Low Countries, the fighter sweeps and escorting roles intensified. No. 124 Squadron carried out 'Rodeos' (ground strafing missions) over many and varied targets, such as barges in the Oise canal and ammunition dumps, 'Rhubarbs', and the escorting of light bombers into northern France and the Dutch islands.

16 August – Close escort to thirty six Marauders to Beauvais. Tough weather, quite a lot of heavy flak – one Marauder went in.

31 August – Led the squadron on an armed recce in the Pas de Calais area, it was rather uneventful. A few ground targets were shot up.

By September, operations were changing. The squadron was escorting Lancaster and Halifax heavy bombers on daylight raids, penetrating deep into the heart of the German fatherland. Targets were concentrated in the German industrial area of the Ruhr. Whenever the bombers made a pass over one of these targets, the area was highly defended by the anti-aircraft crews and the flak was very intense. Peter recalls that the flak was so thick that when the stream of bombers passed over, all you saw over the Ruhr area, which was 30 miles long by 10 miles wide, was just one black cloud. He admits that it was a terrifying experience, not least because pilots just didn't know from where or when the flak would arrive. They could at least take action with an enemy aircraft but the flak was quite literally a case of hit or miss.

> I can't remember hearing the shells burst; I was concentrating on height and location of the nearest bomber. We also had our flying helmet which was a tight fit and that, coupled with the roar of the Merlin engine precluded any sound of flak, thank God.
> 11 September – Withdrawal cover to 400 Lancasters bombing oil installations near Hamm.
> Ten-tenths heavy flak over the Ruhr. Several Lancasters shot down.

Withdrawal cover meant that Peter and the others were flying over the target well above the bombers, giving them protection from enemy fighters. They then waited, hanging around for the bombers to drop their bomb loads before picking them up and heading for home.

Fighter pilots and especially Peter found withdrawal cover missions incredibly nerve-wracking; the heart pounded and the mouth was perpetually dry as the fighters presented themselves as sitting targets to the flak gunners, waiting for the bombers to fly round on their reciprocal heading. He hated these missions. As he says, it started at the briefing:

> We went to the room and all the side-curtains would be pulled and artificial lighting was switched on before the covers were pulled to reveal the huge map on the wall because of the secrecy of the missions. The Briefing Officer said, 'Well now, the trip today is here. You've got to go here, then pick up the bombers there.' They used tape to demonstrate the routes along which we were to escort the bombers. When we saw the tape, we thought Christ! They're

sending us to those highly defended areas? You nearly shit yourself in the briefing room, let alone the mission!

On one occasion, when Peter was involved with close escort for Lancasters and Halifaxes, a Lancaster on Peter's starboard side received a direct hit before the bombs had been released.

It happened so suddenly and there was the most massive explosion in the air. Peter had realised what had happened before he saw the aircraft in pieces falling to the ground. He had been just 50yds away.

In the middle of September, Peter participated in what became known as one of the great battles of the Second World War – that ultimately turned into a British fiasco, Operation 'Market Garden'. The squadron had been briefed for escort duties, supporting glider-towing and supply aircraft over the small Dutch town of Arnhem. The Allies wanted to capture Arnhem Bridge at all costs.

On 15 September, the squadron escorted Mitchell bombers that were targeting German ferries off the Dutch islands. This was considered a 'softening-up' process for what was to come two days later. On 17 September, the Baroda boys flew from Westhampnett to Manston to refuel. It was from here that they flew their first patrol over Holland, escorting transport aircraft returning from the first airborne drop zones. Their role was essentially a rearguard cover to the Dakotas, Halifaxes and Stirlings that had towed gliders and dropped British and Polish paratroopers. In addition, their brief was to ground-strafe anti-aircraft guns, which drew flak away from the main force. Peter witnessed plenty of parachutes and gliders strewn over the ground, close to Arnhem, as he picked up the Dakotas.

The following day, Peter refuelled at Bradwell. The weather was not good in the morning. The fighters had to wait until the cloud cleared in the afternoon.

18 September – 124 Squadron took off from Bradwell to give escort patrol to Liberators dropping supplies to troops near Eindhoven. Also escort to tugs and gliders. Plenty of light flak. Several aircraft hit. To be expected when flying 1000ft over eastern Holland!

The Germans were now fully aware of the Allied flights heading towards Arnhem, and increased and intensified their anti-aircraft defence accordingly. In his words, there were just so many aircraft in the air that day.

Because of the atrocious weather conditions, Peter's squadron was the only RAF fighter squadron to take part in the Arnhem conflict on a daily basis. Much of the fiasco is blamed on the RAF by those who saw their inability to drop supplies on the correct drop zones. Peter is quick to point out that the inability was due to the weather closing in, getting progressively worse over four days; little is mentioned of the fighter pilots' bravery in facing the intense barrage of flak. Indeed, one resupply mission was made during which many aircraft were shot down by flak. In order to hit the drop zones, aircrews flew at an altitude of a 1,000ft!

There was no shortage of aircraft trying! Many Mitchell bombers he escorted to the north of the Dutch islands full of supplies managed to make it through the inclement weather, only to be shot down and destroyed by anti-aircraft guns over the island of Walcheren. Peter is convinced that the weather played the dominant part in the failure of Arnhem. If the weather had been better, more squadrons would have been given the opportunity to provide supplies for the bereft ground troops. As it was, a lack of supplies for the Allies contributed to the failure of Operation Market Garden.

25 September – Escort to Mitchells bombing flak positions near Arnhem.

On 25 September, No. 124 (Baroda) Squadron moved from Westhampnett to Manston.

Early October 1944 brought a change. Three weeks after Arnhem, Peter escorted King George VI and VIPs on a trip to Eindhoven from RAF Northolt, flying in a Dakota. September 1944 saw Peter awarded the Distinguished Flying Cross. Normally such an event would have meant receiving an award at Buckingham Palace, but Peter received his at Manston, from the Squadron Commander, Tommy Balnforth. It was about this time while Peter and the boys were based at Manston, that another squadron arrived with the first RAF jet fighter. No. 616 Squadron had just been equipped with the Gloster Meteor and it attracted interest from both squadrons. Jet aircraft were certainly unusual at this time, so it must have been rather exciting for Peter to witness a historic moment in aviation history – the sights and sounds of the first RAF jet fighter.

No. 616 Squadron was not operational then, but on 12 November Peter was involved with Spitfire affiliation with the Meteors. During the months of September, October, November and December, No. 124 (Baroda) Squadron was heavily involved with bomber escort duties.

5 December – Withdrawal escort to 100 Lancasters bombing Hamm. Intense accurate flak north of the Ruhr. Two hundred plus Me 109s and FW 190s reported. Saw twenty 109s in combat with 91 squadron, but was unable to attack.

Peter and the squadron were escorting Lancaster bombers when a dogfight with No. 91 Squadron broke out away in the distance, where they managed to claim three kills. Tempted as they were to break away and join in, they had their orders. They had flown enough close escort missions to know that once a fighter breaks formation, the bombers are extremely vulnerable.

So far, the ethos in Peter's life had been to work hard, play hard. True, there had been a few dalliances, but it is fair to say that romance had not played a large part in his life. All that was about to change.

His sister, Peg, was getting married in mid-December 1944 and she asked him if he was going to attend the wedding, which was taking place at Westcliff. He told her that he'd take some leave, but unknown to her, he wouldn't reach her until the afternoon because he was flying on a withdrawal escort mission with 100 Lancaster bombers early in the morning, encountering intense accurate flak over the Ruhr. Having successfully landed back at about half-past ten that morning, he had arranged for a few days' welcome leave. Having de-briefed with the intelligence officer, showered and changed, Peter left Manston in his old Ford Eight at about a quarter-past one. By the time he reached Canterbury, he was feeling rather hungry and decided to find somewhere where he could get a beer and a sandwich. He looked at his watch. It was almost approaching 2 p.m. He drove past a hotel called The Three Compasses which he thought looked agreeable, so he decided to stop off before the wedding. The opening and closing times of pubs were different during the war, closing at two-thirty in the afternoon and reopening at six in the evening. Peter had therefore left it rather late; as he walked in, there were just a couple of locals propping up the bar. And there, behind it, stood a very attractive young lady.

'Half of bitter, please. Oh, and do you have any sandwiches?'

'Well, we did have,' the young lady replied, 'but they've all gone.' She looked at him. 'However, if you'd like one, then I'll make you one.'

'All right. What sort of sandwiches would you be making?'

'It'll be a salad sandwich', came the reply.

After a little deliberation, the answer was given. 'Um, no thanks. I don't think I'll have a salad sandwich.'

Food rationing was very much in evidence and Peter knew precisely that a salad sandwich meant one lettuce leaf between two slices of bread, two leaves if he was really lucky.

He was lucky that afternoon. He got talking to the lady behind the bar, noticing several interesting photographs and pictures, including some original Hogarths on the wall. She told him that her husband Lionel had been piloting Halifaxes in Bomber Command. He had set off on a raid, hadn't come back and had been posted missing. (She didn't yet know that he had been killed in December 1942.) Tall and a particularly good rugby player, Peter found out that Lionel had also played for the Harlequins. They chatted about the pictures and photographs. Her name was Betty and she was striking to look at; to Peter, at twenty-two years of age, she was beautiful – high cheekbones, brown eyes that matched her dark brown hair, high eyebrows and a lovely hour-glass figure. She knew how to dress.

After a while, Peter said, 'Do you know, I would rather like a sandwich after all.'

'Would you?' Betty replied, 'You're a bloody nuisance. It's virtually closing time.' She smiled. 'All right, I'll make you one.'

What was it like? He says it was the most fantastic salad sandwich. Yes, it had lettuce, but Betty elaborated and found some egg and salad cream to embellish it which Peter thoroughly enjoyed. It was now well after half-past two; the hotel had closed and Betty had an appointment with a hairdresser up the road while Peter had a wedding to attend. He climbed into the Ford and set off for Westcliff, making a mental note to return to The Three Compasses. He then spent time off at Peg's wedding, enjoying a pleasant three-day leave.

Back on operations, Peter decided to make the fifteen-mile journey to see Betty again one evening.

It took him the best part of half an hour, and things went well. Thereafter, Peter was a confirmed regular. He learnt that Betty had been born into the hotel business – literally. Her family had been involved with running a number of hotels for at least two generations and she was born at the Bull Hotel at Wrotham, Kent. Mr Swift also owned other pubs and hotels in and around Kent, including the Swan at West Malling, the Bull at Larkfield and the Sportsman at Seasalter. Betty had grown up in these environments and consequently she was a good communicator, able to converse with all and sundry in the bar.

Her communication skills made her a natural hostess and she certainly knew how to get on with Peter.

By the New Year of 1945, he had decided that Betty was the girl for him. In January, he broached the subject of marriage.

'You know, I'd very much like to marry you.'

'Would you?'

'Yes. I think you're fantastic. I've never met anyone like you.'

Betty would not be drawn on the subject but Peter maintained their courting. Every now and then he raised the question. He asked her again one evening.

'No bloody fear – I've already lost one husband; while you're flying on operations, there isn't a chance. What do you think I am, a bloody fool?'

'No I don't', Peter said quietly.

'There's no way in which I would ever consider marrying anyone again who is flying operations with the RAF.'

Peter's response, while a little chastened, was sympathetic: 'Well, that's understandable.' However, he was not going to give up; Betty had captured his heart. One day in early February, he had some news to break to her. 'By the way, I've been posted; no matter how long the war continues, I will never get back onto operations. The Group has told me that I'm posted to a company called Vickers-Armstrongs at Castle Bromwich, on the outskirts of Birmingham. I'm now a test pilot. Now, perhaps we can talk more seriously about a closer liaison.'

'Give it time', she said. 'We'll see.'

She was charming, she was witty, she was beautiful and articulate. She also knew how to have fun.

During one of Peter's visits to the pub, he and Johnny Melia took Maj Robert Cain, awarded the only non-posthumous VC two months earlier at Arnhem, to the Three Compasses. Cain had been staying at Manston and Peter chatted about flying escort missions and the problems the RAF were facing. The trio spent much of the evening chatting amiably. The bell rang for last orders and the bar stayed 'open' in honour of Cain's achievement.

Johnny Melia had by this time long since fallen asleep sprawled out in an armchair, his limbs dangling loosely over the arms, his legs splayed out. The temptation was too strong to resist for Betty. She took a flower and carefully arranged it so that it protruded majestically from his trouser flies!

Operational flying was now behind Peter for good and he had scrambled with the Boys of Baroda for the last time. In many ways, it was the end of an era, for the only adult life Peter had ever known was now over. All he had known was operational flying and instructing. True, he'd still be flying but things were going to be different: the camaraderie of the squadron, life in the mess, the buzz, the adrenalin of a dogfight was all history. It was goodbye to the life of a fighter pilot and hello to the life of a production test pilot. He didn't really know what to expect of test flying, though he had had a glimpse back in the desert at No. 1 Air Delivery Unit, where he realised that much would depend on his analytical skills, the same skills he had used when flying the A15 calibration tests. With three and a half operational tours under his belt, it had been a long and unique operational flying career. He had been there from the start, from the outbreak of the war and the first, faltering steps of life in No. 73 Squadron, on to OTU instructing, involvement in the Battle of Britain, where he destroyed the Heinkel He 111, the stemming and turning of the tide in the Libyan desert and what had become Allied superiority with the offensive into western Europe. The tide had turned, the war was virtually over and it was just a matter of time now before all hostilities would cease. The Allied forces had gained superiority and Peter had played his part in many close encounters. Most pilots flew one operation tour, many flew two but Peter does not know of any other fighter pilot who flew *nearly four operational tours – from the outbreak of the war!* Pilots came and pilots went; they arrived and they disappeared, but all but a handful from his early days at Gatwick, Grantham and France survived operational flying.

SEVEN

Test Pilot

The door on one world had closed and Peter made his way from the Kentish Downland of RAF Manston, heading for the Midlands in his recently restored Ford Eight; a new life awaited him at the Vickers factory site at Castle Bromwich.

The call had come through that he was to visit HQ No. 11 Group based at Uxbridge. Facing a panel of officers in well-fitting tunics, he was asked what he wanted to do. What further plans did he have? Peter's eyes searched the room for a moment, then he shook his head. He replied that he didn't know, in fact he didn't have a clue. What was there? 'Well,' one of the panel began, 'there are a couple of things we think you'd be best suited for. The best one is to test-fly Spitfires at the Vickers factory. You see, we think you possess all the necessary amount of experience required for the role. We've had a word with your CO at Manston . . . Scott, isn't it? He recommended you straight away. Anyway, think about it.' Peter mulled it over and decided to accept. He agreed for two reasons: first, the job allowed him to continue his passion for flying Spitfires in an arena that proved interesting, exciting, challenging and motivating. He was well aware that the testing was going to prove . . . testing. He knew what he didn't want to do, and that was ferrying planes back and forth. Secondly, there was Betty. Peter told Scott of his decision, who in turn contacted HQ No. 11 Group. He found it hard to accept the fact that he was no longer an operational fighter pilot. After all, it was all he had really ever known as a career so far. He says that he adopted a philosophical approach to squadron life because it was the only way to survive the fact that some of his friends were never going to return. In his words, you just asked yourself who would be next. In any case, there was nothing you could do about it.

Peter arrived at Castle Bromwich on 13 February 1945, and by the afternoon he was test-flying on two separate occasions, with the legendary Chief Test Pilot of Vickers, Alex Henshaw. Separating the man from the legend was difficult. Henshaw had been fêted for his racing prowess, winning the King's Cup Air Race in 1938. A year later, aged twenty-four, he broke the record flying solo from Britain to South Africa and back in his Mew Gull without navigational aids, in an era when aviators and aviatrices were treated like modern-day pop and sport stars. The record for a solo flight from Britain to South Africa and back has never been beaten. Henshaw's resolve, aircraft-handling abilities and shrewd calculating mind made him an ideal asset to the organisation and running of the testing for a production factory.

It is true to say that Henshaw knew virtually everything about flying the Spitfire. He originally joined the Vickers-Supermarine factory at Southampton in 1940 and had been seconded to oversee the running of the company's sister-factory at Castle Bromwich. Although he had no direct say in the pilots who came to work for him, he proved instrumental in getting rid of those who weren't up to the job. Peter was now part of his team, accountable for the testing of Spitfires as they came off the production line, and the team were soon to match Henshaw's exceptional knowledge of the aircraft. He expected his pilots to put the aircraft through its paces, setting incredibly high standards.

Castle Bromwich was the biggest aircraft factory in the country. At the peak of production (mid- to late 1944), the production rate was 330 Spitfires a month, in addition to the completion of

30 Lancasters. Henshaw was also responsible for overseeing two assembly plants that put together the various wings, fuselages and engines constructed at Castle Bromwich. One was at Cosford near Wolverhampton and the other was located at Desford, near Leicester. Considering the size of the site at Castle Bromwich, the actual airfield was really rather small. It had a small runway, some 200yds from the flight sheds, which the pilots used on take-off. However, they landed on a small grass strip that pointed towards the hangars. Once the Spitfires were back on the ground, caravans of tractors were on hand to tow the planes back to the hangars. In addition to the construction and testing of Spitfires, part of the factory was given over to the production of Avro Lancaster bombers. Any test pilots who joined Vickers-Armstrong were often asked to dinner by the Chief Executive, Mr Dixon.

Peter's first two flights on 13 February were not in a Spitfire but in a Lancaster. Alex Henshaw told him: 'As you haven't flown production aircraft from the factory before, I'll show you the sort of standards we're looking for here, from our pilots as well as our machines.'

Peter had a pad with a pencil in the top of the clip, strapped to his right knee. The pencil was attached to a piece of string, very handy when the pencil dropped out of the clip. The pad consisted of pro forma paper on which the pilots made notes, revs and altitude, etc., for later use in their reports. Sitting in the cockpit of the Lancaster, Henshaw explained to Peter what they were going to do.

'We'll take off, climb up at normal climbing speed, checking the engine temperatures as we go, pressures and so on. Make notes on your pads at various altitude intervals. We'll get to normal operating height with the engines set.'

'Fine, Alex,' Peter responded.

One by one, the four Merlin engines burst alive, adding to the din that was already emanating from the factory sheds. They took off and climbed steadily. When they reached 15,000ft, Alex said, 'We'll do a level run.' He increased all four throttles to maximum so that the Lancaster ran at full power, then adjusted the revs, enabling maximum performance. Peter watched the speed build up. Once the speed had been reached, he noted the pressures on his pad. He also kept an eye on the aircraft controls as the aircraft flew at full speed – checking the ailerons, elevators and rudder. Henshaw's voice was calm and level: 'All right. Now we'll put the Lanc into a dive.' Peter noticed the needle of the airspeed indicator creep up to 390mph, incredibly dangerous for a lumbering four-engined bomber. He also noticed that the angle of attack was steep; probably about 45°. 'Let me tell you why we dive. We need to test the controls in any case but we also need to look for up-float on the ailerons. You'll be aware that at high speeds, you get an up-float on each aileron. See that white painted line on the aileron? We have this line on the inner edge of each aileron to act as a guide. If the up-float comes above that line, it needs to be rectified. The only way we can test this is in a dive.' They looked at the lines on the ailerons. 'That's fine. The up-float's in the designated mark.'

They were still in a dive. Peter noticed that they were down to 7,000ft. Suddenly Henshaw put the Lancaster into a 45° angle of climb. 'Good!' thought Peter, catching his breath, 'he's knocking off the speed.' They continued to climb. In an instant, the Lancaster banked sharply to the right. Henshaw had executed a barrel-roll, while the plane was still climbing.

Peter didn't believe what was happening. It was his first time in a Lancaster in any case, but he never realised that an aircraft as large and unwieldy as this was capable of such manoeuvres. Henshaw had a remarkable understanding of what aircraft could and could not do. To execute a barrel-roll in a bomber was incredible enough, but to perform one without any effect from G-force was something else! Rolling in a fighter aircraft subjected the pilot to the laws of gravity, known as G-force, where unimaginable forces were felt in a fighter pilot's eyes, on his stomach and in his head. It was well known that this was the reason why fighter pilots blacked out in a flight when they had pulled a sharp manoeuvre that changed the forces of gravity so quickly; the body and brain could not adapt quickly enough to these forces. There were no G-forces in a Henshaw barrel-roll. The Lancaster rolled 360° slowly and smoothly.

It was a masterclass in aerobatics. Flight engineers often accompanied Alex Henshaw in the Lancaster. To prove his point to an unsuspecting passenger, he would ask the engineer to stand in the fuselage, holding loosely onto aircraft spars, and stay there as the Lancaster rolled. Not once did an engineer collapse. It says much for Henshaw's skill in a cockpit, and he immediately gained a loyal respect from his test team, not least from Peter.

There were 25,000 personnel employed at Castle Bromwich. As far as the test production team were concerned, Peter was the newest of five test pilots: Ron 'Monty' Ellis, who had been in Peter's old squadron, No. 73, out in the desert; Geoff Huntley; Ron Brown, known as 'Brownie' to avoid any confusion with Ellis; and David 'Mutt' Lamb. All of the team had flown operationally but had joined after the war had begun; ironically, Peter might have been the most recent member to join the team but he had the longest record in operational experience, no doubt a fact that had not escaped Henshaw.

The team explained to Peter that test-flying was far removed from squadron life. Gone were the mickey-taking and ribaldry and the stakes were higher. Looking at it objectively, fighter pilots were ten-a-penny whereas test pilots were few and far between. Few fighter pilots – if they survived – had the combination of experience and analytical mind to carry out test-flying duties. Any fatal mishap to a test pilot was going be keenly felt. The team shared certain aspects: the same analytical approach to flying and taking their roles very seriously, but also enjoyed a laugh and a joke together in the canteen where they took lunch. Peter says that Alex Henshaw would always join them in a natter.

Hundreds of aircraft were lined up on parade, ready for testing. The team would test each Spitfire as soon as it had been completed, straight from the production line. The four would be sitting in the crew room, mulling over paperwork, when an engineer would put his head round the door: 'Morning Gentlemen! We've three Spitfires cleared for testing so far. Here are the serial numbers.'

Henshaw would hand out the honours. 'Fine. Brownie, you take PL 554; Mutt can have PL 567 and Pete can take up PL 570.'

Dressed in white overalls, they would go off to their charges. Testing and flying was only half the job, however. Peter says that much of their time was taken up with writing reports in the test pilots' office from notes made during flights, which they handed to Henshaw on completion. The objective was to conclude with the phrase: 'I consider this aircraft to be satisfactory', meaning that the Spitfire had been passed. Some passed first time but on average Spitfires took three test flights before they were passed. The reports that Peter and the others wrote were collated to make a valuable dossier on each aircraft.

The flight sheds themselves were over a mile away from the factory, and convoys of tractors would tow each brand-new pristine Spitfire from the factories to these sheds ready for testing. When Peter rejected a Spitfire, the aircraft was handed back to the ground crew. He told the line engineers in the flight sheds what he had found wrong with it – the canopy didn't close properly; too much up-float on the ailerons – and the engineers would then set to work repairing the faulty piece of equipment.

The ground crew were well-versed in fixing faults reported by the test pilots. Because of the number of aircraft that Peter and his colleagues had to fly, it was unusual if the same faulty Spitfire was flown again by the same pilot. Once they had been passed, they were placed in a separate holding group for collection by the Air Transport Auxiliary pilots for delivery to an operational squadron.

Peter and the team were also responsible for testing at other sites as well. Cosford and Desford frequently rang the Castle Bromwich office, asking for a pilot to test a Spitfire when it had been completed, and Peter went over to both sites on a number of occasions. The testing process at the two assembly plants was governed by similar procedures to those at Castle Bromwich: Peter would note and explain any faults to the satellite plant engineers. If the problem was minor, Peter would hang about for a couple of hours waiting for the ground crew to remedy the situation. Sometimes he tested a Spitfire that had been assembled at Castle Bromwich *en route* to tests at Cosford. If all went well and the Spitfire passed the testing, it was left at the new assembly plant until Peter was ready to return to Castle Bromwich. He would then fly and test an assembled Spitfire from Cosford, spending the rest of the day with the pilots from the plants and certainly having a spot of lunch with them. At the end of the day he would then climb into the Castle Bromwich Spitfire, returning it to base.

Peter found that Alex Henshaw was professional in everything he did, whether it was flying, writing reports or briefing the pilots on specific items. This professionalism was particularly visible in his flying displays. To those who were lucky enough to see Henshaw flying a Spitfire, it was astounding.

The execution of his manoeuvres were crisp and precise and his performance was breathtaking.

Peter believes that those who haven't seen Henshaw's displays would never have believed that a Spitfire (or for that matter, any aircraft) would be able to withstand such demonstrations; you had to see it to believe it. A continual stream of high-ranking visitors, including Winston Churchill, King George VI and a long list of foreign diplomats, came to see the massive production capabilities of Castle Bromwich and they were treated to Henshaw's flying display as a matter of routine. Peter recalls one move that Alex Henshaw had perfected: a bunt (outside loop), at about 1,500ft. This manoeuvre at such a low altitude was extremely dangerous. With the throttle pulled back, the nose was pulled up, which had the effect of stalling the Spitfire. The nose would suddenly drop towards the ground and Henshaw would then be flying *inverted at house height* adjacent to the spectators, pulling out of it! There were other tricks – diving flat out, then pulling up into a vertical roll and then, at the top, he would stall-turn, drop off and come screaming down again. Peter says he was truly fantastic, a consummate aviator. He believes that no one, including the Chief Test Pilot for Supermarine (Vickers), Jeffrey Quill, could quite match his sheer breathtaking performance and flying prowess in a Spitfire.

Testing procedures for the Spitfire always followed the same pattern: take off, raise undercarriage and stow away correctly, check engine readings, continue climbing speed, set revs and power while holding plane, etc. But things did go wrong. There were a number of occasions when Peter had taken off from the runway, wheeling over the flight sheds, when something went awry – the trim wasn't working or the engine sounded rough. He had been briefed by Henshaw that in these events he was to abort the flight and return immediately. Many test flights in Peter's third and fourth logbooks bear testament to the fact that some flights lasted no more than five minutes, and these cases demonstrate the frequency with which he and the others faced problems daily when flying factory-fresh aircraft. Sometimes there were problems with the airframe. For example, on testing a Mk IX during take-off, the undercarriage had just been raised with one wing flying low. With left hand poised over the throttles, Peter had to fight hard to keep the aircraft flying level at low speed. When his hand gripped the throttles and increased the power, the situation became worse and Peter decided to put the wheels down and come straight back in.

The test-flying day normally started at about half-past eight in the morning, ending at about six.

Most of the flight team retired to the local in Sutton Coldfield to relax and unwind. The art – or science – of test-flying was dramatically different from operational flying. Most squadron flying involved formation-flying towards a specific, defined objective. Test-flying was in many respects harder and it required more discipline and restraint. Up in the air, the testing and analysing was down to Peter and him alone; the buck stopped with him. In addition, the workload was greater and there were a number of objectives to define, test, respond to and analyse.

There were differences between Spitfires too. While operational aircraft benefited from the fitting of radios and other electronic devices, landing systems onto the runway by a ground controlled approach (GCA) when the weather closed in, there were no radios or navigational aids in factory-fresh Spitfires; test pilots had none of these luxuries when they were testing in bad weather. It required a different type of awareness. Peter recalled a feeling of overwhelming awareness in formations, keeping the focus on strict timing when rendezvousing with escorting bombers, but test-flying demanded more of an analytical awareness; not only was he testing the aircraft, but he also had to be aware of and alert to just how the Spitfire ticked; what mood it was in, whether it was going to play tricks on him that particular day. He had to make decisions, potentially fatal ones, in split seconds. His calibration tests in the summer of 1944 over France must have stood him in great stead in achieving the analysis and discipline necessary to make a test pilot.

There was an obvious difference between production test-flying and test-flying prototypes, but both required the same controlled discipline. Peter says that production flying didn't have the element of glamour attached to flying prototypes but there was still a respect within wider aviation circles as well as with the public. He says that the Castle Bromwich pilots knew they were pretty good. They were conscious that there were pilots – and then there were test pilots. This was something that was not confined to Vickers. Those at Hawkers, Gloster, Fairey and Avro considered themselves to be the cream of the cream in aviation. Indeed, it was a thought process necessary for the job, and Peter was aware he had joined an elite force. During the war years (1940–5), there were only thirty production test pilots at Castle Bromwich flying Spitfires. Peter is one of two who still survive. The other is Alex Henshaw. From those thirty, five or six were killed while test-flying, though happily there were no fatal accidents during Peter's time. This was mostly due to experience gained during the war years. Nevertheless, it served as a timely reminder that every test pilot faced potentially fatal hazards as he stepped into the cockpit each day. During the war years, 11,694 Spitfires were flown and tested at Castle Bromwich. By its very nature, test-flying aircraft was and still is a dangerous profession. Pilots were always aware of the potential hazards and dangers of flying in factory-fresh aircraft that had not yet been calibrated, and they knew they were guinea pigs.

The old Ford Eight that Peter had bought at Manston was looking a little worse for wear and he thought it could do with a lick of paint. He thought he had found the ideal solution.

Rather than wash it, he got the ground crew in the workshops to paint it for him. For them, it made a pleasant change from painting Spitfires and they were pleased to do it. In fact, they were a little too accommodating because when Peter came to collect it, the paint work was about 3ins thick! However, his little ruse soon came to an end; the senior managers told him in no uncertain terms that they thought he was visiting the workshops rather too frequently!

He shared a house with Monty Ellis and Mutt Lamb in nearby Sutton Coldfield, paid for by the company. As Brownie and Huntley were both married, they lived in separate accommodation.

A cleaning lady made their beds and prepared breakfast while in the evenings the routine was predictable: head for the nearest pub in Sutton Coldfield and grab a bite to eat. Peter's career had changed dramatically over the past year but his romantic life was still very much on hold, as it had been for the past three months. Up in the air, he spent every moment concentrating on his work, but once on the ground, Peter only had time for Betty. He spent hours on the house phone, making calls to Canterbury. Fortunately, Vickers picked up the phone bill! On the odd weekend he was not required to fly, Peter made the 180-mile trip down to Canterbury. The old Ford Eight protested at doing any more than 50mph on the open road, but as the round trip took ten hours, time was precious. He still remembers the route – he would make his way over to Coventry, travelling down the A5 into London, down the Edgware Road, past Marble Arch and Hyde Park, over Vauxhall Bridge and onto the A2 towards Canterbury. He still finds it hard to describe precisely what it was about Betty that captured his heart – call it chemistry, call it intimacy, but she had touched something in him that other girls couldn't reach.

He says that people know when something is meant to be, and both he and Betty felt something strong for each other. Having known her for fifty years, Jack and Peg, his brother and sister, feel that she could never say an unkind word about Peter. She was immensely proud of and full of admiration for his achievements.

They tied the knot on 5 June 1945 and the wedding ceremony took place at the church of the Holy Cross, Canterbury, in the shadows of the Westgate Towers. It was their spiritual home; apart from meeting Betty there, he had come to know it well. His ancestor was buried in the Cathedral. The couple spent their honeymoon in a pub called The Black Lion at Newquay on the Welsh coast, close to Cardigan. The Lion was run by a couple who were so drunk by early evening that customers happily served themselves. Alan Byfield was there when Peter and Betty arrived. He thinks their wedding night wasn't consummated because all of them spent the night and the following morning downstairs at the bar until 2 a.m.! Although the couple were on honeymoon, rationing was still very much in evidence, but even so, Betty and Peter received large portions at breakfast-time from one of the waitresses.

Peter and Betty met Taffy Jones, the stuttering instructor from Hawarden, there along with his wife.

The honeymoon lasted for two weeks, and by 19 June, Peter was back at Castle Bromwich. Now that they were married, he made arrangements for Betty to join him. She left The Three Compasses and for three weeks or so she lived in a small hotel situated at Sutton Coldfield, before moving to another hotel in Lichfield. Meanwhile, Peter set about finding a house for them.

His task was made easier by the fact that the company paid the rent for the property, including the gas and electricity, which was considered as recompense. Vickers had proposed the renting of property for their pilots because, apart from their RAF pay, they had not been allowed to hand out additional lump sums. The Air Ministry had rejected this scheme outright, saying that this would not be fair to other pilots. A detached house with a garage was found on the Lichfield Road at Four Oaks, just outside Sutton Coldfield. Conveniently, the house was adjacent to the local pub. The house had been owned by a lady who had lost her husband and had decided to let it. Peter recalls that a seven-year-old girl, Nula Poppy Hickey, who lived two doors away, took a shine to Betty. Every afternoon after school, she went to see Betty, who found some cake and drink for her. The couple stayed at Four Oaks until Vickers closed the Castle Bromwich site in 1946. Jack remembers visiting them with his wife at the time, at a party full of test pilots. He says he has only been drunk – really drunk – twice in his life and this event was one of them. Spirits were free; beer was thruppence.

Much to Betty's delight, Peter returned home each month with a sizeable booty of pork. A small pig club was run by the ground crew from the Vickers flight sheds and they let him have a few choice fillets. Their house backed onto a large channel, 400yds wide, where gardens faced them on the other side. As Betty was to discover, the channel was wide enough to get a Spitfire through! On numerous occasions, she heard the throaty roar of a Merlin engine overhead and knew it was Peter trying to attract her attention – sometimes he could see her waving a white tea towel. Not content with frightening her to death, on one occasion he went one better by screaming down the channel – *below the level of the houses* – pulling up and doing an upward roll, waggling his wings as he flew off. She was not best pleased when he entered the door after work. 'You silly sod,' she remonstrated, 'you'll get yourself killed one day!'

He took his last test-flight during wartime on 7 May 1945 and recalls it was uneventful. One day later, war in Europe had finished. The entire nation took 8 May (VE day) off as a holiday, when, Peter says, everyone partied, and Britain ground to a standstill over the next three days. Peter and Betty went to Canterbury. Vickers were still producing Spitfire Mk IXs in 1945 and Peter had flown them both operationally and on test-flights for so long that he knew them inside out. He was soon going to get his hands on the Mk XVI. Reports from squadron pilots flying Mk IX Spitfires in the field suggested that as most encounters were now taking place at a lower height, an aircraft was needed with low-altitude capabilities. The Mk XVI was the answer – virtually a development of the Mk IX, but one that was far more efficient at low altitude. With clipped wings which dramatically increased and improved the rate of roll, a modified empennage and a teardrop canopy, it also included an American-built Packard Merlin, known as a Merlin 266. Different variants of the Mk XVI were still being produced and it was these that Peter was briefed to test. He first climbed into the cockpit of a Mk XVI in August.

It was not a good start: SL 687 was a Mk XVI with various problems and Peter flew it on six separate occasions. It was eventually passed on 13 August and went to 33 Maintenance Unit on 20 August 1945.

Peter's first flight in flying his final Spitfire type, the Mk 22, came on 30 March 1945:

30 March – Experience on type: ten minutes

– not long to gain experience on a fundamentally different aeroplane. The Spitfire Mk 22 – Peter flew PK 314 – was markedly heavier and became the ultimate wartime Spitfire. It was a Spitfire in name only. Their engines needed substantial power and the tried-and-tested Merlins were replaced with the throaty Rolls-Royce Griffon producing over 2,300hp, double the size of the original Merlins. The fuselage was bigger in order to take the engine and the empennage had larger control surfaces to combat the increase in engine performance. The wings were thicker and had lost some of their familiar elliptical 'Spitfire' shape. It had a five-bladed airscrew, giving the plane a tremendous torque effect on take-off. As a result, Peter had to be careful when he opened up the throttle; if it was increased too violently, the aircraft suddenly swung to the right. He realised that he had to keep full left rudder on, the instant he increased the power. As the speed increased, he eased back on the rudders. It was for this reason that the five-bladed Spitfire Mk 22s could not be used on aircraft-carriers.

For a while, he was involved in the testing of research Spitfire Mk 21s in finding a solution to the exceptional torque problem, and thereby a solution in successfully using the Mk 21s for the Royal Navy. Eventually the answer was to be found in fitting a contra-rotating airscrew to the plane consisting of two three bladed screws rotating in opposite directions. As well as flying original Mk 21s, Peter was also involved in the original six-bladed contra-rotating screw tests in a Seafire 45, LA 449, on 5 December 1945. He found it enlightening flying a research Spitfire Mk 21, LA 299, on 12 December. It was a specially modified airframe with a unique engine. In his words, he whammed the throttle open without the need for being too ginger on the controls, while keeping his feet central on the rudder bar – and the aircraft cruised dead straight down until take-off. Peter flew his first production Seafire, LA 451, on 11 July and his second on the 30th, LA 456. He also flew the Seafire 45 (a navalised Spitfire Mk 21) with a Rolls-Royce Griffon 61. On 1 July 1945, Peter was promoted to Squadron Leader. It was not to be his final promotion.

The Spitfire 22 was also Peter's favourite Spitfire to fly, purely because of the sheer volume of power that could be unleashed. For him, it was the definitive aviation experience, the ultimate thrill.

Peter recalls a time when he went to see his friends in No. 124 (Baroda) Squadron at Molesworth on 2 October, which also gave him a reason to test the Spitfire at the same time. The squadron was now flying the new jet Meteors, the second squadron in the RAF to do so.

Peter arrived early in the afternoon to put PK 570 through its paces. In the mess, it was cups of tea all round and the conversation soon got round to the relative merits and differences of flying jet versus piston-driven aircraft. 'You'll like this Pete,' they said; 'we're going to put up a formation of six Meteors and practise some manoeuvres. We'll give you a display of just how fast the Meatbox can go!' The gauntlet of friendly rivalry had been laid down. Squadron pride was at stake.

'OK, fine,' Peter casually replied, 'I'll be leaving round about the same time as you. Who knows, I might even give you a little display of my own.'

The Baroda boys hid their smirks. 'In a Spit? Against a jet? Come on! You've been away from squadron flying too long!'

The Meteors took off in two lines of Vics, line astern. Peter gave them a head's start. 'Right. Let's see what this Spit can do!' He opened up the throttles (keeping his rudder on full left!) as he roared down the Cambridgeshire runway, catching the Meteors up with ease, drawing alongside them and giving them a cheery wave.

The boys' jaws must have hit the bottom of their cockpits as they witnessed PK 570 waggle its wings and accelerate away into the blue towards the direction of Castle Bromwich. From the display, it is fairly safe to assume that PK 570 had passed its test-flight! It was about this time that Peter's good friend Johnny Melia was killed in a flying accident when his Meteor was involved in a collision.

He also had some heart-stopping flights in a Mk 22. He recalls one day when he had been flying full throttle on a full-power level run, the engine suddenly packed up – he had completely lost all power from the Griffon engine at a speed of 450mph! With lighter aircraft it was possible to glide back to ground, but because the Mk 22 was so large and so heavy (all-up weight was 11,000lb), the engine failure meant that gliding in an aircraft as heavy as this back to the site was going to be virtually impossible – Peter's gliding speed was fast, which meant he was going to have to control a near-bullet back to earth! The rate of the descent was also greater. The Griffon 85 engines were relatively new and the pilots found that, in many cases, they were testing the engines as well as the airframes. He looked at his altimeter – 7,000ft and well above cloud; there was no sign of Castle Bromwich. How was he going to get a stricken heavy-weight Spitfire safely down when he couldn't even see the ground? In clear weather, pilots used two massive cooling towers as a landmark. Although the towers were obscured by cloud, Peter saw their smoke emanating through the cloud. It was distinctive, dense smoke that rose in the shape of a mushroom. As soon as he saw the smoke, he knew where he was. Managing to obtain a few additional revs that enabled him to semi-glide the Mk 22, he broke cloud and came over the top of the airfield. Losing height rapidly, Peter was able to land back on the ground, wheels down!

Two days later, Peter experienced precisely the same mishap – engine failure – with another Mk 22.

Coincidence? Two engine failures in Mk 22s in two days? Once again, both cases show Peter's cool-headed approach in near-fatal situations. Such incidents were, of course, part of the job, but test-flying is exhausting and intensive. Accidents do happen . . .

Apart from working with the legendary Alex Henshaw, Peter also worked with the Chief Test Pilot of Supermarine, Jeffrey Quill. Quill had been part of the Spitfire project from its inception – indeed, the design team responsible for the prototype K5054 consisted of Quill and Chief Test Pilot 'Mutt' Summers. Most of the early test-flying in 1935–6 had been performed by Quill. Like Henshaw, Jeffrey Quill was another legend who had reached iconic status. He had phoned Henshaw, saying he was going to be short of a pilot for two weeks at High Post. Could Alex suggest a suitable pilot? Before long, Peter was on his way to High Post. Peter found Quill quiet and serious, with a dry sense of humour.

The contribution that Alex Henshaw made to the production of Spitfires at Castle Bromwich cannot be understated. Peter is still in regular contact with Alex. In one of their many correspondences, Alex wrote on 5 April 1979:

I often think of our period at Castle Bromwich certainly with pride, often with happiness but sometimes of course with great sadness.

It was around this time that Henshaw published his autobiography during his days with Vickers. He gave a copy of his book, *Sigh For a Merlin*, to Peter and inscribed a message:

Success achieved at Castle Bromwich during WW2 was due to the superb teamwork both in the air and on the ground. It was an honour and a great privilege for me to lead this remarkable group of which you were a member.

Looking back, Peter enjoyed taking up new aircraft that had never been flown before. His test-flying days ended when the factory was closed on 11 July 1946. Henshaw had left by this point and Peter was the last test pilot to leave the factory. His final entry is 31 January 1946. For two months, he flitted between HQ Fighter Command and HQ 11 Group at Uxbridge assisting with staff duties.

A deputy station commander vacancy arose at his old base at Manston in late March 1946 and he accepted it for three and a half months. He was now flying a desk in charge of administration. In effect, he says, the role actually took on the task of station commander, as the CO was hardly ever present. Manston was to be Peter's last station in the RAF. Part of the reason for taking the post was to be close to their spiritual home of Canterbury where Peter and Betty were able to live at the Three Compasses. Peter's last day of service was 10 July 1946. He says he should have stayed on; he has one regret – and that is leaving the RAF at this point. In his words, 'I should never have come out because I was offered the opportunity to stay on. I came out because I wanted to – I had had a fair old whack of operational flying without much rest in between.'

It was the end of the era; a real wrench in many ways, and Peter was leaving a way of life, his *raison d'être*. There were two reasons for leaving the RAF: first, he wanted – or needed – to take a decent break; secondly, he wanted to spend more time with Betty and her family in Canterbury. They discussed what he was going to do and it was decided that both of them should run the Three Compasses, which appealed to Peter because he'd be working in an environment away from flying – he'd be meeting different people in the pub and wearing a coat of many colours – from chatting to a coalman to talking to a director of a local company. Last orders in the RAF had been called. Time please, to become a publican.

EIGHT

Dunflyin'

Times were changing. The war had ended and with it the vision for peace. After eight solid years of intense flying, Peter was exhausted; he needed a respite from the RAF. He needed to stretch his wings and do something else. The pub was already there for him; it was already established as a family affair with enough clientèle to make it a going concern, and he and Betty knew it well in any case. Betty's father had died by this time, and so her mother, Cis, needed a hand in running the pub. Peter went from pulling joysticks to pulling pints. It was a much-needed case of recharging the batteries. It is interesting to note that many fighter pilots took a similar path after the war and found that owning and running a pub provided a vital change in pace and lifestyle.

Beer and spirit supplies were purchased from George Beer and Rigden, a brewery located in Faversham, known locally as Kent's Best. Peter was happy with the brewery, and the quality of the beer was excellent, especially its mild and bitter. He recalls that many customers drank a half of each. The brewery also produced a bottled light ale called XXK. At Christmas, small barrels of Christmas Ale were found and tapped on the counter. He believes that eventually the brewery was taken over by Whitbread.

For the first couple of years, Peter and Betty found things were tough because rationing was still in force and this had a knock-on effect for beer supplies ordered on a weekly basis. Beer rationing was applied in much the same way as food rationing in the pub business, although the Three Compasses was given a special allowance because it was considered to be a catering establishment. Many were the times when Peter and Betty had to turn round to customers with a shrug of the shoulders and a philosophical smile, 'Sorry – we've run out until the next delivery.'

One bar would then be closed because, as Peter says, there was no point in wasting lights and electricity. The shortage in beer also applied to a shortage in spirits. He often found that he couldn't get as much whisky, gin or rum from the brewery as he and Betty had hoped for. It was a problem that they faced throughout their time as publicans. Quite simply, you got what was going.

The hardest part that Peter discovered as a publican was putting the firkin barrels on stands known as stillions. When the firkins were ready for use, he tapped them and connected a pipe from the stillions to the pumps in the bar. They managed to get six barrels onto the stillions, and once each barrel was consumed it was rolled off the stand and a new barrel, previously upended, ready for use, took its place. Another shock to the system were the hours; Peter found them incredibly long and hard. The Compasses, as the locals called it, was open for business for eight and a half hours per day, from ten-thirty until half-past-two and six until ten-thirty at night. These were just opening hours to the public; there were many more spent in preparation. Of course, some days were voluntarily lengthened owing to the odd lock-in! Although there were a couple of cleaners who cleaned the bar early in the mornings, it was Peter and Betty who cleaned the glasses. A leftover from his RAF days, Peter preferred glasses with a good shine to them, which he discovered took a great deal of time and discipline. All in all, however, he found it a welcome break.

Learning a new trade, a new way of life, can be difficult. He acknowledges that much of the credit goes to Betty for her organisation. Peter did much of the heavy work in the cellar, and Betty was quick with the maths, totting up the bill as she poured the drinks. It was second nature to her for she had been doing it all her life, and she was very good at establishing rapport with the customers. The hours may have been long but Peter learnt to adopt a 'coat of all colours', as he calls it, when he was dealing with the punters. It opened his eyes to the other side of life, a life beyond the RAF, and he discovered all types of characters came into The Compasses. These years at the university of life were to increase his knowledge of and skills in dealing with people, and for him it was an important stage in talking to and dealing with the public. He says there was the odd awkward punter, but on the whole, most customers were pleasant and interesting. His communication skills were greatly enhanced, and were to stand him in good stead later on.

A Cricket week was held in Canterbury every August and Peter and Betty received visits from Kent county cricketers. He also received calls from the odd pilot friend, who might happen to be in the area and decide to knock up an old mate. One regular who always paid a call was the bookies' runner. Gambling, of course, was strictly illegal, but the runner visited each pub in Canterbury in turn, taking bets and keeping things on the hush-hush. Peter knew several of his customers who were 'well acquainted' with the runner. As mine host, Peter found himself roped in.

'Look, when he comes in, would you put a pound to win on Dark Night?'

'Pete, mind putting a pound each way on Hellfire? It's a dead cert!' The money was strategically left with Peter on the counter. When the runner turned up, Peter acted as mediator. 'Colin wants a quid on Dark Night; here you go.' Every now and again, he had a bet himself, but he never used to win much. In general, the eventual winners had such low odds that it was pointless betting on them. But then, as Peter says, a win at low odds is better than a loss!

He and Betty put their energies into running the Compasses. They had been married for fifteen months; they wanted to enjoy what little spare time they had together. But they wanted children and their daughter Jane was born in May 1947. It happened that when Jane was born, the couple discovered that Betty was suffering from leucopoenia, a disease caused by a lack of white platelets which affects blood coagulation. It meant that Betty picked up infections easily and suffered from nose bleeds. Although she endured these symptoms from time to time, Peter admits that the couple didn't think much about it.

It was all a far cry from his flying days. Banking, diving, climbing, aerobatics . . . the banter, the thrill, the exhilaration . . . he had done flying . . . .

He was running a business, he was with his wife and he now had a young daughter. But deep down, he wasn't happy. As much as Peter enjoyed pulling pints and meeting people, the regularity of running a pub after three years began to pall. He missed flying: the buzz, the adrenalin, the anticipation and the exhilaration. He needed it again. Pilots often compare the thrill of flying to a drug; they crave it if they are grounded, as in Peter's case. He needed a fix and he mentioned it to Betty; he was surprised when she didn't object. So Peter hired a Tiger Moth in 1948, along with a regular customer from the Compasses who had been caught in similar circumstances. Dev Deverson was also ex-RAF, trapped in a job that he loathed, working as a sales representative for Weetabix. He had long been a regular, as had his father, a farmer who had visited the Canterbury market on Mondays and Saturdays throughout the war.

Times were hard and Dev cycled to the pub from his family farm in nearby Bishopsbourne. As he says, when he had just enough for a couple of bottles of beer, he didn't want to waste it on transport. He got to know the then owner, Jim and Cis Swift. Dev recalls Betty's father sitting in his chair in an alcove by the fireplace in the lounge with his cup of 'tea'. Swift's idea of 'tea' consisted of neat whisky. He was also very pro-RAF.

Dev remembers the layout of the Compasses very well. Located in St Peter's Street in the heart of Canterbury, it was found next door to the Arts School, a source of regular patronage. Victorian in style, long and thin in shape, it had a double-fronted exterior with a door on the left, leading to the Four-ale Bar or the Public Bar. The beer was slightly cheaper and there was a dartboard and a billiards table – the Compasses billiards team took on other pub teams in the town. Some stairs rose out of the bar, straight up to the living room and kitchen, where, in addition to the main bedroom, there were two rooms for bed and breakfast. The door on the right led to the Saloon Bar, with chairs and tables scattered along the thin, narrow side. It was more comfortable than the Public Bar (but then the beer was more expensive!), stretching the entire length. In between the two bars lay the serving area to both, where drinkers ordered snacks. A mirror stood guard over the mantelpiece above the fireplace.

There were some terrific parties when Betty made her concoction of fish-house punch. Dev recalls it was lethal – rum as a main constituent, with brandy, wine and lemonade, together with oranges and lemons that Peter had managed to get hold of, now that rationing had ended. Dev says they 'cultivated' local nurses, inviting them to these parties. Invariably the fish-house punch worked its magic and the nurses needed . . . well, a little nursing! He and the others then felt ultimately responsible and took them home. Betty was a leader according to him – she was great behind the bar and she was the motivator. After lunch, when the pub was closed, Peter and Dev took turns in taking other regulars to Herne Bay, where they swam in the summer.

Peter didn't take up flying just because he needed a fix; there were more economic reasons. Dev says he was running on hard times; he knew it and Dev and the others knew it, too, because the pubs in Canterbury were always empty. The truth was that, after the war, the pub business was in decline. During the war years, the towns and cities were heaving with soldiers, sailors and airmen jostling for pints when they were off duty; the breweries had never had it so good. Now, those soldiers, sailors and airmen had been demobbed and the economic austerity of the times forced them to save what little earnings they had.

Dev had gone back to the family farm in Bishopsbourne, but as that was no longer a going concern, he had taken the job with Weetabix. Peter used to change his cheques (£8 per week plus expenses) for him, and Dev remembers Peter being down in the dumps. One day they had a chat about other opportunities:

'I'm fed up with this, Pete, nothing's working', Dev said. 'I'm going to see whether I can get back into the RAF Volunteer Reserve at Rochester.'

'What do you mean? Re-enlist?'

'Why not? The job's hopeless; the farm's shot to pieces . . . Look at it this way, if I go back in, I get paid for flying, something we both love doing, and I'll be paid a damn sight more than I'm getting now. Why not? What have I got to lose?' Peter went to Lympne and hired an old Auster Five and an even older Tiger Moth for £5 an hour.

Dev returned from his refresher courses at Rochester and told Peter how much he enjoyed it, how great it was to have some money again. A lot of people had re-enlisted, everyone was doing it; perhaps Peter should come along to Rochester too? As Dev says, everyone was hard up. Joining the RAF provided a way out, an opportunity to move forward.

Banking, diving, climbing, aerobatics . . . the banter, the thrill, the exhilaration . . . .

The Volunteer Reserve weekends that Peter and Dev signed up for were organised by aircraft companies – de Havilland, Miles, Vickers, in conjunction with the RAF. In the case of Rochester, it was the local aircraft company, Short Brothers, who were always on the look-out for competent air and ground crews. With the wealth of ex-RAF pilots like Peter streaming back into flying, the RAF had the pick of the bunch. The weekend was spent in Volunteer Reserve accommodation at Rochester airfield. Everything had been paid for by Short Brothers, including the food, which Dev says was wonderful. Dev preferred the Auster, which suited Peter because he liked the Tiger Moth, and the pair enjoyed flying together. Dev flew down to Bishopsbourne looking for a cricket match to beat up. The cricketers were well aware that it was Dev who kept buzzing them, and threatened him with physical abuse if he didn't stop ruining their match. Every Sunday during the summer, a cross-estuary steamer took day-trippers from Southend to Margate. Collectively known as 'Richthofen's Circus', Dev and Peter took the Auster and the Tiger Moth to about 3,000ft and dived towards *The Royal Devon*, skimming the steamer at zero feet. Dev says that Peter was a devil for low-level aerobatics, beating up the airstrips of Lympne airfield, possibly an influence from his days with Alex Henshaw. He took Betty up, and together they performed aerobatics: stall-turns, rolls and loops. Although Peter says she would have preferred her flying experience to be straight-and-level, she seemed quite at home. However, when back on terra firma, she turned to Peter and declared, 'I'm not going to come flying with you any more!' Both Dev and Peter were questioned by the police because the two aircraft they flew had not been insured. The owner was duly tracked down.

But to be in the air again; the joy and thrill of flying – feeling the wind on your face at 100 miles an hour and the exhilaration of a dive: Dev wasn't made to sell Weetabix and Peter certainly wasn't cut out to run a pub. Peter applied for a second short-service commission and was accepted immediately. It meant, however, that despite his magnificent record during the war, culminating in his DFC, he had to drop one rank from squadron leader to flight lieutenant. This meant effectively losing twelve years' service. The irony was that all his friends who stayed in the RAF became air marshals, some with knighthoods. It was an immense amount to sacrifice, but he had learnt more about life than those who had continued in the service, and at least he could use his communication skills to good effect both in and out of the RAF. There was nothing that Peter could really do about the situation – he had to rejoin as a flight lieutenant – and he accepted it with good grace.

What, according to Deverson, did Peter have that made him such a good fighter pilot? How did he survive through the war years? Instinct, he had instinct in abundance. Peter knew when enemy aircraft were behind him, he knew precisely where he was in a dogfight and what he needed to do to get out of it. If you don't have these qualities, you are, according to Dev, a dead duck. How did the effect of seeing their colleagues blown up and shot down affect him and Peter?

It didn't. Getting killed never happened to the likes of them; it wasn't going to happen to them.

Deverson went on to fly Vampires and Hunters and became one of a handful of pilots who flew the de Havilland Comet on VIP flights for the Prime Minister, Harold Macmillan, and transport flights. His Comet was often the recipient of the Queen's luggage.

Peter's first commission was to No. 61 Group, covering the administration and control of non-operational squadrons. His posting came through in December 1949 and he was to be based at RAF Kenley, one of the fighter stations that had been badly damaged during the Battle of Britain nine years earlier. Squadrons included university air squadrons, air training cadets and Volunteer Reserve schools, as well as RAF hospitals, recuperation centres and the Central Medical Establishment. The Group covered London and the south-east of England, including East Anglia. He worked in the personnel unit, organising postings, which required a good deal of travelling, inspecting RAF crew and their procedures. He came across some familiar faces at No. 61 Group. One face was Al Deere, the legendary Battle of Britain pilot. They caught up on old times and played on the Kenley rugby field for the Group team. Peter took up his position at centre, Deere resumed his at fly-half. Considering that he had been out of service life for over three years, being with old friends like Deere must have put Peter at relative ease. His ultimate boss was Senior Personnel Staff Officer (SPSO) Wg Cdr Ken Doran, who was one of the first to be awarded a DFC. Doran had piloted twin-engined Blenheims, making one of the first bombing raids in daylight on German shipping during the early days of the war. One of Peter's colleagues was Air Cdre Sir Theobald McEvoy. After work on a Wednesday, Peter and McEvoy paired up with Al Deere and Bob Taylor (Peter's immediate boss), making a foursome on the local golf course at Coulsdon. After the eighteen holes, the nineteenth was held at McEvoy's house nearby. He was to play a significant role in Peter's life later on. Meanwhile, Betty and Jane had moved from Canterbury to Blackheath in 1950, where they purchased a flat and remained for about a year. The move came about through Peter's brother-in-law, Noel Taylor, a senior partner in a chartered surveyors' firm, Jones Lang Wootton. Taylor suggested that flats were going (relatively) cheaply in Beckenham and it might be an idea if Peter and Betty were to rent one. Peter recalls that their Blackheath flat was lovely, but the commuting to Kenley, together with the demands of a young family, would be easier from Beckenham.

He was still managing to hold on to the thrill and buzz of flying, taking off in one of his favourite aircraft, a Tiger Moth, accompanied by another member of the Air Staff, Johnny Forward, who covered ATC Gliding. Peter also flew to their Reserve Command HQ at White Waltham.

He had the opportunity to fly unfamiliar types, such as the Airspeed Oxford, and soloed on the Avro Anson and the Auster Mks 5 and 6. Being back in the RAF gave Peter the opportunity to meet and work with colleagues from a variety of backgrounds. Forward had been in Bomber Command but was shot down and became a POW. After he left Kenley, he married Nancy Wake. The Australian had made a name for herself in France, where she was known as the White Mouse, escaping from the Gestapo on countless occasions. Her story was quite incredible. Married to a wealthy industrialist, she joined the French Resistance, carrying out highly dangerous SOE missions. She worked on an escape circuit through France for Allied forces and her actions were responsible for the exodus of 1,037 Allied lives. She was the leader of 7,000 male Resistance fighters known as the Maquisards. She also drank heavily. Drinking to the French Maquis was similar to duelling – it was a point of honour. No amount of alcohol could knock her out and it was a well-known and proved fact that Nancy drank men under the table, not just due to her constitution but as evidence that she could be taken seriously as their leader. Many are the times when, on the occasions that Nancy and Johnny visited Peter and Betty, Betty handed Nancy a bottle of scotch. 'There you go! That should see you through most of the evening!'

Peter first made the transition from props to jet-powered flight in early July 1952. He had arranged to see Al Deere, who was now CO of RAF North Weald, for lunch. As they finished their lunch, Deere turned to Peter:

'Would you like to go up in a Meteor?'

The eyes widened and a smile spread across Peter's face. 'Not half!'

7 July – Local flying around North Weald.

Deere took Peter up in a Meteor T7, a two-seat trainer version which made him realise for the first time how different jet flying was. The flight lasted for thirty minutes. It was a lovely summer's afternoon and the sun beat down over the Essex countryside as the Meteor T7 turned and climbed and dived, Deere showing Peter what a jet aircraft could do. Peter wondered how he could have done without flying! It was an experience, not least because Peter hadn't flown an operational aircraft for almost six years. He recalls the contrasts between propeller and jet flight, conversely speed wasn't one of them. What this trip had done was to whet his whistle for operational flying. He remained at Kenley until October 1952, but the prospect of operational flying spurred him on, motivated him. The past three years with No. 61 Group were seen as a 'probationary' period; he was going to train for jet-flying.

The standard of flying necessary to pilot operational jet aircraft was, in his words, much sharper than before.

In November 1952, he went to No. 118 Refresher Course, at RAF Syerston, Nottinghamshire.

The circle had turned 360° – here he was back on Harvards as he had been fifteen years earlier, before the war. The course and its instructors showed scant respect for previous combat records. One of the first objectives that pupils had to pass in order to progress was to succeed in the control of instrument flying. Constable Maxwell, a Battle of Britain pilot officer with No. 56 Squadron, had re-enlisted in the same manner that Peter had done, and together the pair took the Harvard in turns, sitting in the rear seat and concentrating on the instrument panel in front of them. Peter passed easily.

From Nottinghamshire thence to Dorset – the refresher course moved on to an advanced flying school based at a station near Tarrant Rushton, where the familiarisation course concentrated on the Meteor. Peter and the rest of the pupils concentrated on exercises like circuits and landings, asymmetric flying (flying on one engine) and asymmetric landings. It also featured ground control exercises, involving the pilot taking a Meteor T7 to a height of 36,000ft with a maximum rate descent and being guided back to base under radio control. As an aside, the first ejector seat trials took place in a Meteor Mk 3. It is interesting to note that at the age of thirty-two and with eight years of first-class flying under his belt, this was the first time he had flown with an ejector seat!

As with his first jet flight with Al Deere in the Meteor T7, Peter noticed a number of differences in jet-flying which came to prominence when he was in full control of the aircraft. The flight was much smoother in terms of vibration and noise – in his words, 'you didn't have a bloody great engine rattling in front of you', but he found that the Meteor was less responsive; when he opened the throttles, there was no immediate acceleration and it took considerable time for the aircraft to respond and climb. Visibility had been improved, which meant he could taxi straight instead of weaving about from side to side as he had done in the Spitfires. The jets were easier to start, by mobile ground battery starters which were plugged into the aircraft. The pilot then gave the signal for contact and the ground crew pushed the button on the battery starter. Once the engines had fired, he would apply the brake and signal the ground crew to remove the chocks. But there were also other compensations, and Peter found that there was wonderful forward vision in the cockpit, partly due to the layout of the cockpit, which was placed in front of the engines. Peter therefore enjoyed flying the Meteor at Tarrant Rushton.

While Peter was away, Betty lived at The Knoll in Beckenham. It was now their spiritual home, and it was very much a home, rather than a base. Jane first went to school in Beckenham and Betty was happy to remain there while her husband was away on courses. Two courses down, one to go – having passed the familiarisation course on the Meteor, on 15 June 1953, Peter went off to No. 229 Operational Conversion Unit (OCU) at Chivenor, Devon.

From Meteors to Vampires – the de Havilland Vampire was the RAF's second generation front-line jet fighter, constructed partly from wood with a single de Havilland Goblin engine behind the short, stubby fuselage connected to twin tail booms. His first experience in a Vampire was in a two-seat T11 trainer on a familiarisation flight, where he became acquainted with the handling capabilities. Despite his experience, the OCU was no pushover; it was the last step before operational flying, and the instructors had to be completely certain that pilots knew what they were doing. It is not unsurprising to discover that Peter found he had to concentrate on the course, which required a good deal of thought and study. There were the same procedures as at Tarrant Rushton – instrument and formation flying, battle formation, gunnery attacks and air firing, and he soloed on the Vampire Mk 5. Peter preferred the Vampire to the Meteor. Although it had one engine, it was far more agile and manoeuvrable. The course lasted just over two months, from 15 June to 22 August 1953.

The Spirit of the Blue was back. It says much for his tenacity and determination that at the age of thirty-three he was prepared to endure three courses with colleagues half his age. It also says much for his marriage that Betty was happy for him to pursue a career away from home when they had a young child, although there were compensations – the pay for an RAF fighter pilot is far better than a publican's! Within ten days of his passing the OCU course, Peter had been posted to Germany, and he was now back on operational flying for real. Initially he spent three days at Cologne airport, home of HQ No. 83 Group, and then he was told to report to No. 16 Squadron, on 7 September 1953. It was based officially at Celle but had moved temporarily to Butzweilerhof, near Cologne, because the runway at Celle was being extended. Peter says that conditions at Butzweilerhof were basic. There was no runway, only PSP metal stripping which the squadron had to land on. Despite the location change, he was told to report at Celle. Peter joined No. 16 Squadron, where he flew the Vampire Mk 5, an extremely good all-round fighter-bomber and all-weather interceptor. Celle was one of many gloriously historic medieval towns with cobbled streets, brightly coloured wooden houses and a town hall with a clock where figures fought each other on the hour, every hour.

No. 16 Squadron was at Butzweilerhof for the autumn of

1953. Peter settled easily into the familiar routine of operational flying and found it similar to riding a bike; you never really forgot the manoeuvres, formations or the thrill of opening the throttles as you raced down the runway in the RAF's latest fighter aircraft; it was matchless. Of course, squadron life had changed for him. He was now married with a six-year-old daughter and arrangements were already under way for them to join him in Celle. He was certain that he had made the right decision; his absence from the RAF had made him realise that operational flying was precisely what he wanted to do in his life. Nothing replaced the camaraderie of formation flying and the anticipation of dives, stalls and spins. It is true that there was an element of danger attached to operational flying, but as this was peacetime, the only dangers came in the form of aircraft that had not been properly serviced.

The runway at Celle had been extended and finished, and No. 16 Squadron was told by HQ that it could return from Butzweilerhof to Celle. Despite his lack of experience of flying jets, Peter led the squadron on the homecoming flight as Senior Flight Lieutenant. The flight lasted forty-five minutes and the Vampires flew in formation at a height of 20,000ft. He remembers there was a great deal of cloud on 31 October 1953. The squadron pilots heard Peter's voice crackle over the radio. 'Right, boys. We'll climb to our given height, then level out.' The formation was lost in cloud. How could they ever find Celle in this? Peter's voice came over the R/T again. 'OK. We'll start to let down . . . NOW!' Although he put a call over to the squadron pilots, he didn't leave a detailed message with ground control at Celle, merely mentioning that the squadron was on its way and would be with them soon. Eventually, the squadron broke cloud and came out underneath at 3,000ft. There, 5 miles in front of them, lay Celle.

'Hellfire!' the control said, when Peter and the squadron had landed safely, 'How the Bloody Hell did you know where to find us in this cloud?' It had been a masterclass in blind flying. Given the horrendous and potentially fatal weather conditions, less experienced flight leaders in Peter's position would have asked ground control for a detailed navigation course to Celle, including height data and, most importantly, a detailed let-down brief. However, Peter had faced situations like this on many occasions, such as the flight from Malta to Constantine, where he had led No. 238 Squadron in blind-flying conditions over the Atlas mountains; it was all down to experience.

Life had become more colourful since his arrival in Germany. He was notified that a married quarter had come available. Peter recalls that the quarters were sizeable and well equipped with an attic, a cellar and a good central-heating system. The kitchens had all mod cons and there was a garden, although Betty and Peter found that there was never enough time to work in it.

Betty and Jane travelled by boat across the North Sea, followed by a train journey. The family were reunited at Celle railway station in November 1953 and stayed in Germany for three years. While Peter was away each day, Betty modified the house to her own taste. One day, Betty heard a knock at the door. There was an eighteen-year-old German girl standing on the doorstep carrying little else but a plastic carrier bag containing her worldly possessions. Were they looking for a maid who could assist them in the housekeeping? She might even help them look after their child. Peter and Betty explained to her that it was not their decision to make: they would have to ask the RAF authorities but, yes, they would request that she work as their maid. The request was granted and Anna-Marie became part of the family. She got on well with Jane and provided company for Betty.

No. 16 Squadron was commanded by Dickie de Burgh. Peter had been posted there as OC of 'A' Flight. It soon became clear to him that de Burgh had some peculiar and hazardous plans for someone who was a commander of a fighter squadron. He had already noted that morale was not at its best – ground and air crews had to prepare and fly every squadron aircraft on a daily basis – and he thought that de Burgh was a little pompous. Squadron strength totalled eighteen aircraft. Peter's flight had nine Vampires as did 'B' Flight. When it came to the management of flying and maintaining these aircraft, it became obvious to Peter that his commander could not successfully organise and coordinate maintenance and support of the squadron. There was a difference of opinion on management control; different views on flights, communication procedures, etc. 'Get them all up, get them all airborne!' de Burgh would cry to the ground crew, who would look at him with bemused and bewildered glances. What de Burgh hadn't grasped, as Peter explains, is that some of the nine aircraft in each flight might have been reported as unserviceable; indeed, a couple might have been on permanent service, which had the net result that neither pilots nor ground crew knew precisely how many aircraft could be flown on a daily basis. It had a negative impact on morale, affecting both Flight Commanders, all the pilots and especially the ground crew, who, as Peter says, didn't know whether they were coming or going.

De Burgh went on leave for three weeks, and as Peter was the most senior officer present, he was left in charge of the squadron. He got the two flight sergeants from both flights together:

'Look, while I'm in charge, we're going to change the system', he told them. 'I want six aircraft per flight each day on the line. What you do with the others is up to you; you can keep them in reserve or service them. All I want is six per flight on the line.' It worked a treat. Everybody knew where they stood. If one of the six aircraft had to break away for whatever reason, there was always another in reserve to keep the full quota. From a flying point of view, it restored morale. Moreover, Peter's system increased the total hours of squadron flying per month. Inevitably, de Burgh returned from his holiday and was less than pleased with Peter's new procedures. There was little doubt which method the squadron preferred: a flight sergeant came to Peter and said, 'I wish to Christ you had taken over the squadron, Sir!' This episode shows Peter's valuable experience in man-management and communication skills. The years spent pulling pints in The Compasses had served him well; he was adept at motivating people and explaining precisely what he required. He stayed with No. 16 Squadron until he was posted at the end of the year.

The year 1954 got off to an excellent start. On New Year's Day, Peter discovered that he had been promoted to Squadron Leader. Betty had held a party the night before to see the New Year in at the officers' mess, and a long lie-in the following morning was necessary. Suddenly, there was a raucous noise outside their house. The temptation to pull the blankets over their heads was overwhelming but the noise grew louder. Before long, it sounded as if it was outside their front door: 'Happy Scraper! Happy Scraper!' Peter managed to crawl out of bed, stagger downstairs and open the door. He was met by a dozen squadron pilots chanting and singing. Even the Squadron Commander, Dickie de Burgh, joined in.

Scraper is RAF-speak for promotion to squadron leader. It is the addition of a thin band in between the two wider bands on the sleeves of a flight lieutenant's uniform. Peter was unaware that he had been awarded his scraper. 'Congratulations!' they shouted, 'you're now a Squadron Leader – again!' Peter didn't leave Celle for another two weeks. On 18 January he found out that he was officially posted to command No. 5 Squadron, based at Wunstorf. Four days later, he was flying a de Havilland Venom.

Peter preferred Wunstorf to Celle, largely due to his promotion, but he was also keen to leave the tensions within the squadron structure. A month later, his family joined him. There were, in fact, three squadrons based at Wunstorf: in addition to No. 5 Squadron, Nos 11 and 266 Squadrons shared the base. The Wunstorf Wing flew the de Havilland Venom. Indeed, No. 11 Squadron had been the first RAF fighter squadron to receive the fighter back in 1952. Similar in appearance to the Vampire, it was a faster, more powerful machine, larger in size and fuel tanks had been attached to the wing tips.

Their squadron commander was Eric Batchelor and his opposite number at No. 266 was Colin Coulthard, whom Peter had known from his No. 124 (Baroda) Squadron days at Manston. Coulthard went on to become an Air Vice-Marshal. The wing commander in charge of flying at Wunstorf was an Australian by the name of Johnny Shaw, who, like most of his fellow countrymen, was direct. Peter recalls that one of his favourite sayings was, 'Aw, there's shit in the hills!' Their station commander was Pat Jameson, now a group captain. It was Jameson who had instructed Peter on Hurricanes in the early days of the war before France. It was Jameson who, together with Kenneth Cross, had endured the sinking of the *Glorious*, heaving pilots' dead bodies into the icy water.

Peter was now Squadron Leader with No. 5 Squadron. He was now accountable for maintaining the general squadron standard of flying training, developing the pilots' proficiency in night-flying as well as upholding the formation of the squadron, making certain that everyone was aware of their role and position in a battle formation, be it pairs or fours, as well as formation in reconnaissance and navigation exercises. In addition to the tactics and logistics of the air crew, there was also the ground crew to oversee. Peter ensured that the engineers had the resources and the support necessary to complete their work. He had a tough job. It was well known that No. 5 Squadron was not in the best shape.

To emphasise this, he had been called to see AVM Hallings-Pott, AOC of No. 2 Group at Gutersloh, who had been chief instructor with Peter at Hawarden fourteen years before:

I don't know what's happened to 5 squadron; they've gone down the drain. They've had a terrible amount of accidents, including two fatals. Flying hours are poor. In short, Peter, they seem to have gone to pieces. The squadron is in rather a mess. I know you of old. I know what you can do. I'd like you to pull this squadron out of the mire. Pick it up!

It transpired that the squadron's previous squadron leader had adopted similar management methods to Peter's commander at No. 16 Squadron, lacking a structured approach to allow pilots, planes and ground crew work effectively.

Slowly, the squadron picked up as Peter implemented the same method of increasing flight hours and running flights that he had adopted at Celle. This had the desired effect, once again especially with the ground crew. Both they and the pilots knew where they were, when they were on and when they were off; they knew precisely was required of them. Within three months, No. 5 Squadron was flying more hours per month than any other squadron in the whole of the 2nd Tactical Air Force. His temporary spell of command at No. 16 Squadron had been a dry run. Nothing was left to chance, everything was now under control, which had a marked improvement on morale. A great spirit between pilots and ground crew emerged; so much so, that a squadron song was written:

> Five squadron for me, five squadron for me –
> If you're not five squadron, you're no use to me!
> Two-six-six are a shower, eleven are too
> If you're not five squadron, you're no use to me!

This was belted out with great gusto after a few beers in the mess, while the other two squadrons sharing the same bar looked on with contempt and disgust.

Perhaps more importantly, there were never any accidents during Peter's spell in the squadron.

It is an immense record and testament to Peter's style of management and command. The squadron were smokin' – literally! One of the methods Peter implemented in improving the pilots' morale was to start twelve de Havilland Ghost engines simultaneously. To start the engine, the ground crew fitted a cartridge which fired into life when the pilot pressed a button. The pilots waited for Peter's voice over the radio: 'Commencing ignition . . . Three . . . Two . . . One . . . NOW!' And, as twelve cartridge buttons were pressed together, twelve Ghost engines screamed into life, belching black smoke into the air.

Twice a year, the squadron travelled to northern Germany for a month at a time. Sylt lay off the coast of Schleswig-Holstein, and it was where Peter and the boys held their armament practice camp. Air firing from the Venoms was an integral part of the course. The pilots aimed at a flag towed by a drogue aircraft. Much to the pleasure of the drogue pilot, the flag trailed well away behind him. After it had served as a target, the flag was then released to the ground and the results were analysed. Much was at stake because the squadron which held the highest score for target practice in the 2nd Tactical Air Force was awarded the Duncan Trophy. In 1954, No. 5 Squadron came second – more evidence of the manner in which Peter had raised the level of pride, passion and determination within the squadron in a short space of time.

A number of Pilot Attack Instructors (PAIs) were based at Sylt, and two were attached to each incoming squadron. One of the instructors attached to the squadron was Ft Lt Ken Goodwin, who, Peter recalls, had a nose for fun, and there were many parties in the Goodwin residence. Peter and Ken struck up a long friendship that has lasted to this day.

The officer in charge of admin for the camp was a well-known bomber pilot who had been AVM Don Bennett's right-hand man in the famous Pathfinder Force. Highly decorated, Gp Capt Hamish Mahaddie was often to be found with the squadron in the bar, and was later to be a consultant on the feature film *Battle of Britain*. Mahaddie managed to locate Spitfires and Hurricanes, as well as Me 109s and Heinkel He 111s in Spain, and after considerable negotiations with the

Spanish authorities, had amassed what amounted to the 25th largest air force in the world.

Why does Peter think he achieved so much with No. 5 Squadron? There are other things besides flying when you're a flight or squadron commander; you're dealing with people. If you don't have the right attitude towards your people, they are not going to support you. Peter had two excellent flight commanders: Tommy Dawkins and Nicky Varanand. Varanand was a Prince from the Thai royal family; His Highness had two gorgeous Rolls-Royce cars in Britain with the number plates NV1 and NV2. While he served in Germany, Prince Varanand didn't bother shipping his cars to Wunstorf; he went out and bought himself a brand new and exceedingly large Mercedes Benz, together with an American station-wagon – just to tide himself over!

In keeping with the Australian habit of not recognising the presence of a Royal, Johnny Shaw often strode up to the Thai Prince, asking for a favour. 'Nicky, can I borrow your Merc? I've got a little business in Hanover to see to.' Varanand grudgingly agreed. Shaw was posted soon after, to be replaced by Frank Woolley, who was an altogether different character: reserved, introverted; another pilot from Peter's days at Manston.

The squadron, including Betty, on one occasion decided to spend a night in Hanover. They found a bar and had a few drinks where, in Peter's words, 'we all got a bit lively'. They moved on. The lively, raucous atmosphere continued until the bar closed for the night and Betty and the boys returned to the cars in a car park just off the main square. As they walked across the square, they saw a German chimney sweep heading towards them. He appeared straight out of a Dickens novel: black top hat and long tailcoats. Peter recalls – with characteristic understatement – that there was a lively scene in the square for the next ten minutes.

He was visibly drunk, shouting at the top of his voice, when he noticed a group of British pilots, and the voice got louder and angrier. From what they could gather, he blamed them for the war; it was entirely their fault. Why were they here? They should go back home! A couple of the pilots rushed up and told him where to go, but he became offensive, throwing his fists around, spoiling for a fight.

Peter realised that discretion was the better part of valour. 'Ignore him, boys, just keep clear! Step round him.' The abuse and aggression continued. Peter then decided that the only way to stop him was to confront him, eyeball to eyeball. 'Careful, Pete!' Betty warned, 'he's probably very strong. I know you; you'll take a pop at him.'

Peter squared up to the chimney sweep, looking at him straight in the eyes. 'We don't want any problems here. You go your way; we'll go ours . . .' The sweep continued to mouth abuse; the eyeballing continued. 'Now, Fuck off!'

The Venom Mk I made way for the Mk 4, particularly efficient at high-altitude flights. Peter recalls sorties made in conjunction with the UK that tested the country's air defences. Many of these sorties began in the early hours. First light had not yet broken as the Venom Mk 4s raced down the Wunstorf runway, their short squat bodies climbing into the dark. The squadron's brief was to climb to a height of 40,000–45,000ft and fly a set course that took it across the continental coast over the North Sea. Once the East Anglian coast had been reached, it was to sweep round over Norfolk and Suffolk and return on a set course bound for Germany. It was over Norfolk that the 'home side', flying Hunters and Meteors, was meant to intercept. Peter and the others from the 'enemy' were told that they were not to deviate from these set courses; no evasive action must be taken. Far below, the 'enemy' could see the Hunters struggling to reach the same altitude as the Venoms, with the Meteors virtually out of the running. The Venoms piled on the power. It was a deceptively agile aircraft and Peter found it very good. As well as exercises like these, No. 5 Squadron practised ground-attack strafes in the Venoms on ranges.

The distance between Wunstorf and Celle is roughly 60 miles. Close by Steinhuder Meer is quite magnificent, stretching as far as the eye can see, but it has a maximum depth of 8ft.

In the winter it froze over completely, and the RAF boys, being RAF boys, drove their cars on it.

One pilot left it a little too late and the lake had begun to thaw as he took his car for a spin. One minute he was on top of the ice and the next he was beneath it. He managed to clamber out unscathed, but not surprisingly the car was a wreck – which didn't matter because, Peter recalls, it was a wreck to start off with! It was rather ironic to think that fifteen years earlier, he and his RAF colleagues had been fighting German pilots, planes and people, escorting bombers that obliterated their economic resources. Times move on. He and a few pilots from the squadron went to Belsen, 20 miles from Celle. The camp itself was still standing when they went there, with the addition of only a memorial stone. He says it was most eerie when you got there; there was absolute silence. 'We noticed that there were no bird calls. They must have had some inner instinct but they never flew above, never landed on the camp.'

The systematic increase in pride and spirit that Peter had instilled in the squadron culminated with the presentation of the Squadron Standard. This meant much to the entire squadron, but especially to Peter, because it was an acknowledgement of the dramatic change; it was symbolic recognition that No. 5 Squadron was now a force to be reckoned with. The Reviewing Officer presiding over the presentation was an old member of the squadron. ACM Sir Leslie Hollingshurst had flown with it back in the twenties. Hollingshurst arrived in a plane used by ACM Sir Harry Broadhurst, AOC 2nd Tactical Air Force in Germany. About 300 guests, including friends, relations and officers, were also present, which meant that everything had to be just right – it was an occasion of immense public relations value. The squadron practised the drill for two months in advance;

everyone was involved – Peter leading with a sword held at chest height, while at his side the two flight commanders led their flights. The Standard itself was carried by Derek Gathercole as guards armed with rifles stood on either side. There were quick-time and slow-time marches. Other personnel from Wunstorf, pilots and ground crew from Nos 11 and 266 Squadrons were included.

The rain clouds held off on 24 April 1954, and the ceremony went ahead with much pomp and circumstance: the march-past by the two supporting squadrons; the arrival of the reviewing officer; ACM Sir Leslie Hollingshurst taking his place on the dais where he was received by a general salute; inspection of No. 5 Squadron as the RAF band played 'Greensleeves'; the uncasing of the Standard draped over drums for the Consecration; the Presentation of the Standard – the reviewing officer presenting the Standard to the Standard Bearer. There followed the address by the reviewing officer; response by the Commanding Officer No. 5 Squadron; the Standard slow marching into the ranks of No. 5 Squadron as the band played 'God Save the Queen'; a general salute, then a march past in slow time while the band played 'Scipio'; a march past in quick time as the band played the 'Middy' while Peter saluted with the sword; then advance in review order and present arms; then the whole parade marched off and the reviewing officer left the parade ground. Then all proceeded to the officers' mess as the Standard carried by Derek Gathercole arrived, carried with great dignity and complete with escort, and was unfurled and put in its casing; there then followed a luncheon. The solid silver trophies won by the squadron over the course of forty years were displayed on the tables for all to see.

It was hard to quell the spirit and morale of No. 5 Squadron, even on a day bound by rigid formality and tradition. Just as Sir Leslie Hollingshurst, accompanied by Harry Broadhurst, boarded the aircraft to leave, Peter says some bright spark slapped a No. 5 Squadron sticker on the port-side fuselage. There was the squadron crest, while someone had chalked up a fat number five alongside it, accompanied by a large white chalky arrow pointing to it. One of the other principal members that day was Keith Sturt. He went on to become a test pilot for Rolls-Royce and flew the new four-engined Avro Vulcan atomic bomber during an Empire Day display! The Vulcan normally carried four Avon engines, but two engines on this particular Vulcan had been replaced with more powerful units. During the display at Syerston, the airframe suddenly disintegrated due to the extra thrust of the additional engines, with the loss of an excellent pilot.

It may have been pure coincidence that Peter had been commander during the Standard presentation, but it is true to say that he had been responsible for putting the squadron firmly on the map. Without his ambition and drive – carried out in a friendly and firm manner – there is every likelihood that the squadron would have continued to wallow in the mire.

The whole family went on leave in July 1955 for a month, embarking on a continental camping holiday. The family car was loaded with so much camping equipment that it was a surprise that the springs held out at all. Peter says it was a wonderful holiday as the family stopped at various locations along the way – Munich, Innsbruck, Bolzano, Trento, Venice, Ravenna, Milan – where Betty's brother, Ted, met them at the airport – Florence, Pisa, Sienna, the St Gotthard Pass, Zurich, Scharfhausen, Triburg, Fraudenstadt, Heidelberg and back to Wunsdorf. Peter had invested in good-quality German camping equipment, including two tents: one for him and Betty and the other for Jane and Anna-Marie. For Peter, it was a satisfying moment to savour. Since his return to operational flying, he had restructured and developed two squadrons with effective results. It was a vindication of his decision to leave Canterbury, and his return into the RAF had been fully justified. Put simply, he could never have done without flying!

The Cold War was reaching its zenith in the 1950s. Western politicians learnt that Soviet countries sent interceptor fighter aircraft over their airspace: tensions were keenly felt on both sides – the war was hotting up. In October 1955, the entire Venom Wing at Wunstorf was moved to Fassberg, situated on the East German border, with the objective of intercepting any Russian air activity over the German borders. In Peter's words, 'The Russians were getting a bit naughty. They erected watchtowers with soldiers spying on your every move through binoculars, training their guns on you if you put one foot across the border. It was a particularly unnerving time.' The Wing continually practised a vital descent manoeuvre termed QGH. If the formation flew above cloud, ground control directed the pilots over the airfield via radar. The formation then lost 10,000ft flying in one direction, immediately turning 180°, doubling back and approaching to land by losing the same amount of height and distance. Carrying out QGH at Fassberg was fraught with problems. When the wind was blowing westerly, which it often did, the squadron had to fly into wind. By flying into the westerly wind and losing 10,000ft, the formation flew over the West German border and into enemy territory. Rather than initiate any tension with the Soviets, an alternative landing solution was devised. The formation flew in the opposite direction, doubled back then had to make a circuit or two around the airfield before landing. Although this method was more time-consuming and less cost-effective, it successfully avoided Russian provocation.

Fassberg was commanded by Gp Capt George Brown. During a conversation one day with Eve, his wife, Betty mentioned that in the days before the war, her brother Ted often went down to Folkestone to the Lees Hall, a well-known dancing club right on the cliff edge. Ted had a reputation for being a bit of a ladies' man; he had an eye for the women and the women had an eye for him. Eve mentioned that she came from Folkestone and she thought she remembered him. 'Was his surname Swift?' she asked.

Betty looked at her incredulously. 'Why, yes. Ted Swift, that's it. Did you know him?' It transpired that Eve certainly 'knew' him; they had 'met' and 'danced' before.

The spirit of No. 5 Squadron at Wunstorf extended to the Fassberg mess and, never a couple to miss the opportunity of letting their hair down, Peter and Betty revelled in the parties that took place. Fancy Dress parties were common and Peter has photos of the Fancy Dress Ball on New Year's Eve 1956, complete with cap, collar, tie and jacket – and no trousers!

NINE

Flying Desks

The days of operational flying were drawing to a close and the time had come to leave Germany. The Air Ministry posted him to the Aircrew Selection Centre at Hornchurch in April 1956. A brief refresher course proceeded for two weeks where he trained as an aircrew selection officer. Working in pairs, Peter and the other selection officers trained in the art and responsibility of selection of aircrew. When candidates first arrived at the Selection Centre in Hornchurch, they underwent a strict medical. Inevitably, there was little point in proceeding with the selection process if they failed the medical.

Peter says that a high percentage of pupils didn't make it past this stage, owing to poor eyesight or lack of height. Those who succeeded were then divided into groups of six, each candidate wearing overalls with a specific number on his back while Peter and a colleague sat facing the pupils, giving them tasks to carry out, individually or together in the group. Group exercises consisted of moving heavy weights from one side of the room to the other using planks and a pole without touching the floor. Peter was responsible for assessing their initiative, marking their results and jotting various notes down on pads.

Aircrew evaluation continued for about six months, until the camp commandant, Air Cdre Teddy Corberley, wanted a new staff officer, and Peter was chosen for the role, organising his routine and programmes. Two years later, Peter was moved on again. He had long realised that operational flying was now no longer possible; flying was for recreational purposes only. Instead, he had made the transition from fighter pilot to staff officer. Pilots had many terms for this change to staff roles, and one of the more respectable phrases was 'mahogany bombing', the other was 'flying desks'. Peter continued flying his desk in the heart of London for the Air Ministry. Later renamed the Ministry of Defence, the Air Ministry was divided into two branches. The Whitehall office covered Air Operations, whereas Adastral House covered logistical support and administration. Located in Theobalds Road, Adastral House was overseen by AM Sir Theobald McEvoy. Much of the support and administration work at Adastral House included the policy for selection of aircrew and ground officers. Peter was posted to a vacancy within the aircrew office because of his relevant experience at Kenley and Hornchurch.

Apart from his short time with W.A. Sparrow back in 1937/8, this was only the second job where Peter had actually commuted to work, travelling from Beckenham. He continued journeying to the Ministry until 1962. He recalls that civilian clothes were worn to the Ministry unless a Selection Unit visit had been scheduled. Every now and again, an opportunity to fly appeared, and when it arrived Peter took it with open arms, climbing into the Ministry's de Havilland Chipmunk based at Hendon twice a month. Looking back, Peter feels his time selecting aircrew has been proved worthwhile because the policies that he drafted and procedures he assisted to implement at the Air Ministry shaped the type and standard of fighter pilot who joined the RAF in the 1960s. These high standards of flying are amply demonstrated in the case of personnel who flew for RAF aerobatic teams during the late 1950s and early 1960s, continuing the mantle of the famous Black Arrows from No. 111 Squadron.

It can be argued that Peter was indirectly responsible for the standards of those aircrew who flew in the Blue Diamonds, the Tigers, the Yellowjacks and the Red Arrows. Every pilot who flew in these teams in the early 1960s had undergone some selection process ultimately covered by Peter.

The desk in Theobalds Road had landed and taxied for good. His three years in the Air Ministry, from 1962 to 1964, were up and it was time to move on again. It was time to move away from the smoke and out into the lush green of the Chiltern countryside, where he was made Squadron Commander of No. 1 Squadron, No. 3 Wing, at Halton. Halton – No. 1 School of Technical Training – had a fearsome reputation within the RAF. Established in 1920 by Sir Hugh Trenchard, it provided essential technical training for boy entrants to the RAF who would become the bedrock of the service in years to come. These boys entered Halton as apprentices and were known as Halton Brats. The officers' mess at Halton was in a building called Halton House, previously owned by the Rothschild family. Peter and Betty's quarters were a little more modest, however. They lived in one of the married quarters and Betty enjoyed going to the mess.

No. 3 Wing consisted of three consecutive entries of apprentices. In addition to Peter's squadron, two other squadrons made up the Junior Wing at Halton. Each squadron took a new intake in turns. As he arrived as Commanding Officer, No. 1 Squadron was half-way through the 97th entry in their first year, but subsequently he received the 100th entry, together with the 103rd and 106th entries. Once the boys had reached their second year, they were considered to be part of the Senior Wing. As Squadron Commander, Peter was responsible for commanding 120 apprentices in the squadron along with eight members of staff – two flight commanders and one flight sergeant who worked in conjunction on both Flights. Each flight commander had a sergeant and a corporal to assist him. In reality, because No. 1 Squadron was part of the Junior Wing, it was a continuation of the school environment, where Peter was guardian and headmaster to pupils who were roughly between the ages of sixteen and eighteen. Some had only just left school, others had worked for a year or two. They came from all over the world, with a variety of characters and attitudes to match and a variety in their education, ranging from the good to the not so good. It was Peter's role to change these boys from civilian to service life, instilling some of the discipline that was required for the RAF but at the same time keeping things light and interesting. They were not in the Air Force proper, and so, in order to maintain their interest, there had to be a level of fun and enjoyment. Despite their different backgrounds, at the end of the first year the pupils were all very much on a par. For many it was their first time away from home and in any case they felt the wrench. Part of his role was to help them through what was obviously a sensitive time.

A lot of time was spent on training. The first thing the boys did when they arrived was to get into uniform. They arrived and were measured up, boots were fitted. Each flight had its own colour, and this was reflected in a band placed around their caps. Once their uniforms had been fitted, they underwent drill practice – how to walk properly, march properly, how to salute – which took about a month.

After that, the boys attended lessons and lectures in various workshops and education centres, some half a mile away from their barrack block. The morning might be spent on drill practice, then in the afternoon they were in the workshops. It was the beginning of an education that would eventually lead to being qualified in a trade in engines or airframes. Other trades, such as radio and instruments, were based at other schools in Locking and Cosford. In addition to education in engines or airframes, Peter and his colleagues were responsible for teaching the boys about general hygiene and cleanliness. There were four dormitories in each block and thirty youngsters shared a dormitory. Beds were placed down each side of the room, with a locker beside each bed containing personal belongings. The boys were taught to fold their blankets on the beds, with their service kit placed on the blankets.

Peter recalls teaching them to arrange their beds in line as you looked down a row. If one was out of line, even slightly askew, the flight sergeants sprang into action. The room had to be kept clean, the floor polished and the toilet and bathrooms spotless. As commanding officer, Peter inspected the rooms once a week, accompanied by his flight sergeant and flight lieutenant. Although he picked out one or two things here and there, he says the rooms were immaculate; the boys worked hard and did their stuff. You could hardly believe it. Evenings were mainly spent swotting up on studies for lessons the following day. There was always plenty of background research to gen up on, especially if they were studying engines. Corporals came round the barrack rooms, calling for lights out, at half-past ten.

One of his sergeants, Sgt Cook, decided to establish a squadron band. Peter says that he taught many lads who had an interest in music to play the bagpipes, which was put to good effect on annual passing-out parades. These parades were carried out with much pomp and circumstance, witnessed by their proud parents. Peter led the parade with his sword, flanked by his two flight commanders leading their flights with the Air Officer Commanding receiving the salute on the dais. Altogether, there were about 250 people as an audience. At the end of the parade, the parents were invited to lunch in the boys' mess. Peter had a female warrant officer who, he says, did wonders with the food. He is particularly proud that they did not lay on anything special for the parents, but ate precisely the same food that he and the boys had regularly eaten, which was excellent. He chatted to parents sitting round the table with their boys, and found it quite gratifying because many of them came up to him after the ceremony, shaking him warmly by the hand. 'You've changed our lad out of all recognition – he's polite and neat and tidy when he's home, he even makes his own bed!'

But there were times when Peter had to be sympathetic with one or two boys who were away from home for the first time in their lives and they were upset and afraid of their new surroundings. They didn't want any part of service life; it wasn't for them. They wanted to go home.

Peter's great skill in communication came to the fore in these circumstances, and being a father himself may have helped. In any case, he dealt with these situations with great sensitivity and empathy. As a breed, fighter pilot aces are not known for their compassion and kindness. Yet, Peter had to demonstrate warmth, understanding and tenderness in attempting to change the boys' attitudes.

He would adopt the manner of a gentle father rather than that of stern headmaster. 'Have you thought about this carefully?'

'Yes sir, I don't think I want to go on with this. I'd like to go home.'

'Well, if that's the way you feel, perhaps you ought to give it some more thought. It might be an idea if you spoke to your parents, see how they feel about it. I think you'll get over this initial strangeness of being away from home and missing your families; you might eventually enjoy it!'

Peter would find their phone number. 'Tell you what. Sit at my desk, sit in my seat, there's the phone; you take it now and I'll walk out. When you've finished the conversation with your parents, come out and I'll be outside.'

After about twenty minutes, they would come out. Peter saw they were visibly happier.

'I think I'm going to try and carry on.'

'Good.'

He knows that some commanding officers in his position would have taken a harder stance in this situation, but feels that adopting this approach would have been counterproductive, driving many boys out of the Halton gates. In three years, Peter lost just one entrant out of a total of 360.

As we have seen during his time with Nos 5 and 16 Squadrons, one element essential to his management approach was morale, and raising this at Halton was no exception. Wherever he went, he felt it was essential to maintain a feeling of well-being in a squadron. Sports were actively pursued at Halton; football and rugby teams played against each other as well as other squadrons in the Junior Wing. Peter was very proud of the high standards that the boys achieved, although they might not have achieved them at all without the support and guidance of his staff.

Despite the drill training and the discipline prevalent in No. 1 Squadron, the old adage that boys will be boys certainly rang true. Each squadron had its own block of buildings, Peter's block facing the parade ground. The boys from No. 1 Squadron crept into the other blocks late one night, taking boots from another squadron and lined them up outside on the parade ground. Come the morning and there were thirty pairs of apprentice boots all lined up for drill and inspection – minus their owners. Peter had to tick them off, with a wry smile. 'Bloody good show – but don't do it again!' On another occasion, his apprentices managed to move an entire airframe of a training aircraft that was being used for teaching purposes onto the parade ground. The same 'stern' reprisal followed!

As he was one of four general-duties officers who were qualified pilots, Peter managed to fly from Halton regularly. Most officers had trained as engineering or ground crew, which meant that the officers who were pilots were responsible for taking up every apprentice in a flight, in order to give them some flight experience. When duties were not urgent or pressing, he ambled down to the airfield and climbed into one of the Halton Chipmunks for a morning's flying with the apprentices. The four pilots flew a number of flights in a morning with up to four or five pupils who were given air experience. It was unlikely that many of these apprentices realised the unique flying calibre of their pilot!

He asked them whether they had flown before. Some had, some hadn't. He told them to put their hands and feet lightly on the controls.

Now, if you move the control column to the left, the aircraft will bank to the left . . . if you want to turn, you'll have to assist with a little bit of left rudder . . . to straighten up, centralise your rudder and control column and we're flying straight and level again . . . if you want to dive, just ease the control column forward and the nose will go down . . . you can hold the column there . . . ease the column back and we're flying level again . . . if you want to climb, ease the control column back and the nose will come back up.

Peter showed them what to do.

'Right, you've had a feel of flying. Now you have a go. I'm going to take my hands and feet off the controls.' He would put his hands above his shoulders to show them he was not in control of the Chipmunk. 'Try flying straight and level . . . try a little turn to the left . . . straighten out again . . .' Quite literally, twenty minutes had flown by. If he saw that the pupils were confident enough, he'd finish off with a couple of aerobatic manoeuvres, a loop and a slow roll. The Gipsy Major engine was still running once they landed, and as one pupil climbed out, another would clamber in while the ground crew strapped him in and gave the thumbs up sign when they had finished. Peter opened the throttles and the Chippie leapt off into the skies once more. The pilots managed about five consecutive flights, totalling about an hour and a quarter, before it was necessary to refuel.

The apprentices also had the opportunity to join a number of societies. Peter was secretary of the Halton branch of the Royal Aeronautical Society, and managed to get some legendary names in aviation to lecture at Halton. Barnes Wallis; Al Deere; Brian Trubshaw, British Chief Test Pilot for the Concorde programme; Bill Bedford, Chief Test Pilot for Hawkers and the Harrier programme; and Wg Cdr Kenneth H. Wallace, the man responsible for the invention of the one-man autogyro; all lectured, thanks to Peter. Indeed, Wallace's invention was featured in the James Bond film, *You Only Live Twice*, as Little Nellie, with Wallace performing his own stunts. Because of the stature of these speakers, the audience was made up of *all* apprentices on the station, not just from the Junior Wing. Often, the lecture room was packed out with some six or seven hundred in the audience, and word quickly spread about the Society lectures, in particular the calibre of guest speakers that the CO of No. 1 Squadron kept finding! The audience didn't stop at apprentices; the air commodore in charge of Halton, along with the group captain in charge of training, were to be found, sitting in the front row!

By 1964, Peter's desk at Halton was approaching finals and cleared for landing; time to fly another desk. In early summer 1964, he was posted as a staff officer to the commandant at the Joint Warfare Establishment at Old Sarum. The Wiltshire HQ was a focal centre for courses run by NATO with the prime objective of members working together, formulating international policies on employing joint tactics and operational policies in exercises. These courses at Old Sarum lasted a fortnight. Where there were courses, parties tended to follow. Betty was in her element and attracted a certain amount of attention, wanted or otherwise! Peter remembers one high-ranking admiral working at HQ Joint Warfare at Whitehall becoming overtly friendly towards her on more than one occasion, catching her eye, chatting her up. She told him outright at each event that he was wasting his time. Peter thoroughly enjoyed working for his commandant at Old Sarum, AVM Ginger Weir.

Unfortunately, he hadn't been there all that long before Weir was posted on. The post for commandant was rotational; each service – Army, Navy and Air Force – took turns in submitting an officer. It had been purely coincidental that an RAF officer was in charge when Peter had arrived. When Weir left, instead of putting forward an admiral, as had been expected, the Navy placed a general of the Royal Marines, Billy Barton.

While based at Old Sarum, Peter was witness to one of the most significant postwar aircraft never to be given the go-ahead, the TSR 2. It was the best aircraft that Britain never had. Undeniably one of the greatest accomplishments in aviation history, it suffered at the hands of various political groups. The project started when Macmillan's Conservative government decreed that in the future, it was unlikely that the RAF would require piloted fighter aircraft! The TSR 2 was based at nearby Boscombe Down and the test pilots put all six aircraft through their paces high over the Wiltshire countryside. It was a truly magnificent sight. Peter thinks it was a great shame it was scrapped.

'I think they should have stayed with the project; from what I saw in the air, it was a bloody good aeroplane. It looked incredibly agile and manoeuvrable.' Unfortunately, the Labour government felt otherwise, scrapping the programme in favour of things American. As a consequence, it sounded the death-knell for the fighter aviation industry in this country. There would never be another all-British combat aircraft. Writing in the magazine *Aeroplane Monthly*, test pilot Roland 'Bee' Beamont wrote, 'Certainly the main roles envisaged for TSR 2 in the 1960s cannot be met by anything in service even today in the western world.'

The post lasted for two years before Peter was selected in September 1966 for a NATO staff appointment back in the smoke of London as adviser to the chairman of the Military Agency for Standardisation (MAS). Because of his experience in dealing with interservices, he was ideal in recommending personnel, as well as managing and developing existing links between international and UK services. He organised joint working parties, one of which was tasked with looking at standardising the use, issue, location and access of fuels and lubricants in different countries.

The MAS had been established to standardise the same type of fuel in Europe. If a pilot landed at an airport in Italy, he knew he would be able to obtain the same fuel and oil as he had in Britain.

Annual meetings of each working party were held either at their Belgrave Square offices or at one of the NATO nations to discuss results and conclusions. Peter found that the elegant and elaborately furnished properties provided an excellent base for locating local pubs in the vicinity. He persuaded his colleagues, a Canadian, an Italian colonel, a Frenchman and an American to join him on these 'fact-finding' missions! During the AGMs, he sat at the top of the table as adviser next to the chairman, taking notes, acting as consultant if required. These meetings were held in either French or English, with an interpreter in a little sound-proof box. Peter travelled to NATO meetings in Belgium, Paris and Rome.

Two years later, his desk had been promoted. Eighteen years after he had been recommissioned, fourteen years after he had last been promoted to squadron leader, Peter was now a wing commander, where, owing to his interservice experience, he was seconded to the Army in the role of Brigade Air Support Officer. The Ministry of Defence had wanted to pursue closer links concerning operations between the Army and the Air Force. Working for Brigadier Edwin 'Dwin' Bramall (later Lord Bramall), Peter was the first incumbent as air adviser from the RAF to take the role, where he was based at HQ 5 Brigade (also known as No. 5 Air Portable Brigade), Tidworth, in Wiltshire. He says, with a wry chuckle, that he was the best Boy Scout in the RAF! If not the best Boy Scout, he was without doubt the Air Force's answer to Action Man. He certainly had to be fit, and no amount of desk-flying would prepare him physically for what was about to begin. Five Brigade sent him to participate in NATO exercises as part of ACE mobile force. Peter's RAF unit was No. 38 Group based at Odiham. NATO saw the ACE mobile force as a premier advanced multiglobal strike force for the late 1960s: able to drop into any country with the objective of gaining and holding territory until the main force arrived. It was an attempt by the organisation to involve and engage individuals from different services and nationalities; Italian generals liaised with Dutch colonels who worked alongside American majors. Peter was there to engage support from the Royal Air Force, if and when required. His brief was to coordinate air support so that resources – dropping supplies, fighter aircraft, aircraft dropping paratroopers, air strikes, as well as a substantial helicopter force – would arrive wherever and whenever. Peter remembers climbing into a uniform of army khaki (retaining his blue RAF beret!) and sleeping out in tents on exercises. Because he was the first member of the RAF assigned to the Army, he was chosen to participate in NATO exercises. Lasting three weeks, these exercises took place all over Europe, from the heat of Thrace in northern Greece to the sub-zero temperatures of the Arctic, as well as operating in mountainous conditions well over 2,000m in height along the border with Greece and Bulgaria.

The Cold War was escalating at this time, and the Task Force had to be certain that it could operate and fight, if required, in harsh Siberian conditions, repelling any threat from Mother Russia.

The exercises took place in February, where temperatures were at an average of below minus 50°C close to Tromsø, 500 miles to the north of the Arctic Circle. Peter flew into the nearest airport at Bardufoss with technical support in the shape of his own Land Rover and trailer, and radios along with a team from the RAF flown out in a Hercules. Although there was no actual opposition, the exercise was very much 'for real', the objective being to move forward and take certain locations with the support of air power. What was the Arctic like? Bloody cold! Sleeping in a tent was dreadful. Peter had a small oil-heater that took the chill off, but despite using a specially designed sleeping-bag on a camp bed with a thick deerskin pulled over for added protection, the biting conditions worked their way through. Peter made sure he slept with his head well underneath the covers – if he hadn't, he would have frozen to death. Bearing in mind that he was approaching fifty, it is remarkable that Peter, as Air Support Officer, was out in the field getting his hands dirty, buried deep in a sleeping-bag in a tent in the biting Arctic cold. Not bad for someone who was entering his second half-century!

The first AOC from No. 38 Group had an impressive pedigree – Australian AM Sir Mick Martin had been a bomber boy and Dam Buster, taking part in the legendary Ruhr dams raid with No. 617 Squadron. Martin was soon posted away, to be replaced by AM Sir Denis Crowley-Milling. The Iron Curtain had yet to be pulled back. To increase communication between East and West, a number of senior officers from the Soviet Bloc had been given permission by the Ministry of Defence to observe a large exercise held by No. 5 Brigade on Salisbury Plain which lasted for a week. There were eight officers in total, including two Russians, a Bulgarian general, a Nigerian admiral and an Italian. Peter was selected to look after them.

He was by now working at an extremely senior level, demonstrated by his colleague for this particular week – Prince Michael of Kent. The Prince had been a major in the Army and was working for the Ministry of Defence in connection with foreign services. Prince Michael met the Soviet senior officers in London before they were brought to a small hotel in Amesbury, their accommodation for the purpose of the exercises.

Peter was introduced to Prince Michael and the guests, then all made their way to the exercise by way of a Westland Wessex helicopter at their disposal.

One aspect of Peter's brief for the visit was successful public relations, which included interesting and entertaining locations during the evenings. Peter recalled that he and Betty regularly went to a particular pub when he had been posted to Old Sarum four years earlier. The food there was fantastic and it was just to the south of Salisbury, in Odstock, where the pub was owned and run by a Frenchwoman, Jeanette, and her English husband. Peter suggested to Prince Michael that it might be an idea if they travelled to Odstock one evening because the food really was out of this world. Prince Michael agreed. Peter phoned ahead to make a reservation and Jeanette was delighted to hear from him.

'I'd like to come down tonight with a party, there'll be about ten of us. Can you have a table ready at eight o'clock?'

'Yes, of course Peter. No problem at all.'

'I'm bringing a mixture of foreign nationals – colonels and generals. Oh, and Prince Michael of Kent will be there too.'

'Of course! Now come on, Peter, be serious.'

'No, really; I am.'

'All right', she replied with a chuckle in her voice. 'Anyway, I'll book you a table tonight. For ten. And one for Prince Michael!'

Her jaw dropped when, at 8 p.m., the party arrived complete with the royal guest.

Peter says that escorting the enemy was a rather strange experience at first; he recalls they were all eyes – they wanted to see everything they possibly could, trying to take it all in – but at the end of five days, he felt that the barriers had been broken down to some extent.

Today, almost thirty-five years later, the Royal Air Force is increasing links with the Army and Navy, finding ways in which support and cooperation can be engaged. Peter was very much one of the early pioneers of Joint-Service Liaison. It must be gratifying that much of the work that he began continues.

He took his desk off for the last flight when he received his final posting in the RAF as Senior Officer in charge of Administration and Deputy Station Commander at RAF Wattisham. Home to Nos 29 and 111 Squadrons, Wattisham was equipped with Lightning interceptor aircraft, Britain's only supersonic fighter. He was responsible for overseeing any administrative support that the station required. He was also accountable for the administrative wing at Wattisham. While the Flying Wing took care of aspects relating to flying on the base, his remit was to supervise the Administration Wing. This included organising supplies, accounts, technical equipment supplies relating to aircraft, uniforms and personnel, which involved managing postings in and out of the station as well as station motor transport. In short, Peter was accountable for the logistical and routine running of Wattisham. He says he had a dedicated team working under him – a squadron leader accountant, a squadron leader in charge of equipment, an RAF Regiment officer and a squadron leader for personnel.

His office in Station HQ was next to the Station Commander's, Gp Capt John Mellors.

Betty and Peter lived in senior officers' married quarters' where their house was adjacent to the Station Commander's house on one side, with the OC of No. 111 Squadron on the other.

Wattisham provided Peter with nine flights that were truly supersonic. The squadron was equipped with Lightning T Mk 5s, and his first flight in the two-seater trainers was with the Station Commander, John Mellors. Peter recalls an unfortunate incident involving one of the Wattisham Lightnings during his stay. Clearance had been given to take one of the Lightnings for an exercise. The pilot had selected the undercarriage up too early on take-off, when the aircraft was not yet fully airborne. After he had selected the wheels up, the Lightning sank back onto the runway and the huge fuel tank, slung beneath the Lightning like a large belly, came adrift, setting fire to both the runway and the aircraft. Although the pilot ejected safely, the Lightning was a write-off and an inquiry was convened while the runway was under repair. The outcome was that both squadrons were moved to another RAF base at Coltishall.

Peter says that the incident shook Mellors to the core. He left the service altogether and emigrated with his Australian wife to her homeland.

What does Peter think of the Lightning, the only supersonic British front-line fighter?

Well, it was one powerful cookie; two Rolls-Royce Avon engines on top of each other. On take-off, if you put them into reheat, you'd get off the ground almost vertically; you'd be standing on the power. Fantastic. And, of course, it went up to 30,000 and 40,000ft – and the rest! It had a high performance at high altitude too. It was supersonic, capable of reaching Mach 2; I've gone through the speed of sound several times! When you compare today's front-line fighters like the Tornado and the Jaguar, their performance speedwise is really no better than the Lightning. Although it was a high-performance aircraft, it was restricted operationally by a lack of range and lack of good armament. Although I was in a two-seater, I flew them most of the time – I wasn't sitting there like a cabbage. We carried out manoeuvres like barrel-rolls and slow rolls. It was one powerful beast.

Mellors was replaced by Ken Goodwin, the Pilot Attack Instructor whom Peter had met and partied with on Sylt. If Sylt provided the platform for the basis of a friendship, then Wattisham cemented it. The photographs taken in the mess show the pair draping their arms over each another in a merry and good-humoured alliance. Goodwin's brother, Dick, who also flew in the RAF, was, in Peter's words, 'quite a boy'. After a particularly raucous party in the mess one night, Ken and Pete were sleeping in the following morning. It was quiet, silent and nothing was stirring – except Dick. Staying with Ken and his wife Sue, 30yds from Peter and Betty, there was a loud bang on the front door at 10 a.m. There he was, in the doorway, holding a silver tray with a bottle of brandy on it.

'Morning!', he said in a horribly chirpy tone, looking very bright-eyed and extremely bushy-tailed. 'I've come to see you!'

The Cold War continued to threaten NATO countries during the 1970s. Wattisham was on the eastern side of England and therefore closer to Russia than other UK RAF bases. As such, it was tasked with intercepting Soviet bombers flying over the

North Sea. In response to these strikes, Wattisham had a Quick Reaction Alert force (QRA) whereby pilots had to stand at Readiness twenty-four hours a day. Peter recalls the QRA Lightnings scrambling several times from Wattisham; scrambling – there was a phrase he hadn't heard for some time. Things had come full circle. The machines were faster and heavier, but the pilots were employing exactly the same principle that Peter had done, sitting at Readiness in the cockpits of the high-altitude Spitfires with No. 124 Squadron nearly thirty years earlier. Indeed, before that, when he was waiting in the Hurricane for that French red flag to wave on the fields of Rouvres in the early days of the Second World War in 1939.

He may not have been flying operationally, but life at RAF Wattisham was all systems go. Peter came into contact with John Baggott, a Lightning pilot who took him up on the odd occasion and eventually married Peter's daughter, Jane.

It was certainly not a station where he could begin to wind down his career, preparing his pipe and slippers by the fire, planning for retirement. The Suffolk airfield was a highly operational station, (especially with QRA units!), and Peter had to remain highly operational with them.

One member of No. 111 Squadron had been at Halton as an apprentice. Cliff Spink made a point of approaching Peter one evening at the bar in the officers' mess, recalling that Peter had been OC during his time. AM Cliff Spink has only recently retired from the RAF. Planned or spontaneous, parties broke out in the Wattisham mess. Betty took the initiative, organising a Saturday evening where everyone could let their hair down regularly. She and Peter decked out half of the dining room with red and white checks in the style of a French bistro, adjacent to the bar, while the other half of the room was set aside for dancing. Betty got hold of a jukebox, laden with records. Betty's hard work became so popular that the parties became a regular Saturday night feature.

The music was close to Peter's heart: a mixture of swing, jazz, bossa nova and easy listening.

All the greats were there: Ella Fitzgerald ('What Is This Thing Called Love?'); Buddy Greco ('You Make Me Feel So Young'); Sammy Davis Jr ('Too Close For Comfort'); Tony Bennett ('Spring in Manhattan'); The Supremes ('Baby Love'); Louis Armstrong, Ray Charles, Anthony Newley ('What Kind of a Fool am I?'); Barry White ('I'm So Blue and You Are Too').

It was music to dance to, either to a quick beat or an intimate slow dance: George Shearing ('Baubles, Bangles and Beads'); Nat King Cole ('The Party's Over'); Frank Sinatra ('Come Fly With Me'); Bobby Darin ('Mack the Knife'); Eydie Gorme ('Separate Tables'); Peggy Lee; Randy Crawford; Dave Brubeck ('Take Five'); Stan Getz; Astrud Gilberto.

Music like this strikes a chord with him, puts more life into him than classical and orchestral does. To him, it has spirit, a feeling, a passion, vitality that other music doesn't have.

26 April 1973

The wheels of English Electric Lightning XS 459 touched down onto the cold, grey tarmac of the Suffolk runway at RAF Wattisham. The throttles were reduced, and in response the scream from the two Rolls-Royce Avon engines dulled to a throaty whine. The aircraft taxied in and slowly, very slowly, it came to a halt.

'Well, I suppose that's it. The last time.' It had been the stuff of Biggles. What years! What flying. And now at fifty-three, his own flying career high up in the blue had come to an end. 'So, Wing Commander, what have you got lined up? Pipe and slippers? Reading the papers and a bit of pruning in the garden? A long and graceful retirement?' 'Not bloody likely . . . . !'

TEN

Finals

Peter retired from the Royal Air Force on 5 May 1973, ten days after his final trip in Lightning XS 459 and eighteen months before his fifty-fifth birthday, the normal retirement date from the Air Force.

While working at Wattisham, he had received a call from his brother-in-law Noel Taylor at Jones Lang Wootton. He had a proposition for Peter. Noel explained that the company was looking to expand in Europe. With established offices in Paris and Brussels, the company wanted to expand further by moving into Holland, Belgium and Germany.

Noel didn't want to misemploy a chartered surveyor who wouldn't have been able to deal with bankers, lawyers and accountants. He knew that Peter had been involved with these countries during his NATO appointments, and although his contacts were not in the commercial sphere, they might still be useful to establish leads and obtain further contacts. 'I know that you have had a lot of experience and dealings with NATO in the countries we want to expand in. Fancy joining us when the Air Force has finished with you?'

'Well, yes – as long as the service will let me go.' But the Air Force wouldn't let him go at first. He felt it was all rather futile because there was no possible hope of further promotion for him. A case of stalemate ensued. In the end, his friends Ivor Broom and Ken Goodwin wrote a few well-chosen letters putting forward Peter's case.

Jones Lang Wootton had two offices in London, one at Mount Street in the West End, where Peter was based, and the other in the City. His brief was to establish offices in Amsterdam and Rotterdam, Antwerp as well as Frankfurt, Düsseldorf and Hamburg. Much of his time was spent in travelling. Taking the first flight out of Heathrow airport at least once a week, he held meetings with bankers and lawyers, setting up satellite offices, and once these had been established, he would fly back for board meetings. In Europe, the regulations for chartered surveyor companies are different from those in Britain. In the UK, under the guidance of the Royal Institution of Chartered Surveyors, businesses have to be partnerships – they cannot be corporate organisations, precisely the opposite on the continent. There is, therefore, a major difference in the corporate structure of establishing companies abroad, and Peter had to be familiar with legislation from each country. During the mid-seventies Britain was suffering from an economic downturn, and this had a significant impact on commercial property prices in Britain, with the net result that the company decided to scale down their European opeations. Peter stayed with Jones Lang Wootton for two and a half years.

Property may not have seemed enticing in Britain, but in the Middle East developers were falling over themselves to purchase property or land. Opulent and affluent, with vast tracts of land ideal for commercial buildings, Iran was considered by many to be the home of the next major boom. Consequently, developers were eager to establish links and contacts with the country. But this wasn't easy; it was a country with a culture far removed from that of Britain, and Iranians had their own way of conducting business. What these developers needed was an insider, someone who already had contacts within the country. Peter's boyhood friend, Alan Byfield, was working for Ronny Lyon, one of the largest UK property developers, and he mentioned that Peter had had influential links with relations of the Iranian royal family. In 1969 his daughter Jane had married His Excellency the Aga Khan Bakhtiar's son, Hedayat. The reception was held at the

RAF Club Piccadilly and many of the groom's family were present, including the Aga Khan Bakhtiar himself. Lyon was particularly interested in Iran. He suggested that Peter might like to search for potential sites around the capital Tehran, negotiating the possibility of obtaining land and commercial properties, and Peter agreed.

It is worth emphasing how important Peter's contacts in Iran were. The Aga Khan was an incredibly wealthy and influential man. Chairman of the National Iranian Oil Company and a government minister for labour, he was also a director of one of the commercial banks. Moreover, the Shah's second wife, Saroya, was his niece and also cousin to Hedayat, and the Aga Khan often discussed personal and commercial matters with the Shah. Peter remembers strolling with the Aga Khan in a park in northern Tehran. A number of Tehranians recognised him, came up to him and stopped, bowing reverently. He in turn removed his hat, acknowledging them, chatting briefly to them in Farsi. Journeys to Iran took the same format. Once Peter had arrived in Tehran (and after his port of call to the British Embassy . . . just in case!), he made his way to the Aga Khan's office in the National Oil Company, where, on the twenty-second floor over a coffee, the pair chatted for an hour or so.

'How were Betty and Jane? How were things in the UK? How would he be getting about?'

'Oh, I shall walk or take a taxi, if necessary.'

'No, no', the Aga Khan replied, 'You don't want to do that. Take my car and my driver.' The car was a huge Mercedes. With a wry smile, Peter recalls the experience was quite good!

His trips to Tehran lasted for about a month at a time, and he stayed in top-class hotels. Although Hedayat and Jane had divorced by this time, the rapport between the Bakhtiars and Peter had remained positive and very amicable.

Peter was developing a skill for handling a number of different and varied business interests while he visited Iran. One of the Aga Khan's relations, Darab Assad, owned a cattle farm 40 miles south-west of Tehran, but Peter says that the term farm was used in the loosest sense; the soil was dusty and the sun was blistering. With a herd of 300 cattle, there were long rows of sheds where the cattle sheltered from the heat, with equally long troughs of food and water. Assad was having problems with his cattle; they were dying from disease and he needed a good professional vet to solve the situation. Did Peter know anyone? As it happened, Peter replied that he had someone in mind, and here his skills in the art of negotiation came to the fore. He wondered whether this vet would take the job for the fee mentioned, and he increased the business terms favourably. After chatting to his veterinary friend, Paul Crossman, about the deal – a three-week job with free flights, free accommodation in a comfortable house and a large fee – Crossman agreed and succeeded in curing the cattle; Assad was overjoyed. On his next visit to Tehran, Assad asked Peter if he could arrange for Crossman's services again – would he be willing to fly out?

'Well,' said Peter, 'I can ask him but whether he's prepared to come out for the same fee, I don't know – he's a busy man with a successful practice.' Those negotiation skills were put to the test once again. 'If you can increase the fee, I'm sure he'd be willing to look at it.' He says it was a pretty nice package – for all concerned. Back in Britain, Crossman was delighted to hear about the fee and was soon on the plane to Tehran. As a vet, he was worth every penny; Peter thinks the cattle were healthier; their diet had been improved and they were vaccinated, which had a direct result on the improved quality and quantity of the milk the cattle were now producing.

The former fighter pilot ace was now a successful business entrepreneur. Other companies got to hear about Peter's Iranian contacts. A Croydon-based engineering consultancy, Mott Hay and Anderson, were anxious to obtain work in the construction of railways in Iran. Could he help?

Peter negotiated a contract on their behalf concerning a

railway line that spread from Tehran to the west of Iran. Some of his trips to Iran were solely on behalf of Mott Hay and Anderson. He also consulted on behalf of an Iranian irrigation company which required a major increase in its irrigation output on local farms. It had been the standard practice for Iranian arable farmers to grow crops around a well. Peter sourced a company that managed to extend the crop range by introducing a huge water-spraying arm about 400m long, standing 10ft off the ground accompanied by eight sets of wheels, driven by a motor. This arm moved slowly round, spraying the plants from the well over a period of twenty-four hours. It wasn't long before nine of these arms were seen spreading their tentacles over the Iranian farmland.

Iran is, of course, a Muslim country, and Peter discovered there were major cultural and religious differences. He was invited to a house owned by an elderly Muslim where, upon entering, he was told to remove his shoes and leave them by the door. The evening was a semi-religious experience as they sat around in a circle on the floor, with the guests drinking wine, but he recalls that there were no women present, except a young girl accompanied by her brother who danced for them to Iranian country music.

The business dealings went from strength to strength. Peter continued to look at centrally located plots of land for commercial use. Almost always, these prices were unrealistic, as Peter says that the Iranians were beginning to get greedy. He relayed this to Ronny Lyon, stressing that he should bide his time for the moment because the costs were proving prohibitive, and suggesting that the next time he was out in Iran, he would go a little further out of the city. 'Just hold on. Keep hold of your money. I have a gut feeling that things aren't quite right.'

'Well, I'll take your advice but I'm very keen to get things going.'

'Yes, I know you are, Ronny, but please – just hold your

horses.' It was sound advice. The revolution to overthrow the Shah succeeded in 1979, bringing the property boom to a halt. Had Lyon ignored Peter, his business would have suffered from major difficulties.

Peter was in Tehran during November when the coup occurred, and he was one of the last Europeans to leave. He recalls the tanks on street corners, the Army with rifles marching along streets, and says it was all a bit tense. The situation had been bubbling under for some time before hand; he remembers a taxi-driver telling him that as a member of the working class, he – and others like him – weren't keen on the Shah; something should be done about him and the sooner the better. It was an early indication of the bitter feeling towards the Iranian royal family. Anti-royalist fervour was in full swing. The Aga Khan and his son, together with their family, were in danger of being hunted down by the new regime. It would be no good explaining to the new mullahs who now held power that they were cousins to the Shah's wife; they were still a threat to the new order. Indeed, the mob was on a witch hunt.

Things became untenable for the Aga Khan and his family after the revolution. At this time, the Aga Khan was already in England for an eye operation and, in fact, never returned to Iran, but Hedayat chose to remain in Tehran with his second wife and daughter. Because he had been educated in Britain, he was considered by the regime to be 'westernised', but that didn't stop them from keeping a very close eye on his whereabouts. One day, Peter received a call from him.

'I've had enough, Peter. I'm getting out. I'm coming to England, but I'm sending my clothing via Geneva in a suitcase where I've also hidden some gold ingots. I'd be grateful if you could pick the suitcase up from the airport, take the gold out and place it in a Geneva bank where you can convert it to English sterling and transfer it to my UK account. [Peter had authority to control the bank accounts for both Hedayat and the Aga Khan.] I'll call you when I've sent the suitcase.'

'OK,' said Peter, 'I'll wait to hear from you.' But the call never came. Strange, Peter thought. What's happened? He phoned Hedayat's wife. She was crying.

'He's in prison. That bag he was going to send to you . . . they've found it; they've confiscated it!'

Prison conditions were harsh; Hedayat was inside for three months. Sharing a barred room with the minimum of food proved to be a salutary experience for him. When he was released, Hedayat told Peter what had happened. He had given the suitcase to a servant, telling him to leave it with a contact at the airport. Unfortunately, this servant could not find the contact and had left it with a stranger, who had opened it and contacted the authorities when he found the gold, which Hedayat had concealed in the soles of a pair of ski boots. When the stranger lifted up the boots, they seemed unexpectedly heavy. The guards had searched his house thoroughly and took him to prison. Hedayat explained that after his release, he went straight to the kitchen and rummaged through a packet of oats. His wife wondered what on earth he was doing. Before he went to prison, he had placed three ingots deep in the oats, which the guards had missed.

The scene in Tehran had changed virtually overnight. Gradually the British returned to the UK and commercial property links with Iran had been severed. Women there were made to wear the chador, covering their faces and bodies. Peter returned to Britain, too, but was asked by Alan Byfield to join him in Dubai, where on behalf of Ronny Lyon, the property developer, he built houses, along with a leisure centre. Peter, as his agent in London, was in charge of procurement of building supplies because of his links in the aviation industry. Everything had to be made to a high finish.

The sands of time were again running out; business in the Middle East had all but dried up, but the restless spirit that Peter possessed still prevailed and he was not ready for the pipe and slippers yet. Peter was asked to consult by a friend, Harry Judd, a chemist who worked for British Airways. The company was becoming rather concerned with the amount of asbestos that had been found in its buildings, and Harry had been asked to investigate and research the problem for it. He was one of only a handful of people who were qualified in the subject. He was also due to retire. 'You know, Pete, I'm thinking of setting up an asbestos consultancy; legislation has tightened recently and it's going to become a major problem area. If BA are concerned about the levels of asbestos, surely others will be too. I can cover the technical side but I haven't got the business contacts. You've got a lot of links with the commercial property world. How about joining us?'

Peter was mildly enthusiastic. 'Well, possibly. But I don't want to become a director. Let's keep it on a consultancy basis.'

'OK, fine.' Peter introduced Harry to a lot of corporate blue chip companies. In order to have the confidence to talk about the subject – and, moreover, sell the business – to other corporate contacts, he needed to gain a basic technical knowledge of the industry. With typical determination and character, he went on site with Harry, learning about microscopy and asbestos analysis so that in time he could chat with ease about the business. He subsequently felt much happier.

The business was expanding and they had taken on an employee to assist in the microscopy, but tragically, Harry died from a massive heart attack. Peter was faced with a dilemma: pack the business in – making redundancies in the process – or take on the challenge of developing his own asbestos analytical business. The spirit of independence and adventure flowed as strongly as ever, even though he was now in his early sixties. He purchased a microscope, pumps and protective equipment and ran the business as a sole trader from a bedroom at his home in Beckenham. (He had since moved from The Knoll and found a quiet semi-detached cottage off the Bromley Road.) He took on another employee, wrote reports and sent out invoices. Realising that he needed some professional development, he signed up for a course at the Institute of Occupational Medicine in Edinburgh, as well as a two-week course at the University of Bristol. There cannot have been too many people in their sixties who had the courage to take themselves off to college. With these courses behind him, Peter was becoming one of the most qualified asbestos analysts in the country. The work continued to increase, and another employee joined the company. Peter went corporate, establishing Ayerst Analysis Ltd in 1985, whereupon he and Betty became directors. Over the next fifteen years, the company grew, becoming a market leader in its field.

In order to receive his pension at the age of seventy, Peter had to relinquish both the directorship and any shares in the company to Betty. Although she became the managing director, he still kept a hands-on approach to the business. Betty died in October 2001. They had been together for fifty-seven years, and right up to her death they had been very much in love. A day does not pass by when he doesn't think of her.

At the age of eighty-one, he came to the conclusion that he had had enough, and the business, together with the directorship, was handed over to his grandson, James, thereby maintaining the company as a family business. The name still lives on but changes have been made and the company is now called Ayerst Environmental Ltd.

At the time of writing, Peter is eighty-three and maintains that restless spirit he has displayed throughout his life. He also retains his love of life the pipe and slippers are only worn metaphorically. He's fit and active, walking 2 miles a day with the same commitment and determination, visiting friends and family all over Britain, with a closely knit group of lifelong and local friends.

Peter is a pilot of incredible skill. He flew genuinely dangerous combat missions over six long years – and survived. He is one of two surviving pilots who flew in France with No. 73 Squadron and is, along with Alex Henshaw, the only surviving test pilot from Castle Bromwich. Charming and amusing, with a warm sense of humour, he retains a philosophical attitude. Not for him any form of navel-gazing self-analysis; life is there to be lived – so live it!

From his first faltering steps in Westcliff, he has balanced an unusual blend of a shrewd analytical mind with a propensity for humour and a *joie de vivre*. There's something both engaging and down to earth about Peter; he is as much at home with the regulars in the local as he is talking to the chief executives of a blue chip conglomerate. He seems to have an uncanny knack in taking a genuine interest in people, be they in their early twenties or his own peer group.

Why does he think he made it through? 'Luck of the draw. I was just bloody lucky on so many occasions.' His close friend Alan Byfield agrees with him: it was whether you were lucky or not. How does he describe Peter? One hundred per cent honest. Alan trusts Peter with his life and thinks it was absolutely coincidental that, after leaving school, they met three times in various parts of the world. Dev Deverson recalls that 'no one said a bad word about Pete. He's a nice bloke, reliable. He likes to progress but he's not self-seeking. He's too modest with his achievements. Most of all, he's a true English gentleman'.

And this sums up Wing Commander Peter Vigne Ayerst DFC rather well. Perhaps it's a combination of all these elements in his character that quantifies his restless spirit, a spirit that kept him alive in the blue skies throughout the dark days of the Second World War, and beyond.

APPENDIX I

Decorations

Peter is entitled to wear the following:

Distinguished Flying Cross
1939/1945 Star
Aircrew Europe Star with France and Germany Clasp
Africa Star with North Africa 1942–43 Clasp
Defence Medal
War Medal 1939–45

Battle of Britain Commemorative Medal, with RAF Bar
Normandy Campaign Medal
Battle of Normandy Commemoration Medal 1994 – 50th
    anniversary of D-Day
The European Cross
Front-line Britain 1944
Cross of the Veterans of HM King Leopold III
Combattants dc la Sommc 1914–1918 1940 Medal
Royal Federation of the Veterans of King Albert I

Ace Combat Record

	Destroyed	Probables	Damaged
6 November 1939	–	–	1 × Me 109
11 March 1940	–	–	1 × Do 17
7 April 1940	1 × Me 109	–	–
7 April 1940	1 × Me 109	–	–
21 April 1940	1 × Me 109	–	–
14 August 1940	1 × He 111	–	–
9 October 1942	1 × Me 109	–	–
	1 × Fieseler Storch	–	–
24 October 1942		1 × Me 109	–
3 November 1942		1 × Me 109	2 × Me 109s
4 November 1942	1 × Me 109	–	–
15 November 1942	1 × Ju 52	–	–
12 June 1944	1 × Me 109	–	–
Totals:	9	2	4

Note: Numerous vehicles, barges and other ground targets
destroyed.

APPENDIX III

RAF Aircraft Types Flown

(in chronological order)

de Havilland Tiger Moth
Miles Magister
de Havilland Leopard Moth
Miles Mentor
Miles Monarch
Gloster Gladiator
Fairey Battle
Westland Lysander
Whitney Straight
Miles Master I
Miles Master III
de Havilland Dominie
de Havilland Dragon
North American Harvard I
North American Harvard II
North American Harvard IIA
Hawker Hurricane I
Hawker Hurricane IIB
Hawker Hurricane IIC
Curtiss Kittyhawk I
Supermarine Spitfire I
Supermarine Spitfire IIA
Supermarine Spitfire IIB
Supermarine Spitfire VB

Supermarine Spitfire VC
Supermarine Spitfire VII
Supermarine Spitfire IX
Supermarine Spitfire XIV
Supermarine Spitfire XVI
Supermarine Spitfire 21
Supermarine Spitfire 22
Supermarine Seafire 45
Supermarine Spitfire 18F
Taylorcraft Auster 3
Taylorcraft Auster 5
Avro Lancaster
Avro Anson XII
Taylorcraft Auster AOP 6
Airspeed Oxford
Taylorcraft Auster T7
Percival Proctor IV
North American Harvard IIB
Gloster Meteor T7
Gloster Meteor 3
de Havilland Vampire T11
de Havilland Vampire 5
de Havilland Venom FB1
de Havilland Vampire 9

Percival Prentice
de Havilland Venom FB4
Avro Anson 19
Avro Anson 21

Avro Anson 17
de Havilland Chipmunk
BAC Lightning

Index